Aligning Perspectives on Health, Safety and Well-Being

Series Editors

Stavroula Leka, University College Cork, Cork, Ireland

Aditya Jain, Nottingham University Business School and Centre for Organizational Health and Development, University of Nottingham, Nottingham, UK

Gerard Zwetsloot, University of Nottingham, Centre for Organizational Health and Development, Nottingham, United Kingdom, TNO InGerard Zwetsloot Research & Consultancy, Amsterdam, Noord-Holland, The Netherlands

Raising awareness of the interdisciplinary and complementary relationship of different research perspectives on health, safety and well-being is the main aim of the book series Aligning Perspectives on Health, Safety and Well-being. Combined research approaches on health, safety and well-being are becoming more and more popular in several research disciplines across and between the social, behavioural and medical sciences. Therefore, Aligning Perspectives on Health, Safety and Well-being stimulates the publication of interdisciplinary approaches to the promotion of health, safety and well-being. Recognizing a need within societies and workplaces for more integrated approaches to problem solving, the series caters to the notion that most innovation stems from combining knowledge and research results from related but so far separated areas. Volumes will be edited by expert authors and editors and will contain contributions from different disciplines. All authors, and especially volume editors are encouraged to engage in developing more robust theoretical models that can be applied in actual practice and lead to policy development.

Kevin Daniels • Olga Tregaskis • Rachel Nayani •
David Watson

Achieving Sustainable Workplace Wellbeing

Springer

Kevin Daniels
University of East Anglia
Norwich, UK

Olga Tregaskis
University of East Anglia
Norwich, UK

Rachel Nayani
University of East Anglia
Norwich, UK

David Watson
University of East Anglia
Norwich, UK

This work was supported by Economic and Social Research Council

ISSN 2213-0497 ISSN 2213-0470 (electronic)
Aligning Perspectives on Health, Safety and Well-Being
ISBN 978-3-031-00664-7 ISBN 978-3-031-00665-4 (eBook)
https://doi.org/10.1007/978-3-031-00665-4

This Springer imprint is published by the registered company Springer Nature Switzerland AG
The registered company address is: Gewerbestrasse 11, 6330 Cham, Switzerland

Preface

Many organizations strive to protect or even enhance the wellbeing of their employees for a variety of reasons. These reasons include meeting regulatory requirements, adopting industry standards, pursuing corporate social responsibility goals and/or because managers think fostering wellbeing can contribute in various ways to superior organizational performance. There are numerous scientific studies on workplace interventions focused on wellbeing. Yet, the current literature indicates that a sizeable proportion of interventions, even those underpinned by robust scientific evidence, still fail to produce anticipated benefits.

Implementation is frequently singled out as the cause of this state of affairs. Moreover, many organizations appear to adopt a range of activities to support workers' wellbeing, rather than relying on single activities. The purpose of this book is to develop a conceptual framework that can explain how specific health and wellbeing interventions come to be implemented as planned or not, as well as how whole programmes are implemented in a manner that sustains workers' wellbeing. The approach we take is purposefully interdisciplinary. In writing the book, we hope to provide a platform to enable researchers in the field to both better understand how specific interventions and programmes of activities are influenced by and influence the organization within which they are embedded.

The first chapter examines the concept of wellbeing and the literature on which interventions improve wellbeing and provides an overview of the model we develop through the course of the book. The second chapter examines existing frameworks focused on implementation and makes the case for an alternative approach. In the third chapter, we begin to examine how specific interventions may come to have effects on workers' wellbeing, including examining why an intervention may have benefits for reasons not connected to the theoretical basis of that intervention and also why some interventions may have adverse effects. In Chaps. 4, 5, 6 and 7, we examine the ways in which programmes of workplace health and wellbeing activities come to be implemented and the interactions between the programme and the wider organization. In the last two chapters, we consider how the ideas conveyed in this book may be developed, in terms of understanding the effects on wellbeing, implications for methods and extensions into other areas of enquiry where organizations seek to create social value.

Norwich, UK

Kevin Daniels
Olga Tregaskis
Rachel Nayani
David Watson

Acknowledgements

This book is a product of the fourth year of research of the Work and Learning programme for the What Works Centre for Wellbeing, funded by Economic and Social Research Council grant number ES/N003586/1.

We are grateful for the support of many colleagues we worked with and alongside on the foundational evidence programmes for the What Works Centre for Wellbeing. From the Centre itself, special thanks go to Paul Litchfield, Nancy Hey, Sara MacLennan, Deborah Hardoon, Tricia Curmi, Ingrid Abreu Scherer, Magdalena Soffia and Marta Morrati. The heads of the other evidence programmes—Louise Mansfield, Rhiannon Corcoran and Paul Frijters—for their support and insights over the years we worked alongside each other.

The research underpinning this book was supported by an excellent project steering group consisting of Cara Maquire, Matt Jayes, Ed Houghton, Jonny Gifford, Rachel Suff, Pamela Keshavarzian, Gemma Comber, Lisa Schulze, Paul Montgomery and Sally McManus. We also thank Nick Pahl and Laura Adelman for their enthusiasm for our research.

Finally, of course, we are tremendously grateful for those we worked with closely on the Work and Learning programme and its spin-off projects: Cigdem Gedikli, Chidiebere Ogbonnaya, Mark Bryan, Alita Nandi, Simonetta Longhi, John Street, Anna Robinson-Pant, Roberta Fida, Ivan Mitchell, Kevin Delany, Martin Hogg, Abasiama Etuknwa, Antonina Semkina, Oluwafunmilayo Vaughn, Sylvester Juwe, Molly Rushworth and most of all Sara Connolly – without whom we would not know the price of anything.

Contents

About the Authors

Kevin Daniels is Professor of Organizational Behaviour in the Employment Systems Group, Norwich Business School, University of East Anglia. He has been researching workplace wellbeing, health and safety for over 30 years and is currently co-editor of Springer's Handbook Series in *Occupational Health Sciences* and an associate editor of the *British Journal of Management*. He was previously editor of *European Journal of Work and Organizational Psychology* and held associate editor roles at the *Journal of Occupational and Organizational Psychology* and *Human Relations*. He has published over 140 peer-reviewed scientific journal articles, book chapters and scientific reports. Since 2015, he has led a multidisciplinary programme of research focused on how organizations manage workplace wellbeing that has been funded by the successive grants from the UK Economic and Social Research Council and has involved 30 staff and PhD students.

Olga Tregaskis is Professor of International Human Resource Management at the University of East Anglia, Head of Norwich Business School and one of the senior social scientists working with the UK's Centre for Climate Change and Social Transformation. A graduate of both the University of Ulster and Cranfield School of Management, Olga's research interests centre on human resource management, management in multinational organizations and implementation of change management. She has held an associate editor role at the FT50 ranked academic journal *Human Relations*, and is editorial board member of a number of prestigious academic journals. She is a member of the REF2021 sub-panel for Business & Management which is the UK's system for assessing the quality of research in UK higher education institutions. She has published over 100 peer-reviewed journal articles, research reports, book chapters and practice tools.

Rachel Nayani is Associate Professor in Organizational Behaviour and Human Resource Management at the University of East Anglia. Rachel teaches the practices and principles of Organization Development. Her research primarily involves understanding organizational process and practices for sustainable change and social value including wellbeing alongside enhanced productivity at work and climate goals. Rachel has undertaken research for the Institution of Occupational Safety and Health and the Economic Social Research Council. She has authored several book chapters on wellbeing and remote working, has published in journals such as *Work and Stress* and is a member of the editorial board of the *European Journal of Work and Organizational Psychology*.

David Watson is Associate Professor in Organizational Behaviour at Norwich Business School, University of East Anglia. He is an interdisciplinary researcher who has carried out research on wellbeing in a number of contexts including education, community organizations and the workplace. He is interested in how organizations' intentions to achieve wellbeing materialize in practice and factors associated with this. Through funded research David has carried out a number of evidence reviews exploring relationships between work, learning and wellbeing and in-depth qualitative fieldwork. He is the author of several book chapters and peer-reviewed journal articles in journals, such as the *European Journal of Work and Organizational Psychology*, *Ergonomics* and *Organization*.

Chapter 1
Introduction

Too often workplace health and wellbeing practices and initiatives fall short of delivering sustained improvements in worker wellbeing, even though these practices and initiatives are based on robust empirical research and sound theoretical reasoning. Frequently, the failure of workplace health and wellbeing practices and initiatives is attributed to implementation processes—that is, the management of the change processes involved in introducing new practices and initiatives. Although researchers have identified a range of factors that could influence the effectiveness of implementation processes, the research literature is fragmented and conceptually under-developed (Biron & Karanika-Murray, 2015).

These issues with the literature create a major obstacle to progress. That is, we simply do not know the regularities in the empirical literature. For example it is widely held that line managers are critical to implementing health and wellbeing practices in the workplace (e.g. Jordan et al., 2003; Nielsen, 2013, 2017), and there are numerous studies that support such arguments (Daniels et al., 2021). On the other hand, there are also numerous studies that indicate line manager resistance can be overcome (Daniels et al.), suggesting line managers may not be so critical after all. Without consistent evidence, it is not possible to develop sound theoretical models to guide research, simply because it is not known which factors are most fundamental to implementation. This obstacle has a consequent effect on organisational practice. Without well-developed and empirically supported models of implementation, there is no basis for evidence-informed practice. Consequently, research is irrelevant to practice, aside from occasional anecdotes from specific studies that may chime with human resources or occupational health professionals.

The purpose of this book is to make progress by addressing this major obstacle—namely developing a conceptual framework based on empirical regularities to inform subsequent research. To identify those empirical regularities, we provide a comprehensive and detailed overview of existing conceptual frameworks and empirical studies of the implementation of workplace wellbeing initiatives. Evidence from existing empirical studies is complemented by qualitative case study evidence from six organisations that had implemented a range of workplace health and wellbeing

K. Daniels et al., *Achieving Sustainable Workplace Wellbeing*, Aligning Perspectives on Health, Safety and Well-Being, https://doi.org/10.1007/978-3-031-00665-4_1

practices. This detailed case study evidence plays a critical role in filling in gaps in the evidence base, as well as providing rich and nuanced illustrations of the various processes involved in implementing workplace health and wellbeing initiatives through the first-hand accounts of organisational stakeholders. The technical appendix provides details on the methods we used to map existing conceptual frameworks, empirical studies and our own qualitative case study research.

Our aim is to develop a model of how organisations achieve and *sustain* workplace wellbeing. Studies that evaluate and describe the implementation of specific interventions involve teams of researchers (oftentimes the researchers are also the implementers) examining specific and discrete interventions—ideally with a control group for comparison purposes, and then retiring from field work after a period of time. This approach is critically important for evaluating the (cost-)effectiveness and implementation of specific interventions, but it reflects neither what sustains the effects of an intervention after the researchers have left the field or how organisations work in practice. Research on the implementation of specific interventions is informative of the wider picture, it does not capture the wider picture. Moreover, engagement with professional researchers in formal evaluations of interventions is the exception, not the rule. Instead, it appears that organisations that sustain wellbeing over an extended period appear to do so through an evolving programme of different initiatives. We come to this conclusion through our own field work, discussions with practitioners, guidance on best practice (ISO, 2018; LaMontagne et al., 2014), and from evidence provided in other case studies and surveys of organisational practices (Batorsky et al., 2016; Johnson et al., 2018; Jordan et al., 2003; Mattke et al., 2015). Therefore, our conceptual work is directed at understanding how organisations manage the whole process, multiple activities and what happens when specific interventions are not formally evaluated. Such considerations justify the need to go beyond the existing literature.

In the later parts of this chapter, we introduce the core elements of our model. However, before we do so, we define our focal concept—wellbeing—and justify why it is the focal concept. We then provide an overview of the literature on those practices that are deemed to be (potentially) effective and describe and define in more detail what is meant by the term 'implementation'.

Wellbeing

Wellbeing has a prominent profile in many academic disciplines. In philosophy, there is Aristotle's conception of wellbeing as associated with human flourishing or 'eudaimonia'. In political theory, Utilitarianism defines the main goals of policy as maximizing pleasure and minimizing pain (Bache & Reardon, 2016). In health sciences, the World Health Organization's definition of health adopted in 1948 states 'health is a state of complete physical, mental and social well-being and not merely the absence of disease or infirmity'. Nevertheless, the dominant view is that wellbeing is psychological in nature (O'Donnell et al., 2014).

In the psychological sciences and the field of wellbeing economics, psychological wellbeing comprises two major components (Waterman, 1993). The first, subjective wellbeing, consists of summative assessments of one's life (e.g. life satisfaction) or life domain (e.g. job satisfaction) and affective wellbeing, which is the experience of positive affective states (e.g. joy, enthusiasm) and the relative absence of negative affect states (e.g. lack of anxiety, feeling calm) (Diener, 1984). The second component is eudaemonic wellbeing which includes feelings of autonomy, mastery, personal growth, learning new things, positive relations with others, sense of accomplishment, sense of meaning, purpose in life and self-acceptance (Huppert & So, 2013; Ryff & Keyes, 1995).

Psychological wellbeing also varies by life domains (Warr, 1990), for example work, leisure and home domains. In relation to work, job satisfaction is one of the core indicators of wellbeing, providing a summative and overall indicator of work-related wellbeing that is highly correlated with other aspects of work-related psychological wellbeing. These other aspects include work-related affective wellbeing assessing how work makes one feel (e.g. Daniels, 2000; Warr, 1990) and work engagement (Schaufeli et al., 2002), which positions positive work-related wellbeing to consist of three elements of vigour, dedication and absorption in work activities. Burnout is also typically conceived as being caused by negative work experiences (Maslach et al., 1986), with the three components of emotional exhaustion, depersonalization and reduced personal accomplishment signifying poor work-related wellbeing.

Focusing on psychological wellbeing as an outcome of various workplace health and wellbeing initiatives has several advantages. First, given the positive relationship between physical health and psychological wellbeing (Reed & Buck, 2009), initiatives targeted at improving physical health (e.g. workplace health promotion) may confer psychological as well as physical benefits. Given that many workplace health and wellbeing initiatives also target mental health and those mental health problems are one of the major causes of sickness absence and disability benefits, focusing on psychological wellbeing means a diverse range of health and wellbeing initiatives and whole programmes of initiatives can be evaluated against the same metrics. Second, psychological wellbeing changes more quickly than many aspects of physical health, and so could be a leading indicator of the success of workplace health and wellbeing initiatives. Third, wellbeing, including but not limited to those elements closely coupled with workplace experiences such as work engagement and job satisfaction, is also associated with positive attitudes to work and workplace behaviours beneficial to organisations, such as organisational commitment, organisational citizenship, lower absenteeism, turnover intentions, proactive behaviours and organisational performance (Baas et al., 2008; Lyubomirsky et al., 2005; Thomas et al., 2010; Thoresen et al., 2003; Whitman et al., 2010). In this sense, workplace health and wellbeing initiatives may be one vehicle through which managers seek mutual gains with workers, whereby workers gain in terms of better wellbeing and health, and through norms of social exchange, reciprocate with higher levels of commitment and effort at work (Guest, 2017). Fourth, initiatives benefitting psychological wellbeing have the potential to improve wellbeing for all, not just people with specific health conditions seeking rehabilitation in workplaces or at risk from specific conditions that may motivate some forms of workplace health promotion (e.g. around smoking or healthy eating). In this sense, wellbeing is democratic that can be used to evaluate the success of different interventions that apply to diverse groups within the same workspace (cf. Layard, 2016).

Nevertheless, although addressing some problems, using psychological wellbeing as a focus also brings complexities. Psychological wellbeing has many components, and so is not a single 'thing'. The choice of which component or components to evaluate, and the measures to do so, could mean that some aspects of wellbeing and the health and wellbeing practices most closely associated with those aspects of wellbeing get higher priority in management decisions than others. Some of these components (e.g. affective elements) are more volatile than others and sensitive to events over which human resources or occupational health professionals have no control—e.g. other organisational changes, the weather or even the performance of football teams (e.g. Gkorezis et al., 2016). This could make it appear as if a practice or programme of practices had no benefits or even adverse effects, when in fact things could have been a lot worse if there were no health and wellbeing practices in place.[1] Third, and related to the former, wellbeing in different life domains spills over into other domains—meaning wellbeing at work can be affected by wellbeing at home and vice versa. This may make some managers feel uncomfortable about encroaching upon workers' personal lives. Fourth, psychological wellbseing is an individual experience, and there exist differences between individuals in 'baseline' levels of wellbeing (Steel et al., 2019), the types of events that trigger changes in wellbeing and abilities to adjust to or cope with negative events or poor mood (Lazarus, 1991). One potential problem here is that managers may be concerned about condescending paternalism through workplace practices focused on wellbeing if workers may feel wellbeing is their own responsibility. On the other hand, individual differences may justify approaches that place the management of wellbeing entirely on individuals (Hancock & Tyler, 2004), and hence also justify decisions to enact practices that are detrimental to worker wellbeing (e.g. casualization of contracts, redundancies, punitive performance management practices, cf. Tomlinson & Kelley, 2013; White, 2017). Moreover, compared to some workplace hazards (e.g. exposure to noxious fumes), the relationships between so-called psychosocial risks (e.g. high work demands) and psychological outcomes can be far less clear cut and difficult to quantify (Rick & Briner, 2000). Correspondingly, regulatory approaches to psychological health and wellbeing may be based much more on employers engaging in voluntary practices and corporate social responsibility (Mishiba, 2020).

Because of, rather than despite, these complexities, we argue psychological wellbeing should remain a key focus for research on workplace health and wellbeing

[1] One of the reasons for including control groups in trials of new practices is to attempt to capture the effects of such 'confounding' events, although many organisations would not attempt this kind of evaluation.

practices. This is because the complexities of psychological wellbeing give different stakeholders considerable latitude in choosing which aspects of wellbeing to emphasize, how to manage it and who should be responsible for managing it (Daniels et al., 2018), thus making wellbeing a contested concept between different stakeholders (Jenkins, 2017; Oman, 2015; Scott & Bell, 2013). Therefore, wellbeing, as a focus of health and wellbeing practices, is located in the social, cultural and political fabric of organisations, and the management of wellbeing is correspondingly tied up in these social, cultural and political factors. This contrasts with the largely rational approach taken in the interventions literature (next section), within which social, cultural and political factors are considered to be 'noise' that interferes with the implementation and effectiveness of scientifically credible interventions. In this book therefore, we focus on the organisation as a social, cultural and political entity is in keeping with the potential for there to be conflict between different stakeholders around how to manage workplace wellbeing. Moreover, if we take the view that the social world (including work organisations) is perceived, produced and reproduced by human actors, understanding different stakeholder perspectives on wellbeing is important for understanding the context within which actions intended to improve wellbeing may actually influence wellbeing (Ackroyd & Karlsson, 2014).

From a practice and policy point of view, acknowledging the contested nature of wellbeing and its management is important if organisations are to be successful in promoting workplace wellbeing. Engagement with stakeholders also may mitigate against the co-option of wellbeing by powerful groups with specific ideological goals (e.g. see Davies, 2015). Moreover, ignoring workers' own views on their wellbeing priorities area in favour of management or consultants' perceptions on what they should be runs a very real risk of implementing practices that are ineffective because they do not address matters of importance to different groups of workers (Nussbaum & Sen, 1993). In part this is because attaining what is important to people influences their wellbeing (Carver & Scheier, 1990; Sheldon & Elliot, 1999). Although understanding the views of different stakeholders in developing workplace health and wellbeing programmes means confronting and dealing with conflicting priorities between different groups of workers, managers and expert implementers (human resources, occupational health, management consultants), the reality is that these conflicts need to be addressed even where the goals are social goods (wellbeing practices). Given finite resources within organisations, understanding the views of different stakeholder groups, especially those to be affected most, allows more inclusive decisions to be taken on how and to whom resources should be allocated.

To conclude this section, although we see wellbeing as a largely psychological and experiential construct, we also acknowledge that it is contested and socially constructed by different stakeholder groups, and that contestation is important for understanding how workplaces influence workers' wellbeing. So far, we have left unaddressed the issue of what constitutes 'sustaining' wellbeing. On the one hand, we could approach 'sustaining' wellbeing as the process through which organisations attain and maintain a given level of 'good' wellbeing amongst their workforces. However, recognizing the contested nature of wellbeing, an alternative approach would be to define sustaining wellbeing as a process through which organisations develop, evolve and continue to address workers' wellbeing priorities and concerns: We view sustaining wellbeing as a continuous process of (re)negotiation, because workers' wellbeing priorities and concerns change and priorities and concerns may differ among different groups of workers. We favour an approach to sustainable wellbeing as one focused on developing and evolving ways in which to address workers' wellbeing priorities and concerns. Such an approach would also encompass attaining and maintaining good worker wellbeing as inherent in the process of developing, evolving and negotiating.

What Works and Why It Works

For the purposes of this book, we favour an approach to wellbeing that recognizes divergence between different stakeholders. This is important because there can exist differences between groups about what to do in a specific instance, where best to allocate resources and who should be responsible. However, scientific conceptions of wellbeing do overlap considerably with lay/public views on what constitutes workplace wellbeing and what is effective for preventing deterioration of wellbeing and enhancing wellbeing (Daniels et al., 2018), for example in relation to workplace wellbeing reflecting job satisfaction, happiness, absence of psychological ill-health, a sense of meaning and purpose in life, as well as the work environment and the behaviour of managers and co-workers as determinants of wellbeing. This overlap is important, because practices shown to be effective in relation to scientific conceptions of wellbeing will have face validity for those affected by the practices.

Workplace health and wellbeing practices are often classified (LaMontagne et al., 2007; Richardson & Rothstein, 2008) by whether their intended target is: prevention (primary prevention, e.g. work redesign, health promotion); providing skills or knowledge for healthy individuals to self-regulate exposure to risk (secondary prevention, e.g. stress management/resilience training); or rehabilitation of those who have developed health conditions (tertiary intervention, e.g. talking therapies). Daniels et al. (2021) differentiated between primary prevention through work redesign, which targets aspects of the work environment that can cause psychological harm (e.g. excessive work demands, abusive supervision) or that enhance psychological wellbeing (e.g. role clarity, being able to participate in workplace decision making), and primary prevention through health promotion (nutrition, exercise, smoking cessation). There also exists the potential for multicomponent interventions, combining elements of two or more approaches (e.g. job redesign coupled with training in problem-solving). Table 1.1 gives examples of each type of intervention according to this fivefold classification.

In general terms, the effectiveness of interventions that are less disruptive to organisations going about their business 'as usual' are more frequently assessed using more powerful randomized control trial designs. Quasi-experimental designs using non-equivalent control groups or even before-and-after designs are frequently

Table 1.1 Examples of specific interventions

Intervention	Specific examples
Primary prevention targeted at work redesign	Training individual workers to make improvements to their own jobs Training managers to make improvements to workers' jobs Leadership development Participatory approaches to work redesign involving teams of workers redesigning their jobs Extensive and organisation wide redesign of jobs Improving social environments through shared social activities
Primary prevention targeted at health promotion	Physical activity promotion Subsidized gym membership Pedometer provision Stair climbing Weight loss programme
Secondary intervention	Problem-solving Mindfulness instruction Coping skills training Meditation training
Tertiary intervention	Employee Assistance Programme Graded/phased return to work Workplace accommodations Return to work planning Web-based self-help for workers with depressive symptoms Cognitive behaviour therapy
Multicomponent	Job redesign coupled with problem-solving training Health promoting leadership, participatory work redesign stress management training e-learning for health behaviours, line manager-led job redesign

Note. Examples drawn from various systematic reviews: Daniels et al. (2021), Daniels, Gedikli, et al. (2017), Daniels, Watson, and Gedikli (2017), Etuknwa et al. (2019), Rojatz et al. (2016), Watson et al. (2018)

deployed to evaluate the effectiveness of all intervention types. Thus, as well as heterogeneity in intervention content within each class of intervention as well as the context of implementation, the literature is uneven in respect of the confidence that can be drawn around the effectiveness of specific interventions, notwithstanding implementation factors. Many of the systematic reviews and meta-analyses reviewed in the following sections involve studies using a variety of evaluation methods. Nevertheless, it is possible to make statements about which types of intervention are most likely to effect changes in wellbeing.

Primary Prevention Through Work Redesign

Multiple epidemiological studies have demonstrated that workplace factors, often referred to as psychosocial job/work characteristics or psychosocial hazards (MacKay et al., 2004), are associated with impaired mental health (Rugulies et al., 2020; Stansfeld & Candy, 2006) and other health problems such as suicide ideation, heart disease and degenerative cognitive disorders (Kivimäki et al., 2012; Milner et al., 2018; Then et al., 2014). Although adverse psychosocial work characteristics increase the probability of developing a health condition, rather than being the sole determinant of health conditions, one approach favoured by legislators and regulators (ETUC, 2004; ILO, 2001; Leka & Cox, 2008; Leka et al., 2003) targets reducing exposure to harmful psychosocial work characteristics (e.g. excessive work demands, conflicting or ambiguous role requirements, abusive supervision) and enhancing exposure to beneficial work characteristics (e.g. job autonomy, opportunity to use/develop skills, socially supportive workplaces). The idea here is that although the relationships are stochastic, at a population level, improving psychosocial work characteristics will improve health (and so reduce healthcare spend and sickness benefits over the longer term and reduce sickness absence, and so contribute to national economic performance) (MacKay et al., 2004). However, these longer term societal benefits may not always be known to or even a concern of employers or investors with a short-term focus on profits and share prices (Symitsi et al., 2018).

There are multiple models of how psychosocial work characteristics come to have effects on health, but a common thread is that they impact wellbeing through psychological processes. One model that subsumes many others is the Job-Demands-Resources model (Demerouti et al., 2001). The basic premises of the model are that: (a) there are workplace demands that impede individuals from attaining personal goals; (b) there are workplace resources that enable workers to attain goals, regulate the aversive effects of workplace demands, and accrue more resources; (c) demands deplete resources; (d) accruing resources is desirable in itself because of their potential to aid goal attainment. Where workplace resources prevail, then positive markers of psychological wellbeing will improve, but where demands prevail over resources, then negative markers of wellbeing will increase. Through a variety of psychological and psychophysiological processes, chronic exposure to work environments where demands prevail over resources will lead to ill-health. Refinements of the model include personal resources as outcomes of job resources (i.e. individual differences such as self-efficacy; Xanthopoulou et al., 2009) and incorporate the differentiation of those demands that require effort to overcome in order to attain (personal growth) goals and those that simply block goal attainment, labelled challenge and hindrance demands respectively (LePine et al., 2005).

Although it is difficult to define demands and resources, because they are defined by their immediate outcomes (i.e. relationships to goal progress or success of self-regulation) (Schaufeli & Taris, 2014), research has established that some psychosocial work characteristics are consistently related to positive markers of wellbeing and health and others to negative markers of wellbeing and health (LePine et al., 2005;

Van Veldhoven et al., 2020). This consistency in the literature therefore enables work redesign interventions to focus on specific aspects of work. However, compared to other forms of intervention, research on primary prevention through work redesign tends to use less powerful research designs and randomized control trials are rare, and so the evidence summarized in systematic reviews (below) is less robust than for other forms of intervention.

In relation to the social environment at work specifically, evidence from a systematic review of intervention studies does indicate relatively simple actions can improve social relationships in work groups, such as improvements in group cohesion, social support and perceived fairness, as well as improving markers of wellbeing (Daniels, Watson, et al., 2017). Examples included establishing dialogue groups, group training and mentoring. However, all of the interventions evaluated in the review included several components and some external facilitation, which would suggest one-off activities have limited or no effects.

The pattern of evidence for interventions focused on aspects of the working environment other than social relationships in work groups is more complex. For example, Fox et al. (2021) reviewed studies of interventions focused on different elements of the working environment. Fox et al. found 50 reported some positive effects on markers of wellbeing, but 15 studies reported no effects on any markers of wellbeing and six studies reported some negative impacts on wellbeing. Fox et al. concluded flexible working practices demonstrated the most consistent and positive impacts on wellbeing, but the effects appeared to be conditional on a range of contextual factors. In a review of 28 job redesign interventions, Roodbari et al. (2021) concluded such interventions were more likely to be successful in favourable circumstances.

Other systematic reviews and meta-analyses of work redesign interventions have identified two major routes through which work redesign may have beneficial effects on wellbeing, reflecting differences in managerial led/initiated job redesign and worker led/initiated work redesign. On the one hand, it appears managerial led/initiated job design has a better chance of improving wellbeing and health markers if extensive changes are made to working practices rather than limiting changes to a small number of psychosocial work/characteristics (Montano et al., 2014) and that the changes need to be supported through improvements in human management practices (e.g. enhanced training, changes to performance management and rewards, Daniels, Gedikli, et al., 2017). On the other hand, training workers to initiate individualized changes to make localized improvements to their own working environment (labelled 'job crafting' interventions, see Van Wingerden et al., 2017) can also lead to improvements in wellbeing (Daniels, Gedikli, et al., 2017; Oprea et al., 2019).

In between these two extremes of extensive 'top-down' management-led change and individualized 'bottom-up' localized changes are interventions focused on specific work groups or departments that engage in participatory processes with managers to make collective changes in the work group or department. Findings from these interventions are mixed, with some indicating benefits for wellbeing and others no or even adverse effects (Daniels, Gedikli, et al., 2017; Fox et al., 2021).

Although worker participation in decisions concerning health and wellbeing practices, including work redesign, is an important element of implementation (Daniels, Gedikli, et al., 2017; Fox et al., 2021; Roodbari et al., 2021), it is not clear why participatory interventions focused on work group environments are less successful than more extensive changes or highly individualized changes to jobs. One possibility relates to individual preferences and goals. More extensive changes are likely to address a multitude of worker concerns, each linked to a different concern for different workers. For example extensive changes may address some workers' concerns in respect of work intensity by reducing demands, other workers' concerns for clarity by eliminating conflicting task demands and other workers' concerns for more interesting work by enhancing the capacity to take decisions and use more skills. Training workers to make individually initiated changes to work necessarily entails workers adjusting working practices to suit their own preferences. However, participatory group level interventions may require compromise between workers (and their managers) on what changes are to be prioritized, potentially leaving some workers (and their managers) dissatisfied with the changes and/or the micro-politics of how those compromises were made.

Primary Prevention Through Health Promotion

As noted earlier, the positive relationship between physical and psychological health suggests workplace health promotion can confer psychological as well as physical benefits. There are many ways in which physical health can contribute to psychological wellbeing, for example through the mood-enhancing effects of physical exercise (Reed & Buck, 2009) and because experiencing symptoms and limitations of chronic physical conditions can lead to mood disorders (Kendall et al., 2015). Components of workplace health promotion can also target psychological health or self-care. Usually, health promotion targets behaviour change in an otherwise (mainly) healthy population, targeted at for example smoking, nutrition, physical activity (including exercise and sedentary behaviour), alcohol and drug consumption. Examples include health education seminars, fitness classes, advice from health professionals, health-goal setting, onsite fitness programmes and pedometer provision (Rongen et al., 2013). Health promotion can also include behavioural nudges, such as easier access to healthy food in work canteens (Proper & van Oostrom, 2019).

From a policy perspective, the workplace is considered a fruitful setting for public health promotion because workplaces provide natural social networks that enable health promotion to a large number of adults in a single physical or virtual space. Health promotion is also more likely to be considered by employers: as less disruptive to 'business as usual' than work redesign; as more clearly aligned to health and wellbeing than work redesign and so more readily sends signals of employer care; and, for employers concerned about intruding into the non-work life of employees, as practices that provide workers with choices on how to behave without necessarily prescribing behaviour. In relation to this last point however, in our research, we have come across employers who strongly encourage engagement in health promotion and healthy behaviours outside of sectors where some unhealthy behaviours (e.g. alcohol consumption) have safety implications.

Research does indicate that workplace health promotion can have benefits for physical health markers and psychological wellbeing, and the conclusions are relatively robust. A meta-analysis of randomized control trials indicated positive effects of workplace health promotion on self-reported health and sickness absence (Rongen et al., 2013) and a review of systematic reviews and meta-analyses indicated evidence that workplace health promotion can improve physical activity, diet/weight, and mental health (Proper & van Oostrom, 2019). Rongen et al. also found that the effects of workplace health promotion were still evident even in the most robust trials (e.g. studies that controlled for potential confounding factors). However, the effects of workplace health promotion on mental health were found to be stronger when mental health promotion was included in the intervention rather than focusing solely on physical health (Proper & van Oostrom), and the effects on self-reported health stronger for more intensive interventions with contact weekly at least (Rongen et al.,). This later finding led Rongen et al. to speculate whether the impact of workplace health promotion has more to do with the frequency of contact rather than the specific components of the intervention.

One concern expressed around workplace health promotion is whether the effects are stronger or weaker in specific groups. Rongen et al. (2013) found no differences between genders, but differences between age groups. Effects of workplace health promotion were stronger in younger workers, although there were still effects in older workers. However, Rongen et al.s' meta-analysis and another systematic review (Van de Ven et al., 2020, which incorporated a systematic review of primary empirical studies and earlier systematic reviews) suggest nuanced differences in respect of socio-economic status. In general, there appear to be no differences between higher and lower socio-economic status workers in the benefits accrued from workplace health promotion, and even that lower socio-economic status workers may benefit slightly more because of differentially high risk (Van de Ven et al.). However, the effectiveness of workplace promotion for lower socio-economic status workers may be undermined if higher socio-economic status workers participating in the intervention are in the majority. The reasons for this differentiation are as yet unclear, and maybe related to social comparison or social identity effects, especially because in the same workplace, lower socio-economic status workers participating in workplace health promotion programmes are likely to be in positions of less structural power than higher socio-economic status workers. However, the possibility of differential effects related to structural issues of power does foreground the importance of understanding micro-political factors in the implementation of workplace health and wellbeing practices.

Secondary Interventions

Secondary interventions aim to provide workers with personal resources that enable them to cope better or regulate the impact of work demands or other psychosocial hazards. Specific interventions will target improvements in different personal resources. The evidence, summarized in multiple systematic reviews, is that interventions focused on improving personal resources to regulate the impact of psychosocial hazards in general promote better wellbeing. Examples include resilience training (Robertson et al., 2015; Vanhove et al., 2016) and mindfulness (Bartlett et al., 2019; Janssen et al., 2018; Khoury et al., 2015; Lomas et al., 2017; Virgili, 2015). The effects of training in better self-regulation are evident across a range of intervention types (Watson et al., 2018), and the interventions appear to be most beneficial for those with either poor wellbeing or working in jobs with high exposure to psychosocial hazards (Eby et al., 2019; Khoury et al.; Robertson et al.; Vanhove et al., Watson et al.). This later finding therefore suggests that the effects of secondary interventions are compatible with theoretical expectations, that is, through improving self-regulation skills. Moreover, the research summarized in systematic reviews does include multiple randomized control trials, meaning the effects can be considered to be robust (Watson et al.).

It could be argued that enhancing professional/vocational skills should improve wellbeing because such interventions would improve the ability of people to cope with the demands of their job by enhancing the ability to do the job, as well as signalling to workers the organisation is investing in their development (Watson et al., 2018). However, the evidence pertaining to deliberate organisational actions to improve professional/vocational skills (i.e. intervention studies compared to surveys of self-reported learning) is surprisingly sparse and ambiguous, although adverse effects appear unlikely (Watson et al.).

For organisations, secondary interventions focused on enhancing workers' ability to self-regulate the impact of psychosocial hazards, or their own wellbeing may be very attractive. First, they are much less disruptive to 'business as usual' than primary prevention through work redesign, and at face value, considerably cheaper. Second, some such interventions can now be delivered through apps and other electronic means, thus allowing flexibility in delivery to accommodate different working patterns (Spijkerman et al., 2016) as well as generating cost savings compared to face-to-face delivery. There is also evidence that online delivery can confer wellbeing benefits, especially mindfulness focused interventions (e.g. Stratton et al., 2017), although Watson et al. (2018) concluded online delivery of interventions were generally less effective than face-to-face delivery because of variable up-take and engagement with the training materials.

For occupations that inherently involve exposure to psychosocial and other hazards (e.g. emergency services, military), secondary interventions focused on enhancing self-regulation skills would appear to be the best option, because they do focus on prevention. However, as noted above, many organisations may consider secondary interventions preferable because they are less disruptive to 'business as usual'. In these cases, it is possible that providing training resources, without other changes, to cope with obviously preventable psychosocial hazards may undermine the potential of the intervention to deliver benefits, because a low-cost 'sticking plaster' approach may signal little concern for employee wellbeing and employees may not engage with the intervention.

Tertiary Interventions

Tertiary interventions occur after workers have experienced some form of harm which then requires some form of treatment as a health condition develops. The workplace may or may not be a cause of the health condition, but the symptoms may be work-relevant insofar as they affect workplace behaviour, performance and absence (Kendall et al., 2015). In some cases, organisations may rely on universal health care provision, for example the National Health Service in the UK. In other cases, organisations will provide access to health services, either through in-house occupational health or through contracted occupational health providers or health insurance. In relation to psychological wellbeing, such services are most often provided through Employee Assistance Programmes (EAPs) that include access to talking therapies. A systematic review of EAPs did indicate some effectiveness in reducing distress and reducing presenteeism, but mixed effects on absenteeism (Joseph et al., 2018).

Notwithstanding, and regardless of the nature of the health condition, the goal of tertiary interventions is successful rehabilitation, which can include return-to-work after a period of sickness absence and in some case staying in work whilst receiving treatment. Indeed, for some conditions, notably common mental health problems and muscular-skeletal problems, staying in work whilst receiving treatment may aid recovery (Karanika-Murray & Biron, 2020; Kendall et al., 2015). Many workplace tertiary interventions are therefore focused on effective rehabilitation (return to work) or more rarely, stay at work: Best practice models incorporate both return to work and stay at work issues, and there is overlap between factors that hinder successful return to work and stay at work, as well as considerable overlap in relation to commonalities across different health conditions (Kristman et al., 2020). These commonalities include implementing workplace accommodations to allow the worker to perform some work tasks (e.g. temporarily removing some designated tasks), a phased return to work, involvement of the employee, managers and healthcare professionals in return to work planning, focusing on what the employee can do rather than what s/he cannot do, maintaining good supervisor/employee relationships, people/health/safety-oriented workplace cultures, and tailoring plans to suit individual circumstances and conditions rather than applying the same approach in each instance (Kristman et al.). What might be particularly problematic for return to work, however, is where workplace factors either caused or exacerbated the initial health problem and those factors remaining in place (e.g. abusive supervision from line managers).

Common mental health problems and muscular-skeletal disorders are the most common reasons for work-related absence, and because of their complexity and potential for developing into chronic conditions and subsequent relapse, are also some of the most difficult to manage in relation to stay at work and return to work (Kendall et al., 2015). A systematic review of studies that examined factors that aided return to work programmes for common mental health problems and muscular-skeletal disorders concluded that the most consistent and modifiable factors associated with successful return to work were support from line managers and co-workers, employees' positive attitudes to work and self-efficacy (Etuknwa et al., 2019).

Multicomponent Interventions

Multicomponent interventions should confer multiple benefits because they address different wellbeing needs and provide a wider range of wellbeing resources, thus individuals and groups are able to benefit from the components that suit their specific needs (cf. LaMontagne et al., 2014), enabling a wider range of individuals to engage with tailored activities than would be possible in single-component programmes (cf. more extensive approaches to work redesign above). Daniels, Gedikli, et al. (2017) concluded there was some evidence in their systematic review to suggest that work redesign accompanied by secondary interventions focused on self-regulation skills did benefit workers' wellbeing: The reasoning here is that redesigning work provides job resources that enable the potential for better self-regulation of wellbeing, and training in self-regulation allows workers to realize the potential of those job resources. However, of the nine multicomponent interventions included in the systematic review conducted by Daniels et al. (2021), only one was associated with benefits to wellbeing that were not contingent on some other factor or limited to a specific group (i.e. Hadgraft et al., 2017). In this study, these benefits were realized through changes in workplace norms around health, although this mechanism was not theorized to be why the intervention should work.

Multicomponent interventions require more co-ordination and resources than many other interventions and therefore may be subject to more problems with implementation compared to interventions with a narrower focus. However, the difference between the conclusions of the two systematic reviews may lie in the level of integration of the components in interventions: For work redesign coupled with training in self-regulatory skills, both components target the same mechanism—improvements in self-regulation of wellbeing. Other multicomponent interventions may have less integration, thus the mechanisms through the intervention works may be less likely to become active and it may be harder to communicate a coherent strategy or purpose for the intervention so that workers know what the overall goal of the several components are. As we shall see later, establishing and communicating a coherent strategy or purpose might be helpful in developing and sustaining workplace health and wellbeing programmes (see Chaps. 2, 4, 6 and 8).

Implementation and a New Model

The implementation of workplace health and wellbeing practices has been acknowledged for some time as a factor that can facilitate or hinder the effectiveness of otherwise theoretically robust and empirically supported interventions (see e.g. Egan et al., 2009, as an early example).[2] Implementation has been defined as 'the dynamic process of adapting the program to the context of action while maintaining the intervention's core principles' (Herrera-Sánchez et al., 2017: 4) and is influenced by a range of actors (Nielsen, 2013: 1030, after Nytrø et al., 2000: 214). Nevertheless, there is a danger for implementation research to focus on narrow considerations related to the actions of a few key implementers (Cox et al., 2007), to see the organisation as an immutable entity that merely provides a context for a study of a specific intervention (Russell et al., 2016) and for this field of research to be under theorized (Biron & Karanika-Murray, 2015).

It might be assumed that workplace health and wellbeing practices that are most difficult to implement are those that interact with or should be integrated with other organisational processes (e.g. work redesign through changing work processes) or have more elements (e.g. multicomponent interventions). However, similar issues with implementation surface with even relatively simple, low-cost interventions and those that can stand apart from organisational practices (Daniels et al., 2021, e.g. wellbeing apps, mindfulness training). Moreover, as noted earlier, many organisations adapt and evolve health and wellbeing programmes that consist of multiple activities that are introduced, maintained or stopped as the programme changes.

In this book, we develop a model of implementation that centres on the organisation as the unit of analysis and that underscores the dynamic relationships between the organisation and implementing the activities that comprise the health and wellbeing programme. Having the organisation as the unit of analysis rather than a specific intervention allows us to develop a model that addresses critical gaps in the implementation literature:

(a) Organisations often introduce multiple health and wellbeing practices simultaneously or successively over a period of time in a managed programme, rather than implementing stand-alone interventions. Therefore sustaining wellbeing in organisations needs to be considered as ongoing practice/process rather than evaluated as a discrete intervention or programme.
(b) At present, there is no model of implementation that can simultaneously explain how management-led changes (sometimes referred to as top-down changes) and employee-led changes (sometimes referred to as bottom-up) can be implemented and integrated into a programme of activities, although some workplace health and wellbeing practices may emerge from employee-initiated actions (e.g. gardening groups, informal changes to working roles) rather than being

[2] This is notwithstanding that the literature does also report evaluations of interventions with limited links to established theories (Burgess et al., 2020).

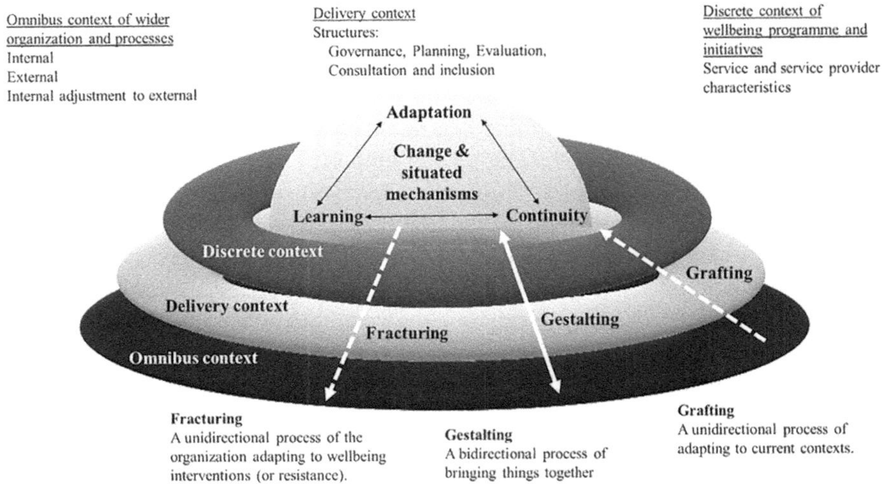

Fig. 1.1 A model of how organisations implement and sustain workplace health and wellbeing programmes

led by senior managers and expert implementers such as occupational health and human resources professionals.

(c) Political and cultural processes that influence organisational change are largely ignored and/or given little detailed, theoretical consideration in the current implementation literature, yet these appear critical in how organisations and their stakeholders go about the process of negotiating and renegotiating the priorities and practices that comprise sustaining wellbeing.

(d) Organisations are dynamic and therefore context is dynamic. Implementing workplace health and wellbeing practices necessarily changes the context. Moreover, as organisations change for other reasons, there is a need to explain how organisations adjust to sustain health and wellbeing programmes.[3]

The model is shown in Fig. 1.1.

Following Johns (2006) and in common with existing models of implementation of specific practices (e.g. Fridrich et al., 2015; Nielsen & Randall, 2013), in our model, we differentiate between omnibus and discrete contexts. The omnibus context refers to the wider organisation and its environment (e.g. prevailing labour market conditions, existing management practices). The discrete context relates to the implementation of a specific practice (i.e. the nature of the specific service being

[3]We have opted to use the term 'programme' in this book because we refer to a managed set of health and wellbeing activities, even where those activities are managed in a largely informal and unplanned manner and when activities initiated by workers in a bottom-up fashion in particular locations or groups are incorporated into that programme, subsuming those instances where bottom-up initiatives are actively encouraged by those responsible for managing the programme. The term 'programme' does not necessarily reflect how practitioners themselves label the range of health and wellbeing activities employed in their organisations.

provided and contextual factors around that service, such as stakeholders' attitudes to the service provider). Organisations adopting multiple health and wellbeing activities will accordingly have multiple discrete contexts corresponding to each of the elements of the entire programme of activities. Here we recognize that organisations adjust their internal environment (e.g. operations, human resources practices) to changes in the external environment (e.g. changes in technologies), which in turn can create opportunities and threats to wellbeing (e.g. training and development opportunities, job insecurity) as well as opportunities and threats to the wellbeing programme. Departing from the dichotomy of internal and external contexts, we insert another layer of context between the omnibus and discrete context: We label this the delivery context that encompasses the processes involved in the management of an entire programme of activities, such as its governance, planning and evaluation, and whether and how stakeholders are consulted/involved in programme governance, planning and evaluation. Each of the three layers of context is dynamic and evolving, and the boundaries between adjacent layers are fuzzy and permeable. For example senior managers involved in the governance of a programme would bring elements of the omnibus context into the delivery context and vice versa: The management of a specific project (e.g. work redesign) would likely involve some of the stakeholders involved in programme governance.

At the centre of the model are three processes that sustain wellbeing (Daniels et al., 2021). These three processes are: (1) learning during implementation in relation to the context of the organisation; so that the practice can be (2) adapted to its context or context adapted to the practice; so that there is (3) continuity of any changes are made. All three processes are interrelated. These are additional to the mechanisms specific to changes in wellbeing brought about by each practice in the programme. For example, at the level of a specific intervention, a group-based mindfulness instruction may improve wellbeing through enhanced mindfulness and/or through enhancing communal activities. These are mechanisms inherent in group-based mindfulness instruction. However, in addition, the group-based mindfulness instruction may need *adaptation* because employees cannot access supporting online materials. This adaptation is based on *learning* on how to provide better access to online materials and so enabling *continuity* in providing the instruction. At a programme level, it may be possible to take this learning about providing access to online resources to other initiatives with online components to enable more rapid adaptation and therefore continuity of these other initiatives.

The last three elements of the model relate to how organisations connect health and wellbeing practices to other organisational procedures, practices and structures. We see these other procedures, practices and structures as both social (e.g. prevailing culture, norms, behavioural routines), administrative (e.g. performance management) and technical (e.g. information systems, production processes). There is highly likely to be tension between the processes of implementing a practice or programme of practices and at least some other organisational processes, practices, structures and actors therein. These conflicts require resolution, which we label:

1. Grafting, which is adapting the practice to be compatible with other organisational procedures, practices and structures. That is the prevailing organisational context influences how a specific practice is adapted. Ensuring compatibility with existing procedures, practices and structures has been recommended in prior reviews focused on workplace wellbeing interventions (Daniels, Gedikli, et al., 2017; Knight et al., 2019; Nielsen & Noblet, 2018). An example would be using existing continuous improvement processes to discuss how to improve health and wellbeing (von Thiele Schwarz et al., 2017).
2. Fracturing, which is changing the organisation to be compatible with the practice by replacing old processes, structures and structures with new ones. That is the prevailing organisational context is influenced by the specific practice. This might be especially important in environments where harmful behaviours and norms are prevalent (Chapleau et al., 2011, e.g. unsafe working practices, abusive supervision, long hours cultures). An example would be to provide training in how to challenge others' harmful behaviours (e.g. Tregaskis et al., 2013).
3. Gestalting, which is bringing different wellbeing practices and other organisational procedures, practices and structures together for simultaneous change in order both to meet common goals or interpretation and hence reduce conflict. An example would be bringing different stakeholder groups together in communities of practice for shared learning (Mabry et al., 2018).

The remainder of the book is structured as follows. In the next chapter, we review existing models of implementation and identify their contributions and the need for explanations of implementation to go beyond a narrow focus on discrete interventions. In Chap. 3, we examine how workplace health and wellbeing interventions may come to have beneficial, adverse or no effects, and begin to examine the role of contextual factors and their influence on whether interventions have effects or not. In Chaps. 4, 5, 6 and 7, we examine implementation in more detail. We examine factors related to the omnibus context in Chap. 4; the role of specific actors and the delivery context in Chap. 5; learning, adaptation and continuity in health and wellbeing programmes in Chap. 6; and the processes of grafting, fracturing and Gestalting in Chap. 7. In the two concluding chapters, we examine how programmes of health and wellbeing activities may come to have effects (beneficial or otherwise) that transcend the effects of the sum of constituent practices (Chap. 8) and the implications of our model for research methods and other areas of enquiry where work organisations may seek to create social value (Chap. 9).

References

Ackroyd, S., & Karlsson, J. C. (2014). Critical realism, research techniques, and research designs. In P. K. Edwards, J. O'Mahoney, & S. Vincent (Eds.), *Studying organizations using critical realism*. Oxford University Press.

Baas, M., De Dreu, C. K., & Nijstad, B. A. (2008). A meta-analysis of 25 years of mood-creativity research: Hedonic tone, activation, or regulatory focus? *Psychological Bulletin, 134*, 779–806.

Bache, I., & Reardon, L. (2016). *The politics and policy of wellbeing: Understanding the rise and significance of a new agenda*. Edward Elgar.

Bartlett, L., Martin, A., Neil, A. L., Memish, K., Otahal, P., Kilpatrick, M., & Sanderson, K. (2019). A systematic review and meta-analysis of workplace mindfulness training randomized controlled trials. *Journal of Occupational Health Psychology, 24*, 108–126.

Batorsky, B., Van Stolk, C., & Liu, H. (2016). Is more always better in designing workplace wellness programs?: A comparison of wellness program components versus outcomes. *Journal of Occupational and Environmental Medicine, 58*, 987–993.

Biron, C., & Karanika-Murray, M. (2015). From black and white to colours: Moving the science of organizational interventions for stress and well-being forward. In C. Biron & M. Karanika-Murray (Eds.), *Derailed organizational interventions for stress and wellbeing: Confessions of failure and solutions for success* (pp. 275–282). Springer.

Burgess, M. G., Brough, P., Biggs, A., & Hawkes, A. J. (2020). Why interventions fail: A systematic review of occupational health psychology interventions. *International Journal of Stress Management, 27*, 195–207.

Carver, C. S., & Scheier, M. F. (1990). Origins and functions of positive and negative affect: A control-process view. *Psychological Review, 97*, 19–35.

Chapleau, A., Seroczynski, A. D., Meyers, S., Lamb, K., & Haynes, S. (2011). Occupational therapy consultation for case managers in community mental health: Exploring strategies to improve job satisfaction and self-efficacy. *Professional Case Management, 16*, 71–79.

Cox, T., Karanika, M., Mellor, N., Lomas, L., Houdmont, J., & Griffiths, A. (2007). *Implementation of the management standards for work-related stress: Process evaluation*. University of Nottingham.

Daniels, K. (2000). Measures of five aspects of affective well-being at work. *Human Relations, 53*, 275–294.

Daniels, K., Connolly, S., Ogbonnaya, C., Tregaskis, O., Bryan, M. L., Robinson-Pant, A., & Street, J. (2018). Democratisation of wellbeing: Stakeholder perspectives on policy priorities for improving national wellbeing through paid employment and adult learning. *British Journal of Guidance and Counselling, 46*, 492–511.

Daniels, K., Gedikli, C., Watson, D., Semkina, A., & Vaughn, O. (2017). Job design, employment practices and well-being: A systematic review of intervention studies. *Ergonomics, 60*, 1177–1196.

Daniels, K., Watson, D., & Gedikli, C. (2017). Well-being and the social environment of work: A systematic review of intervention studies. *International Journal of Environmental Research and Public Health, 14*, 918. https://doi.org/10.3390/ijerph14080918

Daniels, K., Watson, D., Nayani, R., Tregaskis, O., Hogg, M., Etuknwa, A., & Semkina, A. (2021). Implementing practices focused on workplace health and psychological wellbeing: A systematic review. *Social Science and Medicine, 227*, 113888.

Davies, W. (2015). *The happiness industry*. Verso.

Demerouti, E., Bakker, A. B., Nachreiner, F., & Schaufeli, W. B. (2001). The job demands-resources model of burnout. *Journal of Applied Psychology, 86*, 499–512.

Diener, E. (1984). Subjective well-being. *Psychological Bulletin, 95*, 542–575.

Eby, L. T., Allen, T. D., Conley, K. M., Williamson, R. L., Henderson, T. G., & Mancini, V. S. (2019). Mindfulness-based training interventions for employees: A qualitative review of the literature. *Human Resource Management Review, 29*, 156–178.

Egan, M., Bambra, C., Petticrew, M., & Whitehead, M. (2009). Reviewing evidence on complex social interventions: Appraising implementation in systematic reviews of the health effects of organisational-level workplace interventions. *Journal of Epidemiology & Community Health, 63*, 4–11.

ETUC. (2004). *Framework agreement on work-related stress*. European Trade Union Confederation.

Etuknwa, A., Daniels, K., & Eib, C. (2019). Sustainable return to work: A systematic review focusing on personal and social factors. *Journal of Occupational Rehabilitation, 29*, 679–700.

Fox, K. E., Johnson, S. T., Berkman, L. F., Sianoja, M., Soh, Y., Kubzansky, L. D., & Kelly, E. L. (2021). Organisational- and group-level workplace interventions and their effect on multiple domains of worker well-being: A systematic review. *Work & Stress*. https://doi.org/10.1080/02678373.2021.1969476

Fridrich, A., Jenny, G. J., & Bauer, G. F. (2015). The context, process, and outcome evaluation model for organisational health interventions. *BioMed Research International*. https://doi.org/10.1155/2015/414832

Gkorezis, P., Bellou, V., Xanthopoulou, D., Bakker, A. B., & Tsiftsis, A. (2016). Linking football team performance to fans' work engagement and job performance: Test of a spillover model. *Journal of Occupational and Organizational Psychology, 89*, 791–812.

Guest, D. E. (2017). Human resource management and employee well-being: Towards a new analytic framework. *Human Resource Management Journal, 27*, 22–38.

Hadgraft, N. T., Willenberg, L., LaMontagne, A. D., Malkoski, K., Dunstan, D. W., Healy, G. N., Moodie, M., Eakin, E. G., Owen, N., & Lawler, S. P. (2017). Reducing occupational sitting: Workers' perspectives on participation in a multi-component intervention. *International Journal of Behavioral Nutrition and Physical Activity, 14*, 73.

Hancock, P., & Tyler, M. (2004). "MOT your life": Critical management studies and the management of everyday life. *Human Relations, 57*, 619–645.

Herrera-Sánchez, I. M., León-Pérez, J. M., & León-Rubio, J. M. (2017). Steps to ensure a successful Implementation of occupational health and safety interventions at an organizational level. *Frontiers in Psychology, 8*, 2135.

Huppert, F. A., & So, T. T. (2013). Flourishing across Europe: Application of a new conceptual framework for defining well-being. *Social Indicators Research, 110*, 837–861.

ILO (International Labour Organization). (2001). *Guidelines on occupational safety and health management systems*. International Labor Office.

ISO (International Organization for Standardization). (2018). *BS 45002-1:2018. Occupational health and safety management systems. General guidelines for the application of ISO 45001. Guidance on managing occupational health*. International Organization for Standardization.

Janssen, M., Heerkens, Y., Kuijer, W., Van Der Heijden, B., & Engels, J. (2018). Effects of mindfulness-based stress reduction on employees' mental health: A systematic review. *PLoS One, 13*(1), e0191332.

Jenkins, M. (2017). Knowledge and practice mobilities in the process of policy-making: The case of UK national well-being statistics. *Political Geography, 56*, 24–33.

Johns, G. (2006). The essential impact of context on organizational behavior. *Academy of Management Review, 31*, 386–408.

Johnson, S., Robertson, I., & Cooper, C. L. (2018). *Work and Well-being*. Palgrave Macmillan.

Jordan, J., Gurr, E., Tinline, G., Giga, S. I., Faragher, B., & Cooper, C. L. (2003). *Beacons of excellence in stress prevention: Research report 133*. HSE Books.

Joseph, B., Walker, A., & Fuller-Tyszkiewicz, M. (2018). Evaluating the effectiveness of employee assistance programmes: A systematic review. *European Journal of Work and Organizational Psychology, 27*, 1–15.

Karanika-Murray, M., & Biron, C. (2020). The health-performance framework of presenteeism: Towards understanding an adaptive behaviour. *Human Relations, 73*, 242–261.

Kendall, N., Burton, K., Lunt, J., Mellor, N., & Daniels, K. (2015). *Development of an intervention toolbox for common health problems in the workplace*. HSE Books.

Khoury, B., Sharma, M., Rush, S. E., & Fournier, C. (2015). Mindfulness-based stress reduction for healthy individuals: A meta-analysis. *Journal of Psychosomatic Research, 78*, 519–528.

Kivimäki, M., Nyberg, S. T., Batty, G. D., Fransson, E. I., Heikkilä, K., Alfredsson, L., Bjorner, J. B., Borritz, M., Burr, H., Casini, A., Clays, E., De Bacquer, D., Dragano, N., Ferrie, J. E., Geuskens, G. A., Goldberg, M., Hamer, M., Hooftman, W. E., Houtman, I. L., . . . IPD-Work Consortium. (2012). Job strain as a risk factor for coronary heart disease: A collaborative meta-analysis of individual participant data. *The Lancet, 380*, 1491–1497.

Knight, C., Patterson, M., & Dawson, J. (2019). Work engagement interventions can be effective: A systematic review. *European Journal of Work and Organizational Psychology, 28*, 348–372.

Kristman, V. L., Boot, C. R., Sanderson, K., Sinden, K. E., & Williams-Whitt, K. (2020). Implementing best practice models of return to work. In U. Bültmann & J. Siegrist (Eds.), *Handbook of disability, work and health* (pp. 589–613). Springer.

LaMontagne, A. D., Keegel, T., Louie, A. M., Ostry, A., & Landsbergis, P. A. (2007). A systematic review of the job-stress intervention evaluation literature, 1990-2005. *International Journal of Occupational and Environmental Health, 13*, 268–280.

LaMontagne, A. D., Martin, A., Page, K. M., Reavley, N. J., Noblet, A. J., Milner, A. J., Keegel, T., & Smith, P. M. (2014). Workplace mental health: Developing an integrated intervention approach. *BMC Psychiatry, 14*, 1–11.

Layard, R. (2016). *Measuring wellbeing and cost-effectiveness analysis using subjective wellbeing* (Discussion paper 1, measuring wellbeing series, what works centre for wellbeing).

Lazarus, R. S. (1991). *Emotion and adaptation*. Oxford University Press.

Leka, S., & Cox, T. (2008). *PRIMA-EF: Guidance on the European framework for psychosocial risk management. A resource for employers and worker representatives*. World Health Organization.

Leka, S., Griffiths, A., & Cox, T. (2003). *Work organization and stress: Systematic problem approaches for employers, managers and trade union representatives*. World Health Organization.

LePine, J. A., Podsakoff, N. P., & LePine, M. A. (2005). A meta-analytic test of the challenge stressor–hindrance stressor framework: An explanation for inconsistent relationships among stressors and performance. *Academy of Management Journal, 48*, 764–775.

Lomas, T., Medina, J. C., Ivtzan, I., Rupprecht, S., Hart, R., & Eiroa-Orosa, F. J. (2017). The impact of mindfulness on well-being and performance in the workplace: An inclusive systematic review of the empirical literature. *European Journal of Work and Organizational Psychology, 26*, 492–513.

Lyubomirsky, S., King, L., & Diener, E. (2005). The benefits of frequent positive affect: Does happiness lead to success? *Psychological Bulletin, 131*, 803–855.

Mabry, L., Parker, K. N., Thompson, S. V., Bettencourt, K. M., Haque, A., Luther Rhoten, K., Wright, R. R., Hess, J. A., & Olson, R. (2018). Protecting workers in the home care industry: Workers' experienced job demands, resource gaps, and benefits following a socially supportive intervention. *Home Health Care Services Quarterly, 37*, 259–276.

MacKay, C. J., Cousins, R., Kelly, P. J., Lee, S., & McCaig, R. H. (2004). 'Management Standards' and work-related stress in the UK: Policy background and science. *Work & Stress, 18*, 91–112.

Maslach, C., Jackson, S. E., Leiter, M. P., Schaufeli, W. B., & Schwab, R. L. (1986). *Maslach Burnout Inventory* (Vol. 21). Consulting Psychologists Press.

Mattke, S., Kapinos, K., Caloyeras, J. P., Taylor, E. A., Batorsky, B., Liu, H., Van Busum, K. R., & Newberry, S. (2015). Workplace wellness programs: Services offered, participation, and incentives. *Rand Health Quarterly, 5*, 7.

Milner, A., Witt, K., LaMontagne, A. D., & Niedhammer, I. (2018). Psychosocial job stressors and suicidality: A meta-analysis and systematic review. *Occupational and Environmental Medicine, 75*, 245–253.

Mishiba, T. (2020). *Workplace mental health law: Comparative perspectives*. Routledge.

Montano, D., Hoven, H., & Siegrist, J. (2014). Effects of organisational-level interventions at work on employees' health: A systematic review. *BMC Public Health, 14*, 1–9.

Nielsen, K. (2013). How can we make organizational interventions work? Employees and line managers as actively crafting interventions. *Human Relations, 66*, 1029–1050.

Nielsen, K. (2017). Leaders can make or break an intervention—But are they the villains of the piece. In E. K. Kelloway, K. Nielsen, & J. K. Dimoff (Eds.), *Leading to occupational health and safety: How leadership behaviours impact organizational safety and well-being* (pp. 197–209). Wiley.

Nielsen, K., & Randall, R. (2013). Opening the black box: Presenting a model for evaluating organizational-level interventions. *European Journal of Work and Organizational Psychology, 22*, 601–617.

Nielsen, K. M., & Noblet, A. (2018). Organizational interventions: Where we are, where we go from here? In K. Nielsen & A. Noblet (Eds.), *Organizational interventions for health and well-being: A handbook for evidence-based practice* (pp. 1–22). Routledge.

Nussbaum, M., & Sen, A. (1993). *The quality of life*. Oxford University Press.

Nytrø, K., Saksvik, P. Ø., Mikkelsen, A., Bohle, P., & Quinlan, M. (2000). An appraisal of key factors in the implementation of occupational stress interventions. *Work & Stress, 14*, 213–225.

O'Donnell, G., Deaton, A., Durand, M., Halpern, D., & Layard, R. (2014). *Wellbeing and policy*. Legatum Institute.

Oman, S. (2015). Measuring national well-being: What matters to you? What matters to whom? In S. C. White & C. Blackmore (Eds.), *Cultures of wellbeing: Method, place, policy* (pp. 66–94). Palgrave MacMillan.

Oprea, B. T., Barzin, L., Vîrgă, D., Iliescu, D., & Rusu, A. (2019). Effectiveness of job crafting interventions: A meta-analysis and utility analysis. *European Journal of Work and Organizational Psychology, 28*, 723–741.

Proper, K. I., & van Oostrom, S. H. (2019). The effectiveness of workplace health promotion interventions on physical and mental health outcomes—A systematic review of reviews. *Scandinavian Journal of Work, Environment & Health, 45*, 546–559.

Reed, J., & Buck, S. (2009). The effect of regular aerobic exercise on positive-activated affect: A meta-analysis. *Psychology of Sport and Exercise, 10*, 581–594.

Richardson, K. M., & Rothstein, H. R. (2008). Effects of occupational stress management intervention programs: A meta-analysis. *Journal of Occupational Health Psychology, 13*, 69–93.

Rick, J., & Briner, R. B. (2000). Psychosocial risk assessment: Problems and prospects. *Occupational Medicine, 50*, 310–314.

Robertson, I. T., Cooper, C. L., Sarkar, M., & Curran, T. (2015). Resilience training in the workplace from 2003 to 2014: A systematic review. *Journal of Occupational and Organizational Psychology, 88*, 533–562.

Rojatz, D., Merchant, A., & Nitsch, M. (2016). Factors influencing workplace health promotion intervention: A qualitative systematic review. *Health Promotion International, 32*, 831–839.

Rongen, A., Robroek, S. J., van Lenthe, F. J., & Burdorf, A. (2013). Workplace health promotion: A meta-analysis of effectiveness. *American Journal of Preventive Medicine, 44*, 406–415.

Roodbari, H., Axtell, C., Nielsen, K., & Sorensen, G. (2021). *Organisational interventions to improve employees' health and wellbeing: A realist synthesis. An International Review*. https://doi.org/10.1111/apps.12346

Rugulies, R., Aust, B., & Madsen, I. E. (2020). Occupational determinants of affective disorders. In U. Bültmann & J. Siegrist (Eds.), *Handbook of disability, work and health* (pp. 207–304). Springer.

Russell, J., Berney, L., Stansfeld, S., Lanz, D., Kerry, S., Chandola, T., & Bhui, K. (2016). The role of qualitative research in adding value to a randomised controlled trial: Lessons from a pilot study of a guided e-learning intervention for managers to improve employee wellbeing and reduce sickness absence. *Trials, 17*, 396.

Ryff, C. D., & Keyes, C. L. M. (1995). The structure of psychological well-being revisited. *Journal of Personality and Social Psychology, 69*, 719–727.

Schaufeli, W. B., Salanova, M., Gonzalez-Roma, V., & Bakker, A. B. (2002). The measurement of engagement and burnout: A two sample confirmatory factor analytic approach. *Journal of Happiness Studies, 3*, 71–92.

Schaufeli, W. B., & Taris, T. W. (2014). A critical review of the job demands-resources model: Implications for improving work and health. In G. F. Bauer & O. Hämmig (Eds.), *Bridging occupational, organizational and public health* (pp. 43–68). Springer.

Scott, K., & Bell, D. (2013). Trying to measure local well-being: Indicator development as a site of discursive struggles. *Environment and Planning C: Government and Policy, 31*, 522–539.

Sheldon, K. M., & Elliot, A. J. (1999). Goal striving, need satisfaction, and longitudinal well-being: The self-concordance model. *Journal of Personality and Social Psychology, 76*, 482–497.

Spijkerman, M. P. J., Pots, W. T. M., & Bohlmeijer, E. T. (2016). Effectiveness of online mindfulness-based interventions in improving mental health: A review and meta-analysis of randomized controlled trials. *Clinical Psychology Review, 45*, 102–114.

Stansfeld, S., & Candy, B. (2006). Psychosocial work environment and mental health—A meta-analytic review. *Scandinavian Journal of Work, Environment & Health, 32*, 443–462.

Steel, P., Schmidt, J., Bosco, F., & Uggerslev, K. (2019). The effects of personality on job satisfaction and life satisfaction: A meta-analytic investigation accounting for bandwidth–fidelity and commensurability. *Human Relations, 72*, 217–247.

Stratton, E., Lampit, A., Choi, I., Calvo, R. A., Harvey, S. B., & Glozier, N. (2017). Effectiveness of eHealth interventions for reducing mental health conditions in employees: A systematic review and meta-analysis. *PLoS One, 12*, e0189904.

Symitsi, E., Stamolampros, P., & Daskalakis, G. (2018). Employees' online reviews and equity prices. *Economics Letters, 162*, 53–55.

Then, F. S., Luck, T., Luppa, M., Thinschmidt, M., Deckert, S., Nieuwenhuijsen, K., Seidler, A., & Riedel-Heller, S. G. (2014). Systematic review of the effect of the psychosocial working environment on cognition and dementia. *Occupational and Environmental Medicine, 71*, 358–365.

Thomas, J. P., Whitman, D. S., & Viswesvaran, C. (2010). Employee proactivity in organizations: A comparative meta-analysis of emergent proactive constructs. *Journal of Occupational and Organizational Psychology, 83*, 275–300.

Thoresen, C. J., Kaplan, S. A., Barsky, A. P., Warren, C. R., & De Chermont, K. (2003). The affective underpinnings of job perceptions and attitudes: A meta-analytic review and integration. *Psychological Bulletin, 129*, 914–945.

Tomlinson, M. W., & Kelley, G. P. (2013). Is everybody happy? The politics and measurement of national wellbeing. *Policy & Politics, 41*, 139–157.

Tregaskis, O., Daniels, K., Glover, L., Butler, P., & Meyer, M. (2013). High performance work practices and firm performance: A longitudinal case study. *British Journal of Management, 24*, 225–244.

Van de Ven, D., Robroek, S. J., & Burdorf, A. (2020). Are workplace health promotion programmes effective for all socioeconomic groups? A systematic review. *Occupational and Environmental Medicine, 77*, 589–596.

Vanhove, A. J., Herian, M., Perez, A. L., Harms, P. D., & Lester, P. B. (2016). Can resilience be developed at work? A meta-analytic review of resilience-building programme effectiveness. *Journal of Occupational and Organizational Psychology, 89*, 278–307.

Van Veldhoven, M., Van den Broeck, A., Daniels, K., Bakker, A. B., Tavares, S. M., & Ogbonnaya, C. (2020). Challenging the universality of job resources: Why, when, and for whom are they beneficial? *Applied Psychology, 69*, 5–29.

Van Wingerden, J., Derks, D., & Bakker, A. B. (2017). The impact of personal resources and job crafting interventions on work engagement and performance. *Human Resource Management, 56*, 51–67.

Virgili, M. (2015). Mindfulness-based interventions reduce psychological distress in working adults: A meta-analysis of intervention studies. *Mindfulness, 6*, 326–337.

von Thiele Schwarz, U., Nielsen, K. M., Stenfors-Hayes, T., & Hasson, H. (2017). Using kaizen to improve employee well-being: Results from two organizational intervention studies. *Human Relations, 70*, 966–993.

Warr, P. (1990). The measurement of well-being and other aspects of mental health. *Journal of Occupational Psychology, 63*, 193–210.

Waterman, A. S. (1993). Two conceptions of happiness: Contrasts of personal expressiveness (eudaimonia) and hedonic enjoyment. *Journal of Personality and Social Psychology, 64*, 678–691.

Watson, D., Tregaskis, O., Gedikli, C., Vaughn, O., & Semkina, A. (2018). Well-being through learning: A systematic review of learning interventions in the workplace and their impact on well-being. *European Journal of Work and Organizational Psychology, 27*, 247–268.
White, S. C. (2017). Relational wellbeing: Re-centring the politics of happiness, policy and the self. *Policy & Politics, 45*, 121–136.
Whitman, D. S., Van Rooy, D. L., & Viswesvaran, C. (2010). Satisfaction, citizenship behaviors, and performance in work units: A meta-analysis of collective construct relations. *Personnel Psychology, 63*, 41–81.
Xanthopoulou, D., Bakker, A. B., Demerouti, E., & Schaufeli, W. B. (2009). Work engagement and financial returns: A diary study on the role of job and personal resources. *Journal of Occupational and Organizational Psychology, 82*, 183–200.

Chapter 2
Conceptual Models of Intervention Implementation

In this chapter, we present a review of existing reviews and conceptual models of implementing workplace health and wellbeing interventions, alongside a typology of those models.[1] Our purpose is to delineate what existing reviews and conceptual models have achieved, but also what they do not explain, therein justifying an alternative theoretical or conceptual lens to ones currently used. We start by describing models and reviews according to whether they provide guidance on how to conduct research studies of interventions, guidance to practitioners on how to implement interventions or whether they provide a synthesis of evidence on implementation for specific interventions or implementation factors. We conclude the chapter with a summary of existing frameworks according to their features and characteristics, unit of analysis, focus, and contributions, as well as summarizing the case for developing an alternative and complementary conceptual model.

Frameworks to Guide Researchers

Frameworks to guide researchers are focused on what to measure in evaluation research. Outside of research on workplace interventions, Pawson's notion of Context, Mechanisms and Outcomes (CMO) configurations and other concepts from realist evaluation frameworks (Greenhalgh, 2014; Moore et al., 2015; Pawson & Manzano-Santaella, 2012) have been influential in shaping thinking on how to evaluate of complex health interventions involving social processes. However, realist evaluation per se has had little direct influence on studies of implementing workplace health and wellbeing practices and programmes (for exceptions see e.g. Abildgaard et al., 2020; Busch et al., 2017; von Thiele Schwarz et al., 2017). Within realist evaluation, the unit of analysis is the intervention, or more accurately

[1] The methodology for this review is presented in the Technical Appendix.

K. Daniels et al., *Achieving Sustainable Workplace Wellbeing*, Aligning Perspectives on Health, Safety and Well-Being, https://doi.org/10.1007/978-3-031-00665-4_2

the programme theory that describes how the intervention works (Greenhalgh, 2014). CMO configurations refer to the specific mechanism or mechanisms (M) activated in a specific context (C) that cause an intervention to have an effect on some outcome or range of outcomes (O) (Pawson & Manzano-Santaella, 2012). An intervention may have multiple mechanisms activated in different contexts that have the same or different outcomes. Some variants of realist evaluation require CMO configurations to be specified a priori (Moore et al., 2015, see also Nielsen & Miraglia, 2017). One problem here is that complex change may be hard to predict, and it may be difficult to specify a priori how, in any given context, a specific intervention may activate mechanisms (Dahler-Larsen, 2001; Fridrich et al., 2015; cf. Russell et al., 2016): Thus, there remains a need to use inductive as well as deductive methods to detect unanticipated mechanisms. Notwithstanding, realist evaluation seeks to develop theoretical explanation by building upward from the empirical evidence across studies. However, Pawson and colleagues argue this theory-building goal has not been achieved and cite overly localized and a short-term focus in how realist evaluation is used, rather than building a cumulative body of evidence underpinning a more general theory (Pawson, 2006; Pawson & Manzano-Santaella, 2012). At a more general level of analysis, realist evaluation refers to an approach to investigating complex interventions: It does not provide conceptual tools for understanding how changes come about and are sustained in organisations.

Nielsen and Abildgaard (2013) presented an evaluation framework for workplace health and wellbeing interventions that traced some of its development to realist evaluation and CMO configurations. This evaluation framework indicates research studies should focus on four areas of how interventions come to have their effects: The organisational actors who may influence implementation, the mental models of those actors that explain their behaviours, elements of the context that may influence intervention outcomes, and intervention design and processes. Nielsen and Abildgaard propose interventions go through five stepped stages in a linear fashion: (1) initiation of the project, (2) initial screening or baseline assessment, (3) action planning of steps in the intervention, (4) implementation of the intervention, and (5) effect evaluation. The implication of this stepped process is that organisations are expected to follow a sequence of planned activities in a fixed sequence so that the intervention can be evaluated, which does not accord with accepted models of organisational change, which can be far more iterative and unplanned (cf., Alvesson & Sveningsson, 2016; Balogun, 2006; Mintzberg, 1994; Weick & Quinn, 1999), thus a process may be imposed on organisations that bear little or no resemblance to organisational reality. Moreover, in this framework, the wider organisational (omnibus) context is treated as a fixed entity that does not itself change or is changed by the intervention, and the focus is the intervention: 'the framework emphasises the necessity to investigate the whole process, from beginning an intervention programme to post-intervention evaluation' (p. 292). As Nielsen and Abildgaard also acknowledge, the framework neglects 'aspects of organizational life, such as the different interests of various groups (employees/managers), power relations and other factors' (p. 292).

De Angelis et al. (2020) presented a protocol for a study of workplace interventions targeting mental health. Although a protocol for a specific study, the protocol itself could provide a template for evaluation of workplace health and wellbeing interventions because of both the breadth of the study (multiple organisations) and flexibility in the choice of interventions offered to organisations. Like other frameworks, De Angelis et al. specify that organisations should proceed through a sequence of prescribed activities in a given order: (1) needs analysis based on underpinning theories informing the specific interventions on offer to organisations; (2) choice of intervention(s) made by managers/policy makers followed by participatory processes in intervention implementation, with the research team collecting data and providing feedback to allow adaptations as needed throughout implementation; (3) cost-effectiveness analysis. As well as prescribing a series of activities that may be convenient for research design purposes but not reflect how many organisations operate in practice, the research team itself is highly involved in implementation by providing feedback for adaptation. Although this may seem sensible given the complexity of implementation, as noted in the previous chapter, teams of researchers evaluating interventions and helping with their implementation may be the exception rather than the norm for organisational practices targeted at health and wellbeing. Moreover, as found by Tyers et al. (2009), the assistance of stakeholders with a vested interest in intervention success may lead to more positive outcomes than would otherwise be the case if that assistance was not available.

Von Thiele Schwarz et al. (2021) also present a framework to guide researchers in evaluation research that attempts to address the twin aims of rigorous evaluation alongside practical impact. As well as being limited to situations when researchers are actively engaged in implementation, the framework also is based on a linear sequence of activities of design, implementation and evaluation. One of ten principles may apply to one or more of these sequenced activities. These are (1) engagement and participation of key stakeholders; (2) understanding of the wider organisational context; (3) alignment of the intervention with existing organisational objectives (rather than vice versa); (4) developing an explicit programme logic or theory; (5) prioritizing intervention activities that are most cost-effective in terms of the ratio of benefits to resources and effort invested; (6) ensuring the compatibility of the intervention with existing practices, processes and mindsets; (7) observing, reflecting and adapting the intervention as it progresses; (8) developing learning capabilities within the organisation such that (some) knowledge learnt through collaboration with research teams stays within the organisation; (9) evaluating the intervention and its interactions with implementation processes and various elements of the context; and (10) dissemination of learning beyond the intervention site (e.g. scientific publication).

Many other work-specific frameworks focus on lists of more specific factors to evaluate in research on workplace health and wellbeing interventions. Egan et al. (2009) produced a thematic checklist based on a review of the literature. Included in this checklist were: Motivation—reason for intervention/management decision Theory of change—was this incorporated into intervention design?; Implementation context; Experience—competence of implementers, and participants if they were performing new roles; Planning consultations—participative processes during planning; Delivery collaborations—participative processes during implementation; Manager support; Employee support; Resources; Differential effects and population effects. Similar checklists have been produced by Nielsen & Randall (2013, based on a conceptual review, the factors in Nielsen and Randall's framework were subsequently applied in a systematic review by Havermans et al., 2016) and Fridrich et al. (2015, based on conceptual review). Both Nielsen and Randall and Fridrich et al. located their checklist in evaluation frameworks.

Nielsen and Randall's (2013) list of factors to evaluate has three overarching themes: intervention design and implementation, the intervention contexts, and participants' mental models of the intervention and their work situation. Within intervention design and implementation, Nielsen and Randall recommend researchers ask questions around: the actors who initiated the intervention and their goals; the activities targeted by the intervention; the reach of the intervention into the target group; stakeholders and other factors influencing change; the levels of worker involvement in decision-making around the intervention and the information they were provided; the role played by senior managers, middle managers and consultants. Within context and following Johns (2006), Nielsen and Randall differentiate the omnibus context from the discrete context. Questions about omnibus context relate to the participants in the intervention; key actors driving the intervention; where and when the intervention takes place; the fit of the intervention within existing conditions in the intervention group. Questions about the discrete context relate to the events that take place during implementation. Mental models refer to the factors such as understandings of the intervention, readiness for change, experience with similar interventions, and degree of sharedness of mental models.

Fridrich et al. (2015) present an evaluation framework based on Context, Process and Outcomes, which does bear some similarity to realist evaluation frameworks. Context is defined as the underlying frame that influences and is influenced by the intervention. Again, context is further differentiated into the omnibus and discrete contexts (Johns, 2006). Process is differentiated into the implementation process, as the time-limited enactment of the original intervention plan, and the change process of individual and collective dynamics triggered by the implementation process. These processes lead to proximate, intermediate and distal outcomes. Context is seen as something that both hinders or facilitates the implementation process, but something transformable and part of the intervention. The model has a number of phases, the preparation phase, the action cycle phase, and the appropriation phase, which again suggests or imposes a sequence of activities on organisations that usually they may not follow.

One other systematic review (Wierenga et al., 2013) and three other conceptual reviews (Biron & Karanika-Murray, 2014; Nielsen, 2013, 2017) have also focused on what researchers should evaluate. Wierenga et al. identified five main categories that affected the implementation of workplace health and wellbeing interventions: (1) characteristics of the socio-political context, (2) characteristics of the organisation—including management support, (3) characteristics of the implementer, (4) characteristics of the intervention programme, and (5) characteristics of the participant. Biron and Karanika-Murray (2014) discuss possible mechanisms for changes in health and wellbeing, including emotional contagion and shared meaning (identity, psychosocial safety climate, Dollard & Karasek, 2010). Likewise, Nielsen (2013) argues that line managers and workers are active crafters of workplace health and wellbeing interventions and suggests a number of micro-theories may help explain this process: job crafting; social identity theory; broaden-and-build; leadership. Nielsen (2017) suggests the importance of different stakeholder groups in the implementation process (senior managers, line/middle managers, workers) and their readiness for change, perceptions of intervention relevance, skills and resources. Nielsen (2017) also suggests a climate of organisational learning is a facilitating factor for implementation of workplace health and wellbeing interventions.

Despite some attempts to link to different theories that may explain how interventions have effects or how interventions can be embedded, the evaluation frameworks and other conceptual reviews have not been synthesized into a coherent conceptual account of the implementation of workplace health and wellbeing programmes. Rather the evaluation frameworks and conceptual reviews tend to list factors, or classes of factors, to examine rather than specifying how those factors work with recourse to underlying principles and processes of organisation. Many prescribe that interventions go through specific, pre-planned phases in a pre-determined manner, leaving little or no scope for intervention adaptation or abandoning one form of intervention in favour of another as circumstances change.

Frameworks to Guide Practice

A number of sources have presented prescriptions for how best to implement workplace health and wellbeing interventions. Some of these are based on practitioner experience (e.g. Campbell, 2014), some on reviews of the literature (e.g. Kendall et al., 2015) and some on a mixture of literature reviews and empirical evidence (predominantly case studies, e.g. Tyers et al., 2009).

Jordan et al. (2003) produced a 'good practice' model consisting of four components: (1) Top management commitment (and culture change); (2) ongoing risk analysis; (3) multifocal interventions in a comprehensive and continually improving programme that has prevention as a key aim; and iv) a widescale participative approach. Like others (e.g. Dewe & Cooper, 2014), Jordan et al. indicate health and wellbeing programmes should have multiple components (primary preventive, secondary, tertiary) and can have components that are manager or worker initiated and led. Jordan et al. indicate the importance of multichannel communication, involvement of a range of stakeholders (senior managers, middle managers, workers, experts such as occupational health and human resources specialists) and changes in organisational culture as a potential mechanism of change. Elements of culture change can be triggered by senior management speeches and other symbolic acts (e.g. commitment of resources) and setting wellbeing targets (e.g. number of wellbeing initiatives implemented). Jordan et al. also point to the integration of wellbeing into existing systems, such as management development programmes, employee voice mechanisms and appraisal systems.

The UK Health and Safety Executive (HSE, 2017/2019) has also produced its own set of guidance on implementing the HSE's Management Standards for Work-Related Stress. The Management Standards are the recommended approach to meeting UK legal requirements to prevent work-related psychological injury and are focused on job quality and the social environment of work. The HSE recommend a staged, sequential process:

1. Preparation ('Prepare the organisation'): This stage involves activities such as developing a business case, obtaining senior management support, consultation with employees and/or employee representatives, setting up a multi-stakeholder steering group, identifying a project lead and project manager, developing a project plan, obtaining resources, developing a communications plan strategy, and developing a (written) stress policy.
2. Understanding risks ('Identify the risk factors'): This phase involves developing understanding of the HSE approach amongst key implementers.
3. Risk assessment ('Who can be harmed and how'): This involves activities such as analysis of existing data or gathering new data, communicating findings form data analysis.
4. Developing risk management strategies ('Evaluate the risks—explore problems and develop solutions'): This stage includes consultation with employees, developing solutions and action plans for implementation, monitoring and reviewing actions. This stage also involves putting in place procedures that recognize individuals may have different concerns, which relates to developing a social environment where there is support for individuals.
5. Implementing risk management strategies ('Record your findings—develop and implement action plans'): As well as implementation, this stage also involves explicitly recording findings from the previous stage, developing an overall plan and prioritizing different elements of that plan.
6. Continuous improvement through reviewing policies, actions and developing managers' competencies ('Monitor and review').

Two succeeding frameworks to earlier versions of the HSE's approach were based on empirical investigations of the HSE Management Standards (Cox et al., 2007, also included a literature review; Tyers et al., 2009). Cox et al. point to a number of factors that need to be taken into account during implementation: including organisational factors; the intervention strategy—which should be holistic, systemic, clear and planned; involvement of and dialogue with various stakeholder groups; organisational capability—competence and resources; any interference from competing projects and restructuring; the external context; communication; organisational learning; senior management support; already good levels of management practice; corporate values; and sustainability and integration of processes. They also point to factors such as readiness for change, engagement or resistance to the intervention, motivation, having appropriate roles and responsibilities, level of participation and management capacity.

Tyers et al.'s (2009) recommendations were based on 113 interviews in organisations that were initial adopters of the HSE framework, having received additional support for implementation from the HSE and the UK Arbitration and Consultation Service (ACAS, which supports workplace employment relations). Interestingly, of 100 organisations that had volunteered to 'pioneer' the Management Standards approach, 38 dropped out of the trial and most of the rest had not many any changes within an 18-24 month timeframe. These findings underline the need to consider the reality of attempting change in organisations and suggest, even with HSE and ACAS support, the HSE's recommended approach is difficult to implement. Nevertheless, Tyers et al. did identify some facilitating and inhibiting factors for implementation:

1. Existing organisational capability at the start of the process.
2. Adaptation and learning to embed any changes.
3. Full and sustained senior management commitment for progress on implementation.
4. Project managers/champions in more senior positions.
5. Involvement of a motivated/competent key personnel that did not have conflicting priorities/demands on time.
6. Smaller steering groups with senior representation. Senior representation provided credibility. Smaller steering groups were easier to schedule.
7. Maintaining communication, which was difficult over time.
8. Convening focus groups.
9. Involvement of authoritative, outside facilitation (e.g. ACAS), notably for obtaining senior management commitment.
10. Suppression of negative findings in some organisations meant detailed issues were not discussed.
11. Some organisations adopted small-scale changes and/or changes that could easily be integrated into existing initiatives (e.g. incorporating wellbeing into scheduled management development).

Nielsen and Noblet (2018) developed guidance for interventions directed at primary prevention through job/work redesign, and so is related to the HSE Management Standards approach in this and other respects. The guidance was developed from an earlier model (Nielsen et al., 2010) and again prescribes a set sequence of planned activities that organisations should progress through in a linear manner (preparation/ initiation, screening and feedback, action planning, implementation of action plans and evaluation). The last step involves re-initiation of the first in a systematic ongoing process, as is also captured in the idea of continuous improvement embedded in the HSE's Management Standards approach. Nielsen and Noblet suggest effective implementation is built on key principles of participation, management support, building employee readiness for change, a communication strategy and fit of the intervention with existing organisational procedures, practices and structures.

Dollard and Karasek (2010) refer to the concept of psychosocial safety climate that reflects policies, practices, and procedures for the protection of worker psychological health and safety. Dollard and Karasek view psychosocial safety climate as a cultural concept that influences the adoption of health and wellbeing practices and in turn worker health and wellbeing. Dollard and Karasek take a hierarchy of controls perspective, which is a common approach to workplace harm prevention, including primary, secondary and tertiary interventions. Dollard and Karasek argue that targeting psychosocial safety climate represents a whole organisation approach to health and wellbeing practices. Dollard and Karasek see key elements of building psychosocial safety climate as senior management commitment, involvement of all levels of the organisation in decisions and responsibility at all levels, consultation and two-way communication.

Mellor and Webster (2011) presented a 'comprehensive wellbeing strategy implementation framework', involving enablers, key stakeholders, communications and worker involvement, needs analysis, choice of intervention and evaluation. Mellor and Webster listed enablers as: Strategic alignment of programme, including incorporation of wellbeing into the organisational mission and regular reporting to board on wellbeing; senior leadership support; line manager support; and readiness for change—commitment from all stakeholders and capabilities to implement change. Mellor and Webster recommended multidisciplinary teams of key stakeholders co-ordinate the wellbeing programme, and that these key stakeholders should ensure buy-in and support. Communications and worker involvement were argued to be important to ensure programmes were tailored to worker needs. Needs assessment included risk assessments as well as provision of self-assessment and advice for healthy lifestyles. Choice of interventions was made through consultation and involvement with employees.

Ammendolia et al. (2016) provided an example of how intervention mapping can be used in practice for workplace health promotion and to reduce presenteeism. Intervention mapping (Bartholomew et al., 2016) is a staged process for implementing complex health interventions in social settings. Intervention mapping has six steps: (1) Development of a logic model of the problem (including, e.g. needs assessment); (2) Development of a logic model of outcomes and a logic model of change (including, e.g. a statement of change objectives; (3) Programme design (including choice of behaviour change methods if appropriate); (4) Programme production (including, e.g. drafting communications); (5) Developing a programme implementation plan (including, e.g. identifying users); and (6) Developing an evaluation plan (including, e.g. developing indicators for assessment). Intervention mapping should involve a multi-stakeholder steering group, including end users, and so has participatory processes embedded in the approach. As well as following a sequence of pre-defined stages, Ammendolia et al. also recommended mandatory training for managers on priority health conditions; regular and effective communication between senior management and managers through webinars or video conferencing; having a highly notable and respected champion; incorporating health objectives into annual performance plans, and action plans for senior managers focused on improved communication using multimedia and multi-pronged approaches.

In a systematic review of intervention mapping in occupational health interventions, Bakhuys Roozeboom et al. (2021) noted that in practice, not all steps of intervention mapping were followed in every study. Bakhuys et al. noted particular problems with mapping of change objectives, which Bakhuys et al. considered to be too complex, difficult or time consuming in organisational contexts. Bakhuys et al. also concluded there was no clear relationship between how closely organisations followed the prescriptions of intervention mapping and implementation, except that implementation seemed to be greatest when a theory based/logic model approach was adopted (cf. Burgess et al., 2020). Bakhuys et al. also suggested that intervention mapping as a process for implementing workplace health and wellbeing interventions could be developed to focus more on organisational context and that being able to adapt the intervention plan during implementation may contribute to success.

Like many others, von Thiele Schwarz et al. (2016) developed a staged process (Dynamic Integrated Evaluation Model, DIEM). Unlike other practice-based approaches, DIEM focuses on co-creation of knowledge between organisational stakeholders and researchers (thus rendering academic independence in evaluation difficult and requiring a great deal of reflexivity on the part of research teams). In this respect, it is unclear whether the model, as it is intended to be used, would be appropriate in the majority of situations when expert research teams are not present in organisation. However, the co-created approach means extensive consultation with multiple stakeholders through the process and the approach does recognize intervention activities evolve and are adapted over time in unpredictable ways.

DIEM has eight steps. There are some feedback elements, but the process is mainly a linear sequences of activities. Steps 1 and 2 are concerned with determining objectives and outcomes. Step 3 is about designing the intervention. Step 4 contextualizes the intervention, which entails consulting with stakeholders to identify potential moderators in the relationship between the intervention and outcomes (as defined by stakeholders in earlier steps). At this stage, it may become apparent that further interventions are needed to augment the effects of the intervention designed in Step 3 (e.g. adding individual assertiveness training to a group-level activity aimed at increasing job autonomy). Step 5 concerns iterative improvement cycles, which involves initial implementation and then adaptation of the intervention—these adaptations are held to be rapid and data driven. Steps 6, 7 and 8 entail evaluation of how the intervention was implemented and intervention outcomes For Steps 5 through 8, von Thiele Schwarz et al. recommend using data that is already routinely collected by organisations as much as possible.

Another staged process has been recommended by Herrera-Sánchez et al. (2017), who propose ten steps that lead to successful implementation of interventions at the organisational level: (1) Problem definition; (2) Analysis of resources and support; (3) Clarification of goals and objectives for the intervention; (4) Investigation of existing and effective interventions that can be adapted to the current context; (5) Clarification of the intervention to be implemented and its components; (6) Building and empowering implementation teams; (7) Establishing an organisational infrastructure for implementation, for example leadership support and resourcing; (8) Piloting and adapting the intervention; (9) Further adaptation of the intervention during full implementation; (10) Achieving sustainability through embedding the intervention into organisational routines. Herrera-Sánchez et al. also indicate potential importance of alignment with organisation mission and values for intervention maintenance, sustainability and institutionalization. They also note there has been limited investigation of achieving sustainability of workplace interventions.

Based on a scoping review, Rasmussen et al. (2018) suggest 11 practice-based components that lead to successful implementation:

1. Engaged, competent and active management.
2. Initiatives that are meaningful to end users, supported by easy to access and simple, practical tools.
3. The initiative must be developed in such a way that a focus is maintained on core work tasks.
4. A clear, structured process that is appropriately resourced (e.g., people, time, finances).
5. Organisational perseverance with the initiative and understanding of the initiative in the organisation.
6. The initiative should address current workplace needs.
7. The initiative must be easy to maintain and easy to communicate to relevant stakeholders.
8. Multi-stakeholder participation/involvement.
9. The initiative is focused on the workplace community, there is an expectation that the initiative will be beneficial, and there is a project champion or 'pioneer'.
10. Support from the occupational safety and health system and co-operation with employee representatives.
11. Innovative and attractive content/presentation of the initiative.

Other sources directed at factors associated with successful implementation include Biron and Karanika-Murray (2014), Morris and Morris (2014), Campbell (2014), Kendall et al. (2015) and Lehmann et al. (2019). Biron and Karanika-Murray listed a range of factors that would lead to successful implementation, including ongoing monitoring of implementation processes, specific achievable and measurable goals, allocation of roles and responsibilities and clear communication plans. Morris and Morris listed a number of necessary but not sufficient conditions for workplace health promotion interventions, including awareness and knowledge; financial incentives for participation which should be mixed with factors directed as promoting intrinsic motivation to participate; effective goal setting—including breaking larger goals into smaller goals, building self-efficacy through mastery experiences, role modelling, improving physical or psychological states, verbal persuasion; comprehensive planning and programming of an integrated package; providing support networks.

Campbell (2014) recommended:

1. Early establishment of goals and success criteria.
2. Building momentum by first aiming first for 'low hanging fruit' targeting potential early adopters in order to influence later adopters.
3. Using existing processes/resources in the organisation for implementation.

4. Sponsorship from senior leaders to signal the organisational importance of health and wellbeing.
5. A multi-stakeholder steering group, including a project manager, end users, a co-ordinator, someone to spread wellness ideas, someone with appropriate skills in designing promotional materials, and a health professional to advise on evidence-based practices.
6. Programme branding that is appealing and novel.
7. Using of multiple channels to communicate a single and clear message.

Kendall et al. (2015) developed a practitioner toolbox with four major modules: (a) Preparation, (b) Developing good jobs, (c) Developing supportive workplaces, (d) Organisational learning. Kendall et al. recommend that the choice of actions in each module are subject to three tests before implementation: (a) responsive to worker needs yet flexible enough to be implemented; (b) acceptable to all relevant stakeholders; (c) choosing the option(s) that give(s) the best return on investment compared to other options as well as being consistent with other policies and practices. Kendall et al. also noted that implementing health and wellbeing practices required multi-stakeholder commitment, involvement and co-operation.

Like frameworks to help researchers evaluate interventions (previous section), frameworks and guidance for practice are prescriptive accounts that are largely atheoretical and are not anchored in theoretical processes of organisational change, which can be non-linear, unplanned and highly iterative (although Morris and Morris' (2014) prescriptions are based partially on individual behaviour change theories rather than collective organisational change). Although Dollard and Karasek (2010) propose a theoretical concept that influences the adoption of health and wellbeing practices (psychosocial safety climate), they do not provide details of the processes through which psychosocial safety climate can be changed. There is also a great deal of overlap between the content of evaluation frameworks and the content of practice frameworks (indeed von Thiele Schwarz et al., 2016 could be placed in either category). Both sets of frameworks, for instance, highlight the roles of multiple stakeholders and highlight the use of planned sequences of activities and tend to portray workplace health and wellbeing interventions as progressing in a linear sequential fashion. There are also elements in some of the models of integrating new practices into existing systems, which we label 'grafting' (Chaps. 1 and 7), some do hint at the importance of establishing a coherent narrative around the interventions in respect of communications, but there is very little if anything in practice models in respect of replacing existing practices with new ones ('fracturing') and the political/cultural processes involved in enacting such fracturing activities (Gersick, 1991; Johnson, 1987, 1990; Westover, 2010).

Prior Systematic Reviews

There have been systematic reviews oriented towards providing researchers with checklists of variables/concepts to assess in implementation research (Havermans et al., 2016; Wierenga et al., 2013) and a scoping review designed to guide practice (Rasmussen et al., 2018). There have been six other systematic reviews that have sought to provide evidence on implementation of specific types of workplace health and wellbeing interventions or specific factors.

In a review of process evaluations of workplace stress management interventions, Murta et al. (2007) identified support from management and supervisors as important to implementation, along with positive attitudes towards the intervention, intensity of intervention and feedback on behaviour change.

Rojatz et al. (2016) reviewed factors influencing the implementation of workplace health promotion interventions. As well as methodological issues, they identified five main substantive categories of factors that could influence implementation:

1. Factors at the contextual level comprising, for example wider economic conditions and project management of the intervention.
2. Factors at organisational level referring to factors such as management support and resourcing for the intervention.
3. Factors at intervention level referring to characteristics of the intervention, such as how the intervention was promoted.
4. Factors at implementer level (e.g. trainers and peer-leaders), such implementer personality.
5. Factors at participant level such as participants' commitment to the intervention.

Hoefsmit et al. (2012) examined factors influencing the success of return to work (RTW)/rehabilitation interventions. They found that the characteristics of successful RTW interventions were: Early intervention, involvement of multidisciplinary care professionals and employers, targeted interventions for specific health conditions. For physical conditions, there was evidence that involving employees in decision-making about return to work was associated with intervention success, but there were no studies in the review that examined employee involvement in RTW decisions for people with psychological health conditions. Also, in relation to psychological health conditions, Hoefsmith et al. found no consistent evidence linking the success of an intervention to following a prescribed sequence of activities in the intervention or intervention intensity.

Moran et al. (2014) reviewed evidence in relation to a specific form of intervention for a specific population (mentoring support for healthcare practitioners). They identified several relevant implementation factors, including: involvement of stakeholders from design through implementation; organisational/leadership commitment and support; access to training for the intervention; needs analysis; feedback and evaluation; intervention promotion; appropriate resources, including external facilitation; methods for improving supportive relationships such as networking.

Similar to Moran et al. (2014), Kletter et al. (2021) examined a specific form of intervention, namely workplace positive psychology interventions, for health workers. Kletter et al. identified a range of barriers and facilitators, which were summarized as facilitators (i.e. barriers were reversed) as follows (see Table 2 of Kletter et al.):

- *Stage 1: 'Before design and implementation of intervention'*. Factors listed here included trust in management; staff morale; workers receptive to changes; perceived need for intervention; past success of other interventions.
- *Stage2: 'During design and initial implementation of intervention'*. Factors listed here included buy-in from leadership and workers; clarity of communication around the intervention; committed intervention champions; organisational support for the intervention; feasibility of the intervention feasible given existing work demands.
- *Stage 3: 'During the intervention'*. Factors listed here included authentic and optimistic intervention delivery; adequacy of training workshops and other materials in respect of factors such as quantity, duration and access; reminders to participate and reinforcement for participation.

Kletter et al. (2021) developed a logic model for workplace positive psychology interventions based on realist evaluation principles, in which contextual factors influence the activation of mechanisms. However, the logic model again followed a linear progression through stages and did not incorporate any feedback loops that would allow for iterative development of a given intervention or change of approach. However, the logic model did make explicit links between activated mechanisms and improvements in organisational performance. These links indicate at a conceptual level at least, an acknowledgement of the potential for health and wellbeing practices to influence aspects of the organisational context.

Passey et al. (2018) concentrated specifically on managers' support for employee wellness programmes. They identified the following as influences on managers' support for such programmes: management involvement in implementation, senior management support, role expectations and demands, training on employee health, and managers' attitudes towards employee health. Passey et al. also found that managers' support for employee wellness programmes may be an influence on organisational culture, managers' own support for wellness programmes and employees' behaviours.

In summary, existing systematic reviews have, like many frameworks and models developed to guide researchers or practitioners, tended to focus on specific variables rather than providing explanatory accounts of how interventions come to be implemented and then sustained over time. Although Kletter et al. (2021) developed a logic model from their systematic review, like all other models, there is a prescribed series of steps to go through in implementation, and like most of other models, these steps proceed in a linear manner with no scope for iteration.

Categorizing Existing Frameworks and the Case for an Alternative Approach

So far, we have treated the different frameworks and models as falling into three categories: Those derived to help researchers understand implementation processes; those derived to aid practitioners with implementation; and summaries of evidence derived from syntheses of existing research on implementation of workplace interventions. A more nuanced picture of these frameworks has been presented by Daniels, Watson, et al. (2021), who categorized the various frameworks and models in a five-fold typology, which in turn can be divided into frameworks that seek to evaluate the factors that contribute to intervention success (implementation frameworks, appraisal frameworks, realist frameworks) and models that specify best practice (best practice models, and a sub-set of best practice models focused on achieving regulatory compliance). This typology is reproduced in Table 2.1. Of these realist frameworks have been discussed in more detail above, although the other categories have not been summarized, rather constituent exemplars have been described in detail.

Implementation frameworks focus on providing best practice guidance on how to undertake workplace health and wellbeing interventions, what should go into a successful intervention and why the content should look as it does for intervention success. These frameworks have been generated from systematic and conceptual reviews, scrutinized for mapping of the content, structure and process of intervention implementation. The temporal nature of implementation comes to the fore in implementation frameworks, represented through planning models and rational action models that segment the implementation process into phases, e.g. preparation, action cycle and appropriation (Fridrich et al., 2015; Nielsen & Randall, 2013). Implementation is conveyed as dynamic in that these frameworks identify a vast array of possible mechanisms for changes in health and wellbeing, such as psychological (e.g. emotional contagion, shared meanings or readiness for change, identity; Biron & Karanika-Murray, 2014; Nielsen, 2017); organisational support (e.g. climate for organisational learning, skills and resources; Nielsen, 2017); job crafting (Nielsen, 2013, 2017); and, occupational group (senior managers, middle managers or workers; Nielsen, 2017). A key strength of the implementation frameworks is the breadth of concepts that they are able to encompass. However, an acknowledged limitation from this community is the lack of theory development (Biron & Karanika-Murray, 2015).

Appraisal frameworks focus on providing researchers with a route map for planning and designing interventions for effectiveness evaluation. As such, they take an analytical approach to reviewing empirical evidence and conceptual arguments through a focus on identifying factors that may restrain the anticipated effectiveness of a planned intervention and the efficacy (or omission) of metrics. The resulting normative frameworks are designed as learning platforms that pull together the checklists of features that appear most likely to support intervention effectiveness. Consistent categories emerge as intervention effectiveness enablers

Table 2.1 Typology of workplace health intervention frameworks

	Implementation frameworks	Appraisal frameworks	Realist frameworks	Best practice models	Regulatory compliance guidance
Framework features	1. Normative: How to undertake a single intervention; what content should go into a successful intervention and why 2. The frameworks represent a descriptive and empirical mapping of the literature	1. Normative: Identifying the gaps and conflicts that restrained intervention effectiveness and identifying constraints and enablers as a learning platform for better-informed interventions 2. The frameworks represent a route map for robust interventions evaluation	1. Methodological: Aimed at identifying the underpinning configurations of Context, Mechanisms, Outcomes (CMO) that generate effective interventions 2. The framework is aimed at explanation, but restricted to be applied as a methodology for building theory through creating an empirical evidence-base focused on intervention configurations	1. Normative: List of factors to take into account during intervention implementation 2. The frameworks provide prescriptive, usually linear, sequenced activities	1. Normative: List of factors to take into account during intervention implementation, incorporating best practice for regulatory compliance 2. The frameworks provide prescriptive staged models of intervention implementation
Unit of analysis	Intervention implementation process; single interventions	Intervention features associated with effectiveness	Interaction of context, mechanism and outcome in an intervention and/or implementation	Intervention implementation, organized around (mainly) linear stages	Intervention implementation, organized around prescriptive linear stages

(continued)

Table 2.1 (continued)

	Implementation frameworks	Appraisal frameworks	Realist frameworks	Best practice models	Regulatory compliance guidance
Characteristics	Dynamic: Process variables and participatory processes	Evidence-based implementation appraisal	Dynamic: Context-Mechanism-Outcome (CMO)	Activity focused. Issues to consider and actions to undertake. Some accommodation of dynamism	Activity focused incorporating standards: Issues to consider and actions to undertake
Temporal features	Focus on pre- and during intervention features; linear staged	Focus on post-intervention appraisal	Focus on micro-temporal features of mechanisms that generate outcomes	Focus on pre-and during intervention actions; predominantly linear staged prescriptions (or stage-gates, i.e., feedback loops for adaptation)	Focus on linear staged prescriptions during intervention implementation
Disciplinary focus/theory level	Intra- and inter-personal psychosocial micro-theory (primarily micro)	Not specified	Can vary according to CMO configuration, however, in application, this is predominantly micro	Universal best practice principles	Regulatory compliance through universal best practice principles
Main contributions	• Acknowledges dynamism • Proposes contextual influences • Acknowledges influence of key actors/and social systems	• Identification of weakness in reporting implementation effectiveness • Identification of measurement and methodological weaknesses	• Provides a method for theorization that incorporates context, mechanisms and outcomes • Provides a method for analyzing dynamics in relation to context, mechanisms and outcomes	• Typologies or categorization of organisational resources, structures and process to aid intervention success, configured round roles and activities of practice-actors	• Guidelines that represent regulatory and compliance best practice, configured around activities

Calls for action arising/ research gaps	Theoretical explanations are fragmented and there is a need for greater integrative theory building to underpin the frameworks	Theory and implementation need to pay attention to dynamism. Lack of integrative theory to explain effective implementation. More detailed reporting post hoc to provide basis for evaluation of longer-term and systemic effectiveness Improved longitudinal designs	Requires accumulation of body of empirical evidence of theorized configurations in order to make theoretical progress	Refinement and development required of staged models, mapping and assessment techniques in practice settings	Call for application of guidance by organisations
Exemplary papers	Biron and Karanika-Murray (2014); Fridrich et al. (2015); Nielsen (2013, 2017); Nielsen and Randall (2013); Havermans et al. (2016)	Egan et al. (2009); Hoefsmit et al. (2012); Moran et al. (2014); Murta et al. (2007); Passey et al. (2018); Rojatz et al. (2016); Wierenga et al. (2013)	Pawson and Tilley (1997)	Ammendolia et al. (2016); Herrera-Sánchez et al. (2017); Jordan et al. (2003); Rasmussen et al. (2018); von Thiele Schwarz et al. (2016)	Health and Safety Executive (2017/2019)

Source: Reproduced from Daniels, Watson, et al. (2021) (https://doi.org/10.1016/j.socscimed.2021.113888) under a CC-BY creative commons license. © Elsevier

(e.g. support of powerful stakeholders; employee involvement; appropriateness of competencies and resources to support the initiative; Egan et al., 2009; Wierenga et al., 2013). However, like implementation frameworks, appraisal frameworks are limited in their development of theoretical explanations.

There is considerable overlap between the content of the three types of evaluation frameworks (implementation, appraisal, realist evaluation) and the content of best practice and regulatory compliance models (as noted von Thiele Schwarz et al., 2016, for example could be placed in either category). Both sets of frameworks, for example highlight the roles of multiple stakeholders. For example Jordan et al. (2003) produced a 'good practice model' that recognizes a widescale participative approach to engaging the variety of stakeholders alongside engagement of top management as a key strategic stakeholder group. Best practice and regulatory compliance models likewise highlight the use of planned sequences of activities and tend to portray workplace health and wellbeing interventions as progressing in a linear sequential fashion. For example Ammendolia et al. (2016), Herrera-Sánchez et al. (2017), von Thiele Schwarz et al. (2016) and the UK Health and Safety Executive (HSE, 2017/2019) amongst others have developed explicitly staged prescriptions of how to implement workplace health and wellbeing practices. Von Thiele Schwarz et al.'s model is different from other staged models in that it allows extensive feedback loops and has a particular emphasis on co-creation of knowledge between organisational stakeholders and research teams that can allow intervention activities to be adapted over time in unpredictable ways. Overall, the practice frameworks focus on providing prescriptions based on assumptions of universal applicability across contexts and progression through stages in a given order. However, as Hoefsmit et al. (2012) note, some of the prescriptions from the practice-oriented literature about following a defined sequence of activities may not always be applicable, for example in the case of complex conditions such as psychological health problems.

Despite the overlap between research-oriented frameworks, practice-oriented frameworks and findings from systematic reviews, there remain problems. One of the key problems identified in this field is the lack of theoretical models, or indeed conceptual principles, of how to affect change in organisations. This lack of a theoretical or conceptual basis for the research is acknowledged (Biron & Karanika-Murray, 2014, 2015; Martin et al., 2016; Nielsen, 2013). Therefore, although previous frameworks and guidance are able to guide us in respect of what information to extract from empirical studies of interventions, they are not able to guide us on underpinning principles of organisational change that may form a conceptual explanation on how change occurs and how change can be made to occur.

Alongside the need for a strong conceptual foundation for understanding implementation, there are two other salient conclusions from this chapter that has reviewed existing frameworks, models and evidence syntheses on the implementation of workplace health and wellbeing. First, many, if not all, existing approaches treat the implementation of health and wellbeing practices as planned activities that follow prescribed stages, and by and large, do not consider if and how implementation may iterate between stages. Second, frameworks, models and evidence syntheses have focused on specific interventions and neglected the wider organisation. Focusing on specific interventions is important in order to build an evidence base on what kinds of interventions work and knowledge of how they work and can be made to work more effectively. Our argument for an alternative approach is that it should be complementary to intervention-focused research and not be used to replace intervention-focused research using realist evaluation frameworks, for example.

Ignoring the wider organisation has several implications. First, as noted in the first chapter, organisations may adopt several different initiatives to protect and enhance worker wellbeing (Batorsky et al., 2016; Johnson et al., 2018; Jordan et al., 2003; Mattke et al., 2015), and indeed different interventions may have synergistic effects if combined into a coherent and managed programme of activities that signals a commitment to worker wellbeing (Daniels, Fida, et al., 2021; Huettermann & Bruch, 2019). What else an organisation may or may not be doing for wellbeing may influence implementation of any specific practice (Dollard & Karasek, 2010). Moreover, even if one element as a programme fails to deliver benefits, other elements may confer benefits, and the unsuccessful element may be replaced. Second, implementing some interventions can entail or require extensive organisational change, and therefore readjustment of other organisational procedures, practices and structures—not least those interventions directed at job/work redesign, that some define as 'organisational level interventions' (e.g. Nielsen & Noblet, 2018, p. 1). In this respect, the organisation can be de facto the unit of analysis because it is the focus of the intervention. Third, neglecting the organisation, and tendency to treat it as a fixed entity that provides a contextual backdrop to a specific intervention (Russell et al., 2016), misses the dynamism of organisations: Organisations are socio-political entities that adjust their procedures, practices and structures to changes in the external environment as well as to new health and wellbeing practices, and are populated by actors with their own frames of reference, interests and power bases. Actors' frames of references, interests and power bases also shift over time, and differing interests can lead to conflict between actors, including those involved in the implementation of health and wellbeing practices. Fourth, there is no explicit consideration of the different ways in which any health and wellbeing practice comes to 'stick' and be sustained in an organisation. Many frameworks and models indicate implementation is aided by making health and wellbeing practices consonant with existing structures, systems and processes, but other approaches to implementation are possible and may even be desirable in some instances, as noted in Chap. 1.

Treating implementation as a planned, staged activity with limited iteration is problematic. This does not accord with how change in organisations plays out in practice, where unanticipated events may derail one intervention, yet at the same time make another intervention feasible and/or more appropriate (Fuller et al., 2019). Further, treating implementation as a planned activity provides no way for accounting for practices that occur spontaneously from the actions of specific workers or groups of workers with or without tacit or explicit support from managers, for example informal walking or mindfulness groups. Yet, such informal practices do occur (Braganza et al., 2018), even in the realm of job redesign, as the extensive literature on the concept of job crafting demonstrates (Rudolph et al., 2017).

In the following chapters, through an in-depth review of existing research and our own empirical research on the implementation of a range of workplace health and wellbeing initiatives, we develop in detail the elements of the model introduced in the first chapter that addresses these key limitations.

References

Abildgaard, J. S., Nielsen, K., Wåhlin-Jacobsen, C. D., Maltesen, T., Christensen, K. B., & Holtermann, A. (2020). 'Same, but different': A mixed-methods realist evaluation of a cluster-randomized controlled participatory organizational intervention. *Human Relations, 73*, 1339–1365.

Alvesson, M., & Sveningsson, S. (2016). *Changing organizational culture: Cultural change work in progress* (2nd ed.). Routledge.

Ammendolia, C., Côté, P., Cancelliere, C., Cassidy, J. D., Hartvigsen, J., Boyle, E., Soklaridis, S., Stern, P., & Amick, B. (2016). Healthy and productive workers: Using intervention mapping to design a workplace health promotion and wellness program to improve presenteeism. *BMC Public Health, 16*, 1190.

Bakhuys Roozeboom, M. C., Wiezer, N. M., Boot, C. R., Bongers, P. M., & Schelvis, R. (2021). Use of intervention mapping for occupational risk prevention and health promotion: A systematic review of literature. *International Journal of Environmental Research and Public Health, 18*, 1775.

Balogun, J. (2006). Managing change: Steering a course between intended strategies and unanticipated outcomes. *Long Range Planning, 39*, 29–49.

Bartholomew, L. K. B., Markham, C. M., Ruiter, R. A., Fernández, M. E., Kok, G., & Parcel, G. S. (2016). *Planning health promotion programs: An intervention mapping approach*. Wiley.

Batorsky, B., Van Stolk, C., & Liu, H. (2016). Is more always better in designing workplace wellness programs?: A comparison of wellness program components versus outcomes. *Journal of Occupational and Environmental Medicine, 58*, 987–993.

Biron, C., & Karanika-Murray, M. (2014). Process evaluation for organizational stress and well-being interventions: Implications for theory, method, and practice. *International Journal of Stress Management, 21*, 85–111.

Biron, C., & Karanika-Murray, M. (2015). From black and white to colours: Moving the science of organizational interventions for stress and well-being forward. In C. Biron & M. Karanika-Murray (Eds.), *Derailed organizational interventions for stress and wellbeing: Confessions of failure and solutions for success* (pp. 275–282). Springer.

Braganza, S., Young, J., Sweeny, A., & Brazil, V. (2018). oneED: Embedding a mindfulness-based wellness programme into an emergency department. *Emergency Medicine Australasia, 30*, 678–686.

Burgess, M. G., Brough, P., Biggs, A., & Hawkes, A. J. (2020). Why interventions fail: A systematic review of occupational health psychology interventions. *International Journal of Stress Management, 27*, 195–207.

Busch, C., Koch, T., Clasen, J., Winkler, E., & Vowinkel, J. (2017). Evaluation of an organizational health intervention for low-skilled workers and immigrants. *Human Relations, 70*, 994–1016.

Campbell, Q. (2014). Developing and implementing corporate wellness programs: Lessons from the firing line. In R. J. Burke & A. M. Richardsen (Eds.), *Corporate wellness programs: Linking employee and organizational health* (pp. 257–276). Elgar.

Cox, T., Karanika, M., Mellor, N., Lomas, L., Houdmont, J., & Griffiths, A. (2007). *Implementation of the management standards for work-related stress: Process evaluation*. University of Nottingham.

Dahler-Larsen, P. (2001). From programme theory to constructivism: On tragic, magic and competing programmes. *Evaluation, 7*, 331–349.

Daniels, K., Fida, R., Stepanek, M., & Gendronneau, C. (2021). Do multicomponent workplace health and wellbeing programs predict changes in health and wellbeing? *International Journal of Public Health and Environmental Research*. https://doi.org/10.3390/ijerph18178964

Daniels, K., Watson, D., Nayani, R., Tregaskis, O., Hogg, M., Etuknwa, A., & Semkina, A. (2021). Implementing practices focused on workplace health and psychological wellbeing: A systematic review. *Social Science and Medicine, 227*, 113888.

De Angelis, M., Giusino, D., Nielsen, K., Aboagye, E., Christensen, M., Innstrand, S. T., Mazzetti, G., van den Heuvel, M., Sijbom, R. B. L., Pelzer, V., Chiesa, R., & Pietrantoni, L. (2020). H-WORK Project: Multilevel interventions to promote mental health in SMEs and public workplaces. *International Journal of Environmental Research and Public Health, 17*, 8035.

Dewe, P., & Cooper, C. L. (2014). Occupational stress and work: From theory to interventions. In A. R. Gomes, R. Resende, & A. Albuquerque (Eds.), *Positive human functioning from a multidimensional perspective: Promoting healthy lifestyles* (Vol. 2, pp. 15–36). Nova Science.

Dollard, M. F., & Karasek, R. A. (2010). Building psychosocial safety climate. In J. Houdmont & S. Leka (Eds.), *Contemporary occupational health psychology: Global perspectives on research and practice* (Vol. 1, pp. 208–233). Wiley.

Egan, M., Bambra, C., Petticrew, M., & Whitehead, M. (2009). Reviewing evidence on complex social interventions: Appraising implementation in systematic reviews of the health effects of organisational-level workplace interventions. *Journal of Epidemiology & Community Health, 63*, 4–11.

Fridrich, A., Jenny, G. J., & Bauer, G. F. (2015). The context, process, and outcome evaluation model for organisational health interventions. *BioMed Research International*. https://doi.org/10.1155/2015/414832

Fuller, P., Randall, R., Dainty, A., Haslam, R., & Gibb, A. (2019). Applying a longitudinal tracer methodology to evaluate complex interventions in complex settings. *European Journal of Work and Organizational Psychology, 28*, 443–452.

Gersick, C. J. (1991). Revolutionary change theories: A multilevel exploration of the punctuated equilibrium paradigm. *Academy of Management Review, 16*, 10–36.

Greenhalgh, J. (2014). Realist synthesis. In P. K. Edwards, J. O'Mahoney, & S. Vincent (Eds.), *Studying organizations using critical realism: A practical guide* (pp. 264–281). Oxford University Press.

Havermans, B. M., Schelvis, R. M., Boot, C. R., Brouwers, E. P., Anema, J. R., & van der Beek, A. J. (2016). Process variables in organizational stress management intervention evaluation research: A systematic review. *Scandinavian Journal of Work, Environment & Health, 42*, 371–381.

Health and Safety Executive. (2017/2019). *Tackling work-related stress using the management standards approach: A step-by-step workbook*. http://www.hse.gov.uk/pubns/wbk01.pdf. First published 2017, updated 2019.

Herrera-Sánchez, I. M., León-Pérez, J. M., & León-Rubio, J. M. (2017). Steps to ensure a successful Implementation of occupational health and safety interventions at an organizational level. *Frontiers in Psychology, 8*, 2135.

Hoefsmit, N., Houkes, I., & Nijhuis, F. J. (2012). Intervention characteristics that facilitate return to work after sickness absence: A systematic literature review. *Journal of Occupational Rehabilitation, 22*, 462–477.

Huettermann, H., & Bruch, H. (2019). Mutual gains? Health-related HRM, collective well-being and organizational performance. *Journal of Management Studies, 56*, 1045–1072.

Johns, G. (2006). The essential impact of context on organizational behavior. *Academy of Management Review, 31*, 386–408.

Johnson, G. (1987). *Strategic change and the management process*. Blackwell.
Johnson, G. (1990). Managing strategic change; the role of symbolic action. *British Journal of Management, 1*, 183–200.
Johnson, S., Robertson, I., & Cooper, C. L. (2018). *Work and well-being*. Palgrave Macmillan.
Jordan, J., Gurr, E., Tinline, G., Giga, S. I., Faragher, B., & Cooper, C. L. (2003). *Beacons of excellence in stress prevention: Research report 133*. HSE Books.
Kendall, N., Burton, K., Lunt, J., Mellor, N., & Daniels, K. (2015). *Development of an intervention toolbox for common health problems in the workplace*. HSE Books.
Kletter, M., Harris, B., & Brown, C. (2021). Outcomes, mechanisms and contextual factors of positive psychology interventions for health workers: A systematic review of global evidence. *Human Resources for Health, 19*, 1–14.
Lehmann, A. I., Brauchli, R., & Bauer, G. F. (2019). Goal pursuit in organizational health interventions: The role of team climate, outcome expectancy, and implementation intentions. *Frontiers in Psychology, 10*, 154.
Martin, A., Karanika-Murray, M., Biron, C., & Sanderson, K. (2016). The psychosocial work environment, employee mental health and organizational interventions: Improving research and practice by taking a multilevel approach. *Stress and Health, 32*, 201–215.
Mattke, S., Kapinos, K., Caloyeras, J. P., Taylor, E. A., Batorsky, B., Liu, H., Van Busum, K. R., & Newberry, S. (2015). Workplace wellness programs: Services offered, participation, and incentives. *Rand Health Quarterly, 5*, 7.
Mellor, N., & Webster, J. (2011). *A process review of a corporate health and well-being strategy. DWP case study*. Health and Safety Laboratory.
Mintzberg, H. (1994). *The rise and fall of strategic planning*. Free Press.
Moore, G. F., Audrey, S., Barker, M., Bond, L., Bonell, C., Hardeman, W., Moore, L., O'Cathain, A., Tinati, T., Wight, D., & Baird, J. (2015). Process evaluation of complex interventions: Medical Research Council guidance. *British Medical Journal, 350*, h1258.
Moran, A. M., Coyle, J., Pope, R., Boxall, D., Nancarrow, S. A., & Young, J. (2014). Supervision, support and mentoring interventions for health practitioners in rural and remote contexts: An integrative review and thematic synthesis of the literature to identify mechanisms for successful outcomes. *Human Resources for Health, 12*, 10.
Morris, C. W., & Morris, C. D. (2014). Increasing healthy habits and health behaviour change in corporate wellness programs. In R. J. Burke & A. M. Richardsen (Eds.), *Corporate wellness programs: Linking employee and organizational health* (pp. 215–240). Elgar.
Murta, S. G., Sanderson, K., & Oldenburg, B. (2007). Process evaluation in occupational stress management programs: A systematic review. *American Journal of Health Promotion, 21*, 248–254.
Nielsen, K. (2013). How can we make organizational interventions work? Employees and line managers as actively crafting interventions. *Human Relations, 66*, 1029–1050.
Nielsen, K. (2017). Leaders can make or break an intervention—But are they the villains of the piece. In E. K. Kelloway, K. Nielsen, & J. K. Dimoff (Eds.), *Leading to occupational health and safety: How leadership behaviours impact organizational safety and well-being* (pp. 197–209). Wiley.
Nielsen, K., & Abildgaard, J. S. (2013). Organizational interventions: A research-based framework for the evaluation of both process and effects. *Work & Stress, 27*, 278–297.
Nielsen, K., & Miraglia, M. (2017). What works for whom in which circumstances? On the need to move beyond the 'what works?' question in organizational intervention research. *Human Relations, 70*, 40–62.
Nielsen, K., & Randall, R. (2013). Opening the black box: Presenting a model for evaluating organizational-level interventions. *European Journal of Work and Organizational Psychology, 22*, 601–617.
Nielsen, K., Randall, R., Holten, A.-L., & Rial-Gonzalez, E. (2010). Conducting organizational-level occupational health interventions: What works? *Work & Stress, 24*, 234–259.

Nielsen, K. M., & Noblet, A. (2018). Organizational interventions: Where we are, where we go from here? In K. Nielsen & A. Noblet (Eds.), *Organizational interventions for health and well-being: A handbook for evidence-based practice* (pp. 1–22). Routledge.
Passey, D. G., Brown, M. C., Hammerback, K., Harris, J. R., & Hannon, P. A. (2018). Managers' support for employee wellness programs: An integrative review. *American Journal of Health Promotion, 32*, 1789–1799.
Pawson, R. (2006). *Evidence-based policy: A realist perspective*. Sage.
Pawson, R., & Manzano-Santaella, A. (2012). A realist diagnostic workshop. *Evaluation, 18*, 176–191.
Pawson, R., & Tilley, N. (1997). *Realistic evaluation*. Sage.
Rasmussen, C. D. N., Højberg, H., Bengtsen, E., & Jørgensen, M. B. (2018). Identifying knowledge gaps between practice and research for implementation components of sustainable interventions to improve the working environment—A rapid review. *Applied Ergonomics, 67*, 178–192.
Rojatz, D., Merchant, A., & Nitsch, M. (2016). Factors influencing workplace health promotion intervention: A qualitative systematic review. *Health Promotion International, 32*, 831–839.
Rudolph, C. W., Katz, I. M., Lavigne, K. N., & Zacher, H. (2017). Job crafting: A meta-analysis of relationships with individual differences, job characteristics, and work outcomes. *Journal of Vocational Behavior, 102*, 112–138.
Russell, J., Berney, L., Stansfeld, S., Lanz, D., Kerry, S., Chandola, T., & Bhui, K. (2016). The role of qualitative research in adding value to a randomised controlled trial: Lessons from a pilot study of a guided e-learning intervention for managers to improve employee wellbeing and reduce sickness absence. *Trials, 17*, 396.
Tyers, C., Broughton, A., Denvir, A., Wilson, S., & O'Regan, S. (2009). *Organisational responses to the HSE management standards for work-related stress. Progress of the sector implementation plan—Phase 1. Research report 693*. HSE Books.
von Thiele Schwarz, U., Lundmark, R., & Hasson, H. (2016). The dynamic integrated evaluation model (DIEM): Achieving sustainability in organizational intervention through a participatory evaluation approach. *Stress and Health, 32*, 285–293.
von Thiele Schwarz, U., Nielsen, K., Edwards, K., Hasson, H., Ipsen, C., Savage, C., Abildgaard, J. S., Richter, A., Lornudd, C., Mazzocato, P., & Reed, J. E. (2021). How to design, implement and evaluate organizational interventions for maximum impact: The Sigtuna Principles. *European Journal of Work and Organizational Psychology, 30*, 415–427.
von Thiele Schwarz, U., Nielsen, K. M., Stenfors-Hayes, T., & Hasson, H. (2017). Using kaizen to improve employee well-being: Results from two organizational intervention studies. *Human Relations, 70*, 966–993.
Weick, K. E., & Quinn, R. E. (1999). Organizational change and development. *Annual Review of Psychology, 50*, 361–386.
Westover, J. H. (2010). Managing organizational change: Change agent strategies and techniques to successfully managing the dynamics of stability and change in organizations. *International Journal of Management and Innovation, 2*, 45–51.
Wierenga, D., Engbers, L. H., Van Empelen, P., Duijts, S., Hildebrandt, V. H., & Van Mechelen, W. (2013). What is actually measured in process evaluations for worksite health promotion programs: A systematic review. *BMC Public Health, 13*, 1190.

Chapter 3
Tangible Changes and Activated Mechanisms

In the first chapter, we saw that a range of interventions *could* have beneficial effects on wellbeing and health outcomes, and also that there exist interventions that are predicated upon well-developed theoretical models of factors that influence wellbeing. For an intervention to work, two conditions need to be satisfied (Daniels et al., 2021): First, there are changes to the status quo of how the organisation operates, ranging from more minor changes to more extensive changes. Examples include introducing flexible working policies (primary work design), communications to leave the office for a walk at lunchtime (primary health promotion), introducing training in self-regulation skills (secondary prevention), training for managers on how to make reasonable work adjustments for those returning to work after illness (tertiary intervention) or some combination of these kinds of changes (multicomponent interventions). Second, the changes activate mechanisms that bring about changes in wellbeing (cf. Pawson & Manzano-Santaella, 2012), which in relation to wellbeing can include, for example changes in cognition, social relationships, physiology.

The purpose of this chapter is to examine in detail whether (a) workplace health and wellbeing interventions are implemented as intended and (b) whether those interventions activate the mechanisms that the underpinning programme theory of the intervention indicates *should* bring about improvements in wellbeing. Examining both conditions enables us to determine if the success or failure of interventions is related to whether interventions are implemented as intended, either partially or in full, whether failure is connected to contextual factors that prevent the activation of mechanisms, or both. An example of the former would be where a resilience training programme is terminated when only half-completed because of cuts to training budgets. An example of the latter would be where flexible working practices are introduced to allow people with childcare responsibilities to start work at a later time but are undermined by line managers calling departmental meetings at 8.30 am.

In their systematic review, Daniels et al. (2021) have already indicated failure to implement an intervention or failure to activate mechanisms can explain why interventions have no effects on wellbeing. However, the picture for interventions

K. Daniels et al., *Achieving Sustainable Workplace Wellbeing*, Aligning Perspectives on Health, Safety and Well-Being, https://doi.org/10.1007/978-3-031-00665-4_3

that provide wellbeing benefits is more nuanced. In this chapter, we will explore some of these nuances in more detail. Daniels et al. were not able to find any evidence on how implementation may bring about adverse effects. We will address the issue of what may cause adverse effects in this chapter. We examine, in turn, five different scenarios: Where there are no effects on wellbeing because changes are not implemented; where changes are made, but mechanisms are not activated; where changes are made and mechanisms are activated as planned; where changes are made, wellbeing improves, but effects cannot be attributed to mechanisms that reflect theoretical principles underpinning the intervention; and where adverse effects occur.

This is the first chapter to draw on some of our empirical work based on interviews with 41 informants in six case organisations.[1] A summary of each case is provided in Table 3.1.

No Effects: Implementation

This is the most straightforward scenario of intervention failure: An intervention is planned but it is not implemented as planned. Because the intervention is not implemented, the theoretical mechanisms assumed to underpin the intervention cannot be activated, leading to null effects. In Daniels et al.'s (2021) systematic review, there were 21 studies with no adverse effects on wellbeing markers. Fourteen of these 21 were studies where the intervention was not implemented as planned. In two of the more extreme examples from their review, both work redesign interventions, initial risk assessments were received badly by senior managers, leading to termination of the intervention in one case before any implementation had taken place (Coffey et al., 2009) and, in the other, resulting in apathy towards the intervention that slowed any progress on implementation (Schelvis et al., 2017). In a study of a workplace health promotion programme, the intervention was withdrawn from two participating work sites considered by the implementation team to be unreceptive contexts, for reasons including employee hostility to the programme, lack of vision from management and high staff turnover (reported in Zhang et al., 2015, 2016). A less extreme example of implementation failure comes from a study of a rehabilitation programme for workers with minor mental health problems (reported in Andersen et al., 2014; Martin et al., 2012, 2013). In this study, some of the professionals involved with implementation did not follow the protocols of the intervention.

The reasons for lack of implementation of interventions will be explored in more detail in the following chapters. The examples given indicate: The power of expert implementers (Zhang et al., 2015, 2016) or senior managers (Coffey et al., 2009), who can terminate interventions seemingly by their own fiat; the competence of

[1] The Technical Appendix provides further details of this empirical work.

Table 3.1 Case summary and interviewees

Case study	Case description	Interviewees	Summary of approach and initiatives
Large infrastructure and construction	Large construction and infrastructure firm. Early adopter of new international standard for health and safety. Two mental health first aiders on site, various signs/leaflets of wellbeing toolbox around site office and facilities. Very transient and shifting workforce, also highly international	Leader/sponsors: Wellbeing lead; Human resources director; Health and safety director Manager/Agent: Senior Safety Adviser; Site Manager Worker: Groundworks Worker; Site Engineer; Electrician	Many different initiatives, but most high profile is mental health, which has dominated wellbeing activities. Also employee perks/rewards, employee assistance programme, health surveillance organized around an evolving strategy and seven key enablers: (1) leadership, (2) education, (3) communication, (4) healthy working environment, (5) standards in design, (6) engagement and (7) improvement. Continuous improvement group on occupational health & wellbeing
Medium construction	A family-owned construction and civil engineering company with 300 employees. Workforce is mainly male, middle-aged. Mobile workforce and multi-site locations, with around 100 'live' sites at any one time	Leader/Sponsor: Human resources director Manager/Agent: Contracts director; operations manager; head of assurance Worker: Bid co-ordinator; financial controller; marketing officer	Cultural value of doing the right thing by employees embedded in family ethos of the firm. Provision includes various resources (e.g. employee assistance programme, educational/training and support tools and information) and initiatives (e.g. employee-led volunteering, embedding wellbeing training within managerial training). Core is an appraisal and personal development programme using coaching techniques and designed to foster personal health and wellbeing alongside work-based competencies
Large, multinational law	An international law firm with over 2500 employees and 25 offices globally	Leader/Sponsor: Human resources manager Manager/Agent: Health and safety manager; facilities compliance manager; policies and projects manager; responsible business	Approach articulated around three pillars of wellbeing: Health, financial and environment. Informed by the pillars, a mental health and wellbeing strategy, and

(continued)

Table 3.1 (continued)

Case study	Case description	Interviewees	Summary of approach and initiatives
		associate; assistant rewards manager Worker: Partner	governance structures co-ordinate and mobilize action including a health and wellbeing steering group. Wellbeing resources organized through an intranet hub, which includes policies and procedures as well as advice and signposting to support. External partners and provider organisations are important in delivering wellbeing services and understanding employee need. Employee interest groups inform bottom-up initiatives, but emphasis on integrating localized actions into comprehensive practices across firm
Medium accountancy practice	An audit and accounting partnership, employing over 300 employees across multiple sites and run by 20 partners. Working at client site, in office, some travel. Not highest payers in industry	Leader/sponsor: Head of human resources; managing partner Manager/Agent: Senior manager; wellbeing coordinator Worker: Auditor; auditor	Broad range of activities organized under six different strands: Financial, social, mental, physical, career and community. Examples of activities include wellbeing champions, mental health awareness training, healthy eating initiatives, debt management advice, charitable and community work as well as a social fund for team-based social activities. Existing human resources policies and processes re-configured under the six strands. Employee wellbeing seen as fundamental to core business services and in supporting their talent framework
Large care	A commercial business for social purpose. Group organisational structure, encompassing a wide range of 20 businesses,	Leader/Sponsor: Human resources director; health and safety director Manager/Agent: human resources business	Wellbeing strategy across groups within organisation is configured around five pillars (employee physical wellbeing,

	including leisure centres, care and support services, facilities management, property management, construction (e.g. social housing), housing associations. Total 13,000 employees, 9000 in leisure centres. Company is acquisitive, pursuing growth strategy—need to be competitive in attracting workers ('future-proof') as well as 'driving productivity'	partner; head of corporate facilities; human resources business partner Worker: Payroll manager; payroll manager; human resources business partner; managing director of subsidiary business	employee mental wellbeing, employee safety and external facing: community wellbeing and place making wellbeing). Attempting to generate a joined-up wellbeing strategy, delivery and governance structure, while also accommodating subsidiary-led and tailored wellbeing initiatives and facilitating cross-group learning. Consistency across organisation through strategic communication and establishment of mental health first aider/champions. Partnering with wellbeing service providers to ensure there is evidence to make informed decisions about wellbeing priorities and assessment of initiatives
Small care	A learning and disability care home under the umbrella of care provider. The home is single site, with around 20 residents and 22 staff (full and part time). Management structure is manager, deputy manager, 2 seniors. 24-h shifts	Leader/Sponsor: Care home manager Manager/Agent: Deputy Manager Worker: Support worker; Support worker	Recruitment according to fit and mindset aligned to the inclusive and supportive culture. Role modelling by leadership, consideration, and support for staff alongside no tolerance of bullying or power plays. Other-career encouragement and support for individual progression beyond the organisation and sector. Employees encouraged to bring own interests into work and integrate caring for residents' wellbeing with their own

those charged with making specific changes (Andersen et al., 2014; Martin et al., 2012, 2013); and the attitudes of workers towards the intervention (Zhang et al., 2015, 2016). However, although there is evidence from other studies that barriers such as those listed here can be overcome (Daniels et al., 2021), what is not yet clear is how those barriers may be overcome.

Another reason why an intervention may not be implemented is that it may simply (be perceived) not to be needed (see next section). This is illustrated in the following quote from a senior manager in a care home for adults with learning disabilities that formed one of our case studies. Here both a workshop and a counselling intervention around staff mental health are not perceived as relevant because the culture of the workplace enables staff to deal with mental health issues without a formalized intervention.

> We wouldn't do like a workshop, but everybody is quite open actually about their mental health. I don't know whether it's the job we do but we tend to talk in a group. I mean we've had these conversations that somebody's feeling a bit down or we'd talk about going to the doctors about it. Yes, it's quite open actually. Especially when we've had deaths here of residents. Because the relationship is quite intense with our guys, and they're dying as younger adults as well, and it's quite difficult to avoid... Like a lady that died last year at 60, but she'd developed Alzheimer's with her Down Syndrome, but she sort of died in her bedding that was all princess Disney, surrounded by her toys, and it's a really difficult thing. But everybody does then talk about that. I'd have to say we were offered bereavement counselling by palliative care, which apparently is never really offered to care homes, it's generally families, but everybody said no, we'll just go out for the night and have a few drinks together and do that. It might not be the healthiest way to address it, to go out and have a few drinks, but it works for us again. But everybody would talk about how they're feeling. I've had staff had a cry about somebody dying, none of that is discouraged, do you know what I mean, it's more encouraged. We'd make every effort to get as many people as we could to the funerals, that sort of thing. We've arranged funerals here for people that have had no family and all the staff have been involved in that. So I think, you know, it's just very open about that sort of thing. (**Small care provider, manager**)

This quote also raises another issue that is not clear in the literature. Because the unit of analysis is the intervention in the literature, what the organisation does after failing to implement an intervention is not explicitly considered in the research literature. One organisational response to fail to implement an activity that could have benefits for employee wellbeing would be to investigate why the intervention failed, and then incorporate this learning into future efforts to implement other interventions (cf. von Thiele Schwarz et al., 2016).

Data from our case companies indicates at least one other reason why interventions may not be implemented: This is that planned interventions never move beyond initial discussions and/or planning because the scale of the problem and what is required are not recognized, as touched on in the following quotes from a partner in a large, multinational law practice and a senior manager in a medium-sized accountancy practice. The first quote relates to the scale of changes required and that it needs to be recognized at very senior levels of the organisation. The second relates to a recognition to move beyond discussions about wellbeing and onto tangible action, otherwise wellbeing benefits would not be realized.

> It would involve a shift in culture because that's typical of a law firm, we are simply how all the others are, so we would need to make a decision that we are not going to behave like other law firms for lots of very good reasons. And that is way beyond my pay grade making those kind of shifts in culture. (**Large, multinational law firm, partner**)
>
> I think the first thing was for... We can always talk about wellbeing and we can talk about it purely as a headline issue or we can actually see we're doing something about it. What we did was we had a really good engagement process with third parties who came in and talked to us. People who are specialists in that particular area came in and talked to the managers about what we should be spotting and what we should be doing. We really needed to get engaged with the whole thing, it's not about a box ticking exercise and trying to promote yourself to try and win awards, it's actually about doing something properly. (**Medium accountancy practice, senior manager**)

No Effects: Context

In this scenario, an intervention is implemented as planned, but the intervention fails to have a positive effect on wellbeing. There are three potential explanations for how an intervention that is implemented may produce null effects. In each case, elements of the context limit the effectiveness of the intervention. The explanations are not mutually exclusive, and for any given intervention that is implemented, one or more explanations might apply. First, mechanisms are activated, but they are simply not strong enough to produce benefits for wellbeing (within the timeframe of the evaluation). Second, mechanisms replicate existing practices, so the mechanisms through which the intervention is meant to produce benefits have already been activated. Third, for whatever reason, any mechanisms that may produce beneficial effects appear not to be activated at all. In the rest of this section, we will provide examples of each of these explanations.

Two studies provide illustrations of where interventions activate intended mechanisms, but the mechanisms are not necessarily powerful enough to generate wellbeing benefits. An intervention provided participants with an activity tracker to mitigate muscular-skeletal risks from sedentary office behaviours and poor sitting positions (reported in Brakenridge et al., 2016, 2018). Although there was evidence that the key mechanism was activated (increased physical movement indicated by step counts), markers of wellbeing did not improve. Kidger et al. (2016) describe an evaluation of an intervention that combined a peer support service with Mental Health First Aid training (MHFA, Kitchener & Jorm, 2004) in three schools (with three other schools in a control group). MHFA aims to provide individuals with the skills to help those with mental health problems, and this support was to be delivered through the peer support service. Participants that underwent MHFA reported the training was useful for improving their knowledge, skills and confidence in helping a colleague with mental health problems, and so there is evidence that one of the mechanisms in this multicomponent intervention was activated. However, the intervention did not have any overall effects on wellbeing markers on staff in participating schools, partly because many staff did not engage with the peer support service: One of most common reasons given by participants for this was that they did not need to engage with the peer support service because help was not needed. In both of these illustrations, it may be the case that the activated mechanisms were not powerful enough across an entire sample to effect changes in wellbeing because the numbers of people with significant muscular-skeletal or mental health problems to require help was too low. That is, neither intervention may have been targeted sufficiently.

The Kidger et al. (2016) study also provides an illustration of when multiple explanations of why an implemented intervention failed to have an effect on wellbeing. One other reason cited by participants for not engaging with the peer support intervention was that existing networks already provided support, and in some cases, the trained peer-supporter already provided informal support within schools. The Kidger et al. study therefore also provides an illustration of when an intervention replicates existing practices that have already activated appropriate mechanisms (see previous section and the example of bereavement counselling). Therefore, the context is not conducive to a given intervention because the need for the intervention is less than would be the case where informal practices were not already in place.

The third scenario is where an intervention is implemented but *appears* not to activate appropriate mechanisms. This case can be further sub-differentiated into cases where we can be more confident that the intervention did not activate mechanisms after implementation, and cases where it may be the case that mechanisms were activated but were then nullified by other contextual factors. An example of the former case is provided in a study by Carolan and colleagues (Carolan & de Visser, 2018; Carolan et al., 2017). Using a passive control group, Carolan and colleagues evaluated a web-based programme on self-regulatory skills (e.g. a module was focused on problem-solving) and the same web-based programme supplemented with access to an online guided discussion group. Although the web-based elements appeared to confer wellbeing benefits, the online discussion groups were not differentially effective, and participants in this condition reported dissatisfaction with the groups, indicating social support mechanisms were not activated. There were some indications in this study that the online nature of the intervention may have inhibited the activation of mechanisms. An example of where mechanisms may have been nullified is provided in one of three case studies reported by Greasley and colleagues (Greasley & Edwards, 2015; Greasley et al., 2012). The specific case was set in a call centre and involved a multicomponent intervention, with elements focused on improving working practices (e.g. through management development), return to work processes and healthy behaviours. Many contextual factors were positive, including employee engagement, senior management support and a promotional campaign. There was evidence of activation of some mechanisms around healthy behaviours and perceptions of a supportive environment, but no clear impact on absence or work satisfaction. In this case, there were concurrent organisational changes, including a takeover, that may have offset any activated mechanisms.

As with implementation failure, studies of interventions rarely, if ever consider what happens after an intervention fails to have effects. In some organisations, it may be the case that no more initiatives are implemented. However, in others, it is the case that attempts are made to adapt practices targeting wellbeing where mechanisms are not activated or offset by other contextual factors, as illustrated in the following two quotes from managers in a construction firm and large, multinational law firm respectively. The first quote relates to being responsive to feedback from workers on how well provision is working (in this instance onsite welfare facilities). The second relates to educating (as well as learning) from clients on what constitutes good practice for worker wellbeing, wherein client expectations may act to inhibit the effects of the organisation's approach to wellbeing.

> But yeah I think they are quite, I think as a company they're quite active, open, engaging with our workforce. There are various things that are available like we've had different depending what we've done we've had two mental health different toolbox talks here welfare facilities I think are quite of a high standard for them. If there's ever any issues with the welfare obviously as soon as we're alerted it is promptly solved. If we don't think that the, we run at the beginning we had, before we had the setup that you see here today, we had smaller units and the guys were complaining that they weren't adequate and so we got extra ones in for them, bits and pieces to try and make sure that that's OK within in the wellbeing side. (**Large infrastructure and construction, site engineer**)
>
> So I think working with our clients to try and make sure that their, they obviously they see this as an important topic as well is quite a big challenge. So you've got clients that are maybe coming to some of our staff and saying right we expected you to send this response straightaway which again is going against this you know having a healthy work life balance if they're expected to reply to an email at 11 o'clock at night. So it's all about messaging and making sure that we're helping you know to share that practice with our clients and that we're taking on-board best practice from them as well. But that's, I think that's probably the biggest issue is the expectations around billable hours. (**Large, multinational law firm, responsible business associate**)

Effects as Planned

This is the most straightforward scenario to explain intervention success: Everything worked as planned and according to theory.[2] For evaluation research, this may also be the ideal scenario: Through introducing a planned change, ideally in a randomized control design, not only is there evidence that the intervention worked, but also that the theoretical mechanisms underpinning the intervention are sound, thus providing ecological valid data on the underpinning theory. However, what also needs to be investigated is whether there are additional implementation factors that are also required for the intervention to confer wellbeing benefits, and therefore important qualifying factors for the underpinning theory. Investigating qualifying factors potentially places boundary conditions on the theory or theories underpinning a specific intervention.

In Daniels et al.'s systematic review, out of 24 studies of interventions that conferred benefits to wellbeing, 15 provided evidence that interventions worked

---

[2] A high-level classification of mechanisms planned as part of the intervention could map onto the classification of different interventions types outlined in Chap. 1.

according to the theoretical mechanisms designed into the intervention. Of these 15 studies, all intervention types were represented. Examples include integrating work redesign into existing continuous improvement processes (reported in Augustsson et al., 2015; Tafvelin et al., 2018; von Thiele Schwarz et al., 2015, 2017); a staged health promotion campaign tailored to individuals' readiness for change (Haslam et al., 2018); a mindfulness intervention (Byron et al., 2015); and a problem-solving approach for return to work (reported in Arends, Bültmann, et al., 2014; Arends, van der Klink, et al., 2014).

Some of these studies provide examples of the kinds of factors that could promote the effectiveness of an intervention that goes beyond the theoretical processes underpinning the content of the intervention, and therefore indicate qualifying factors for intervention success. These include processes for developing shared understandings about the intervention, establishing trust between stakeholders, establishment of learning processes (Augustsson et al., 2015; Tafvelin et al., 2018; von Thiele Schwarz et al., 2015, 2017), modifying interventions as they are implemented, integrating the service provider into the work group (Byron et al., 2015) and good relationships between different stakeholders involved in intervention implementation or closely related working practices (Arends, Bültmann, et al., 2014; Arends, van der Klink, et al., 2014). These studies, and others, indicate that finding supportive results for an intervention is insufficient, and that further exploration of factors that could be responsible for intervention success are important to progress knowledge. These implementation factors will be explored in subsequent chapters. However, our cases did indicate the importance of wellbeing practices being able to address individual needs, illustrated in different ways by three quotes from a care home worker (adjustments for an individual's education and social life) and human resources directors in a construction firm (development of personal wellbeing plans) and accountancy practice (whole person focus):

> Well there was no support at all, bearing in mind I was at college full time. They would always put me down for shifts when I was at college, I had let them know that I was at college and they would still expect me to work. And they didn't really care about what you do. I know [name of manager] tries here with the younger staff, like myself included, she tries to give us Friday and Saturday evenings off or an early shift. Just so that we can go out and do what we usually would do. But there was no regard for any ones' social life at other places. (**Small care provider, support worker #1**)
>
> And actually that led to this thinking which became [name of wellbeing programme] but around this concept of whole person development. So if you are going to be the best version of yourself if you are going to be the most productive successful person you have got to have the right skills to do the job. You have got to have the right procedures or resilience and you have got to be physically and mentally well. So only when those three things are working at their maximum are you going to be your best are, we going to see the highest productivity, are we going to see the highest engagement. And you can't not act on one you have got to look at all three of them. So we want to come up with a process that is going to help us to analyse where each person was in each of those areas and come up with a personal plan. Put that plan into place and then review if it was actually making a difference to that person. (**Medium construction, human resources director**)
>
> And the first thing I got the partners to do, was commit to a wellbeing commitment. So we haven't got a policy, it's not a, you must do this or there is trouble. It was a commitment that we would look after, at the moment it's six strands, we're just looking at whether or not

> we had a seventh strand, but six strands of employee wellbeing, which, basically, when added together, look after the whole person, be that at work, at home, in their social situation, with their families, financially, etc. So it was kind of a total thing. It wasn't just focusing on what we do in the workplace. And I got the partners to sign up to that. (**Medium accountancy practice, head of human resources**)

In summary, there is evidence that interventions that confer wellbeing benefits for workers do so because there are implemented in ways that are generally consistent with original plans and that activate mechanisms that are predicted from the theories underpinning the interventions. This finding is significant because it does indicate evidence-based interventions with sound theoretical footing can be beneficial. However, there are two caveats. First, some studies indicate that contextual factors and the manner in which interventions are implemented can contribute to their success: It is not just implementation failure and inconducive contexts that explain the pattern of null or positive results, but implementation and context can be significant factors in intervention success that transcend the theory underpinning the intervention. Second, around 38% (nine out of 25) of the beneficial interventions in Daniels et al.'s systematic review (2021) attributed intervention success to factors that were not hypothesized to be part of the intervention.

Beneficial Effects Not as Planned

The unanticipated and beneficial mechanisms that link an intervention to improvements in wellbeing, regardless of their theoretical focus and intended mechanisms of the interventions, have been labelled *emergent mechanisms* (Daniels et al., 2021). Karanika-Murray and Biron (2013) have indicated that one way in which health and wellbeing interventions can have beneficial effects through these emergent mechanisms is through social processes embedded in the process of implementation. Indeed, in all nine studies in Daniels et al.'s (2021) systematic review where mechanisms were activated that were not predicted from the underlying programme theory, the success of the interventions for improving wellbeing was attributed to social processes linked to implementation through means such as group workshops and group exercises. As indicated by another systematic review (see Chap. 1), shared social activities in workplaces are a relatively easy way of improving wellbeing, provided the social activities are ongoing and involve some external facilitation (Daniels et al., 2017).

There was some variation in the nature of the social processes that effected change, indicating a single theoretical perspective cannot account for these unanticipated mechanisms attached to shared implementation processes. In some cases, these related to support for changes in health behaviours, such as changes in workplace cultures and norms around health and wellbeing (one study reported in Edmunds et al., 2013; one study reported in Hadgraft et al., 2017 and Healy et al., 2017), peer support for behaviour change through social modelling (one study reported in Chau et al., 2014, 2016) and opportunities for peer-to-peer learning

(Foureur et al., 2013; Page & Vella-Brodrick, 2013). In other cases, the processes related more to needs for social contact, through enhanced interaction (one study reported in Saksvik et al., 2015, 2018; Undebakke et al., 2015; one study reported in Moll, Patten, et al., 2018; Moll, VandenBussche, et al., 2018), creating a sense of belonging (Edmunds et al., 2013; Menzel et al., 2015) or improving perceptions of social support (Allexandre et al., 2016).

It might be tempting to conclude that only social processes can account for mechanisms that promote wellbeing that are not formally part of the underpinning theories of interventions. However, there is also evidence that workplace health and wellbeing interventions promote wellbeing simply through enhancing self-awareness of health and wellbeing. For example Biron et al. (2010) report on a work redesign intervention based on psychosocial risk assessment implemented by line managers: Although the intervention did not produce any benefits for worker wellbeing, and workload and absence generally deteriorated, one manager who used the psychosocial risk assessment tool reported better personal mental health. Kitchener and Jorm (2004) also reported that Mental Health First Aid training can improve the mental health of those who have received the training, even though the focus of the training is helping others with mental health problems. In an evaluation of an online mindfulness resource, Fitzhugh et al. (2019) make the explicit link between improved knowledge of health and wellbeing and improvements in self-care, so that not all of the positive effects of the intervention could be explained by improvements in mindfulness.

The data from our case studies, like the research literature, indicates that the predominant emergent mechanisms are social in nature, but a wider range of social processes was evident in our case data. Table 3.2 provides illustrative quotes around these emergent processes. These social processes included changes in behavioural norms around health, social contact, belonging and support, as indicated in the literature. More specific forms of interaction and support were also indicated in the interview data. These included wellbeing programmes as forming a means of establishing common ground between people (as also indicated in the quote around health norms), a feeling of being invested in the organisation, and some practices that promoted inclusivity. Related to inclusivity was a feeling that wellbeing initiatives promote open discussion of health and wellbeing issues and can reduce stigma. Our data also indicate that health and wellbeing programmes can promote self-care, which as in the research literature, was the only non-social emergent mechanism.

It seems, therefore, that although a range of social processes may be able to account for some of the unanticipated benefits of workplace health and wellbeing interventions, they may not be able to do so exclusively, and some benefits may accrue simply from improved knowledge of health and wellbeing leading to better self-care.

Table 3.2 Emergent mechanisms

Social processes	
Health norms	*Yes some people have started to look fitter, quite a few of us have slimmed down quite noticeably. I don't think I have particularly but I think, a few people have said to me have you lost weight so there is definitely a lot more fitness around. We talk a lot more about exercise and steps than we used to so I suppose it has created a bit of that, a bit of a banter as far as that's concerned. So some days I will look at what some people do and the steps and there is no way you could have done that and done a full days work!* ***[Interviewer] So you think there is a bit of cheating going on!*** *Yes you get bit of banter going. And then we discover that the cyclists if they wear the watches it shows them as so many thousands of steps and we go alright OK we get it now.* **Medium construction, contracts director**
Contact and belonging	*Well I think especially the ones that have worked here a long time, they're just happy to be working in a happy atmosphere now. They've worked, some of them, in other care homes years and years ago and have said they wouldn't work anywhere else in care other than here, I'm guessing just because they're happy. We do a lot together as well. We do socialise together and support each other, especially like us older lot, we have a little bit more in common, although the youngsters come out with us for a night too.* **Small care provider, manager** *I think encouraging people to take the time to know the person that sits next to them and to be kind. We have each month we publish like a little calendar, it's part of our wellbeing newsletter, but what tends to happen is people print it off and put it on the walls and that. And, you know, it might say, you know, today might be, say something nice to three people you've never met before or, you know, smile at a stranger or leave a note for someone telling them they've done a good job, you know, little things like that. Just to encourage people to focus more on their colleagues as people and, potentially, friends.* **Medium accountancy practice, head of human resources**
Common ground	*We in [name of town] are quite big on social things. We don't go out all the time but a lot of us, so for example park run on a Saturday, there's probably five or six members of staff that go to that. It's not something that the firm organises but because we've all, you know, we had a wellbeing week, I think it was last year or the year before, and we had a step challenge and we had teams and everyone was getting into that groove, and I think that's kind of just naturally carried on here. I think that's quite a [name of town] thing, there are a lot of people that like to be active, that like to be healthy and that kind of thing.* **Medium accountancy practice, auditor #2**

(continued)

Table 3.2 (continued)

	Support network groups, I guess they are not really, I wouldn't see it through the prism of wellbeing. I think it's a way of bringing together people with like-minded interests of connections. And so the family network will provide sessions about supporting your children during their transition to secondary school education or something like that. But it's just part of that overall feel that people get that there is more to just coming to sit at your desk, go home again. There is a network there. **Large, multinational law firm, partner**
Support	*It's an organisation where yes tough decisions sometimes have to be made but people are looked after. I will give you an example, people get cancer and one of the things that we have done as a business is anyone who gets cancer gets paid in full and they get to stay on as an employee even though they are never coming back. And if they stay we provide six times someone's salary death in service benefit so obviously everybody knows that they are going to be able to stay on and get that financial benefit for them and their family or their family because it's not necessarily going to be for them.* **Medium construction, human resources director** *I think probably the people who have suffered over the years a bit from you know low mood, slumping into sort of depressive state. And I think people once they've gone through that kind of do recognise it a lot more and tend to be much more aware of it and much more tuned into it. And also more helpful towards others as well that are, they can see are suffering. And there's one of the guys downstairs who we all know he's quite low quite a bit of time, his family circumstances have changed, not for the better over the last few months. And we do all try and gee him along a little bit you know it's a little bit of carrot and stick, a little bit of banter. But there's also a little bit you know if you fancy going for a pint after work you know just shout up kind of thing. So there is quite a bit of support within the guys themselves and I think that is from an understanding of what wellbeing is and recognising people who are struggling a little bit.* **Large infrastructure and construction, groundworks worker**
Invested in	*Yeah well I think my working patters are more flexible so I mentioned I went for a run at lunchtime just before this call, I ran at lunchtime 35 minutes and then ate my lunch at my desk whilst I was doing bits and pieces of work. I might do some work, I've got a laptop so occasionally I'd be working at home just to, there's a bit more flexibility around the working pattern. If I cycle to work I might get in a little bit later so you know there's a, I think for nobody in [name of company] in my experience are clock watching but for me there's a sense of I have been invested in by the company therefore I need to do my bit. So if I'm not arriving on the dot of half 8 and leaving at 5 then that's not a problem but*

(continued)

Table 3.2 (continued)

	you still need to get the work done. So I think there's a more of a flexible approach to working life than there would have been before. **Medium construction, head of assurance** *I think I expressed an interest in that's what I wanted to do, and the sector that I wanted to work in, and everyone kind of just supports each other to make it happen really. So, yes, I think it depends a lot on who it is and where they want to go and who they're speaking to. But I would say I can probably email any partner and say I'd really like half an hour of your time to go through where I want to go and what I want to do and they'd facilitate it to be honest. I think it's really quite relaxed in that respect.* **Medium accountancy practice, auditor #2**
Inclusivity	***[Interviewer] And do the older people, would they learn stuff from the…*** *Yes they will. Yes, they're brilliant like that. Say if one of the youngsters has got... So sometimes the longer you've been in care you get more set ideas, but then all the older lot are really good. If one of the youngsters says look I've found this works best, this and that, then they do listen and take it onboard. There's no, you know, don't tell me what to do when you're only 21. Everybody, with age wise, is very respectful towards each other.* **Small care provider, manager** *the LGBT group has to be seen alongside the idea of this firm being truly inclusive, the Stonewall stuff speaks for itself and so people are able to come to work and be what they are. And that seems to me it surely has a wellbeing element to it as well. So these groups shouldn't just be seen as they are groups that you can join or not join, they are allied to those other wider initiatives which the firm absolutely is living and breathing. I don't think anybody could possibly counter say that.* **Large, multinational law firm, partner**
Open discussion of health issues and removal of stigma	*I think there's a groundswell of interest in this. We've had no end of feedback, either verbally or written, from people in and around Head Office, to me personally, that says we're so pleased you're doing this, we're really pleased, it's really helping. And we did a wellbeing day around mental health last week, last Thursday, and the first time I did it, it was two years ago, I had three people come and talk to me, this time I've had 40 or 50 just come in the room and take leaflets, talk to me about their stories, their experiences. So that to me is the anecdotal effect of what we're doing, people are far more willing to talk about it. People come and talk to me, you know, in an open plan office or we'll go to a coffee shop and they'll talk about their experiences. But people generally are talking about it, particularly mental health, but now we've got to get that out as being wellbeing, let's talk about wellbeing openly rather than just mental health. So that's my focus for this year.* **Large**

(continued)

Table 3.2 (continued)

	infrastructure and construction, wellbeing lead *I think obviously not just from a business perspective, but mental health awareness is coming to the forefront a lot more. And I think when I have had responses from people there are a lot of people that said actually I would be really interested in doing this because I have had a personal experience with mental health or one of my family members has experienced issues. And I have had some experience with that and I would really like to give something back to the company and help colleagues and share my experiences and the support that they have had. So I think that's quite a lot of it. I think the stigma of mental health is reducing and people are much more willing to talk about it and wanting to talk about it. And help other people if people are going through similar issues.* **Large care provider, human resources business partner #1**
Personal processes	
Self-care	*Also, we've made all the current training courses, forced isn't the right word, we've encouraged people to volunteer for these things and we've been overwhelmed by how many people have volunteered, for instance, for the mental health first aiders course. We've created a profile around that particular course saying these are the sort of attributes you should have before you go on it. We haven't stopped anybody going on it but there are some individuals that have done the course that I suspect will never talk to anybody about their mental health, they've probably done it for their own personal reasons but we didn't want to stop them doing it.* **Large infrastructure and construction, wellbeing lead**

Adverse Effects

Daniels et al. (2021, Table 2) labelled mechanisms activated by an intervention that cause adverse effects '*negative mechanisms*'. Research on these negative mechanisms is more sparse, partly because most interventions tend to have beneficial or no effects (Daniels et al.). However, some interventions do appear to produce negative effects, but the classification of negative mechanisms is necessarily more speculative and tentative than the classification of emergent mechanisms. Even so, it is possible to delineate four potential routes through which interventions may produce or seem to produce adverse effects on wellbeing. The first of these has been discussed in studies of change in terms of methodological 'noise' but pertains to shifts in frames of reference, which themselves may be real effects on those participating in interventions. The second pertains to the other side of social processes, connected to conflict and micro-politics. The third pertains to processes that engender employee cynicism. The fourth pertains to side effects in how the intervention was implemented that can have adverse effects on some or all of a targeted group.

The first category reflects how researchers define change in intervention studies. In quantitative assessments of any intervention or change based on individual reporting experiential or behavioural data on rating scales (e.g. Likert scales), three different forms of change have been identified (Golembiewski, 1986). These are alpha, beta and gamma change. Alpha change is normally what is assumed in intervention studies, and this pertains to the degree of change on the rating scale accurately reflecting *real* change in the construct being measured. That is, a change in reports of anxiety reflects changes in feeling of anxiety. Beta change occurs when individuals change their interpretation of a rating scale. For example following an intervention, an individual may change his/her interpretation of what it means to 'agree strongly' with a statement, thus rendering inferences on the degree of change in a focal construct problematic. Gamma change occurs when an individual or individuals change their conceptualization of a construct. For example an individual may change how s/he defines the experience of anxiety following an intervention. Again, this renders interpretation of changes in rating scales problematic if the intervention was directed at alpha change.

However, as noted by Golembiewski, gamma change implies 'complex and patterned decision-making processes' (1986: 554). Given the socially constructed nature of wellbeing that can be contested and subject to different understandings of what 'wellbeing' is, then alpha change in interventions may not be a realistic assumption in intervention research.[3] Beta change may reflect changes in expectations that individuals have of workplace health and wellbeing programmes, and gamma change reflects changes in how individuals make sense of their experiences of wellbeing (and consequently what practices should be included in workplace wellbeing programmes and how they should be managed). In short, adverse or null effects that appear on the surface to reflect a harmful or ineffective intervention may reflect something far more profound in how individuals have changed their understandings of wellbeing.

Gamma and beta change may be prevalent in intervention studies because change in how people make sense of themselves or their work environment might be one process necessary for certain kinds of intervention to work (Nielsen & Randall, 2013), as the following quote from a manager in medium-sized construction firm illustrates. In this quote, benchmarking and feedback are used to promote self-awareness of responses to work demands and an appraisal of how the informant could change his behaviour.

> So in regards to self-control, my mark was two percent below the company average. So [name of coach] was, basically, asking me, you know, because, obviously, our job is very stressful and we're working to a deadline and there's maybe like a multi-million pound project and that's the nature of the job. But he was saying to me, would you, you know, have a short fuse whenever you're under pressure? And I said, yes, I have to hold my hands up

[3]There do exist statistical techniques to assess whether beta or gamma change has occurred in intervention studies (e.g. Meade et al., 2005). However, our review of the literature suggests these techniques are rarely used.

there. So he was then talking about, how could you work on this? (**Medium construction, bid coordinator**)

Adverse effects may also be a product of conflict between stakeholders in the implementation process. In Chap. 1, we noted that the adverse effects caused by some participative interventions may be the result of intra-group conflict between the goals and needs of different group members. In one study of a Danish participatory intervention focused on redesigning working practices (reported in Abildgaard et al., 2016, 2018; Nielsen et al., 2014; von Thiele Schwarz et al., 2017), intra-group conflict was more evident in some groups of workers that were tasked with developing action plans. The potential for conflict had been recognized and experienced at one of our case companies, an accountancy practice, where a senior human resources manager left because she did not proactively pursue a wellbeing agenda, as illustrated in the following quotes from the managing partner of an accountancy practice:

So that was a difficult time. I spent quite a lot of time trying to persuade my HR (human resources) Exec(utive) at that particular point in time, that that was where we needed to go. She believed it absolutely but just never made time for it. So it was very much a question of sort of trying to put out the fires here, when I'd much rather sort of stop the fires at source, rather than anything else. So I think it was really important to have just, you know, the whole thing, not being sort of shrouded in some form of mysticism. So people could find out basic details like salaries, like personal data and those sorts of things, to be able to manage their team. So in the end, we agreed to go our separate ways. And then it was very much a question of finding somebody who I was convinced was going to be a finisher, as opposed to a thinker (**Medium accountancy practice, managing partner**)

Relatedly, and as reported in the Danish study, workers may become cynical about interventions if they are not perceived to address salient wellbeing needs (also reported in one study described by Greasley & Edwards, 2015; Greasley et al., 2012; Stansfeld et al., 2015) or if there are doubts about whether the intervention truly reflects the genuine intentions of management or whether there is a hidden agenda (reported in one intervention group in Albertsen et al., 2014; one study reported in Fridrich et al., 2016; Jenny et al., 2011, 2015, see also Danford et al., 2004). Other sources of cynicism may stem from failure to implement an intervention as planned or at all. The potential for cynicism and suspicion to undermine interventions were also evident in our case studies. The three quotes below illustrate cynicism and suspicion linked to requiring proof attending to worker wellbeing has benefits, scepticism of underlying motives and antipathy towards change:

Well realistically some areas are better at it than others so some line managers have been very slow to catch up and up until a year or so ago refused to do it at all because they didn't believe it worked. These sorts of things certainly in a construction businesses I have found people watch for other people to try it and see. And you know this is a journey we have been on for three nearly four years now, so how we have diffused it is really getting those people who lead by example, show that it works, who really believe in it and role model it. And then the people are more cynical tend to follow. So there is no rocket science in my answer I am afraid but it's really been a slow burn and focused on behavioural change and people showing that it can be successful with others following (**Large infrastructure and construction, human resources director**)

> Well I would say, but then I stand at partner level, but sitting there the perception I have is that the teams the guys in the teams don't just see this as some sort of hogwash that's there to make the firm look better, but actually it really means it. And I think there has been a high level of engagement. So you may be aware of the Purpose Initiative that the firm is engaging on to become a Purpose Led Business, and I think at anecdotal level I get the sense that people aren't seeing that as just window dressing and they are suspending their lawyers' natural cynicism about that (**Large, multinational law firm, partner**)
>
> But you'll always have people who are sceptical at the start but it's like with anything when there's change, not everybody likes it (**Medium construction, financial controller**)

Related to suspicion is the idea that health and wellbeing are private concerns and not the concern of individual's employer, as illustrated in the following two quotes.

> I remember a colleague saying actually whenever [name of wellbeing programme] was launched and we were in a meeting about that and it was all about you know your physical health, and my colleague was outraged that the company would even be interested in her physical health. She's just like it's private to me, it's got nothing to do with my work. And some people would have that attitude that hang on it's not, it's outside you leave that alone. (**Medium construction, head of assurance**)
>
> I think one of the big challenges we've got is a lot of this impacts on their life outside of work and it's, I've not so much found it within [name of company] but when I've talked about some of the things we're doing to other events, other companies, or other people, they've said well it's none of your business what I do outside of work. You've got no right to ask me to do these things (**Large infrastructure and construction, senior safety adviser**)

The final way in which interventions may come to have adverse effects is through interventions being implemented but being done so in a way that creates side effects. This can create problems across the entire target group or just for a minority in the target group. Tregaskis et al. (2013) report on an intervention that involved significant redesign of work and human resource management practices (e.g. training, performance management). Overall, the intervention appeared to have a beneficial impact on job satisfaction and organisational commitment, while at the same time improving safety and productivity. However, as well as improvements in skill use and decision latitude of workers (which should improve wellbeing in most cases, Karasek & Theorell, 1990), the intervention did also increase the intensity with which workers were required to work. For some workers, this may have adversely affected their wellbeing, although many commented that improvements in development opportunities and pay offset the impact of increased work demands. Another direct example comes from one of the three cases reported by Greasley and colleagues (Greasley & Edwards, 2015; Greasley et al., 2012): Overall, a multicomponent intervention seemed to have no effects on wellbeing. One component of the intervention included a change to performance management practices to emphasize customer service but did not in reality replace existing performance targets focused on call time, effectively meaning workers had two sets of performance criteria instead of just one. Although our case studies did not explicitly reveal any instances of unintended side effects, the potential for adverse side effects was recognized, and strategies put in place to reduce the potential. The following quotes illustrate such strategies. One quote was provided by a human resources manager in a medium-sized construction firm, and two were provided by a human resources manager in a large, multinational law firm. The strategies were adapting the initiative, making it voluntary and being aware of needs and sensitivities at different organisational locations.

> But actually employees were a bit flummoxed so we ended up providing a workshop for employees as well so they could understand how this personality profiling worked and what it meant and how they interplayed with [name of wellbeing programme] and with their day-to-day work. And then managers themselves get coaching and they get access to things, emotional intelligence, mindfulness bit, they are getting probably a higher level of intervention. (**Medium construction, human resources director**)
>
> the thing is, we were talking about healthy eating and healthy food in the canteen, in the middle of the office, the thing is though, not everyone wants to eat, you know, vegan food or vegetarian food. And I think it's about being really clear that, if you don't want to, that's fine, there are other options. It's the same as, if you don't want to be involved in alcohol awareness month, you know, if it's not something that you're interested in, that's absolutely fine. It's not a kind of one size fits all. It's just about saying, these are the different things on offer and if any of these resonate with you and you'd like to be involved, that's fine. I think it's an important point, that we don't kind of force it down people's throats, if you like, because I think once you, you know, if you create that culture, then people feel, god, there's always something going on and I'm always being pressured to attend and get involved, then I think you can kind of lose it early on.
>
> There are challenges and, in truth, a lot of them are around cultural, local cultural sensitivities, things that just wouldn't work elsewhere. And what we've said, is, you know, as much as possible, we will roll things out across all of our global offices, but we also have, there's budget for Dubai to do something that's local to them. And, likewise, Singapore and, likewise, you know, Beijing. So we are kind of realistic that, yes, we want to be inclusive of everyone, but there will be certain nuances that, in truth, you know, are only going to really be known sort of to the local business market. (**Large, multinational law firm, human resources manager**)

In summary, a range of factors could explain any adverse effects of workplace health and wellbeing interventions, relating to conflict, cynicism or side effects in the implementation of practices. However, if workers change their construal of what wellbeing is as a result of an intervention, then what appears to be an adverse effect may in fact reflect something else entirely.

Conclusions

One important conclusion from this chapter is that in order for an intervention to have a beneficial effect, tangible changes have to occur, and mechanisms must be activated that are either embedded in the theory of how the intervention is meant to work and/or emergent from how the intervention is implemented. The importance of making tangible changes cannot be overestimated, even if interventions do not work through the anticipated mechanisms. This is because, practically, simply getting senior managers to talk about wellbeing as a priority without coupling this with practical action may lead to employee cynicism and a deterioration of wellbeing. Elements of the organisational context may serve to stifle implementation or activation of mechanisms: The evidence indicates both of these are possibilities. There may also be several ways in which an intervention can come to have adverse effects. What is clear however, regardless of whether an intervention is implemented as planned or not or works in the manner it is intended to or not, contextual factors around in the intervention and in the wider organisational environment are important as much for intervention success as they are for failure. In the next chapter, we begin to explore the contextual factors in more detail by focusing on the wider organisational context within in which interventions are implemented.

References

Abildgaard, J. S., Nielsen, K., & Sverke, M. (2018). Can job insecurity be managed? Evaluating an organizational-level intervention addressing the negative effects of restructuring. *Work and Stress, 32*, 105–123.

Abildgaard, J. S., Saksvik, P. Ø., & Nielsen, K. (2016). How to measure the intervention process? An assessment of qualitative and quantitative approaches to data collection in the process evaluation of organizational interventions. *Frontiers in Psychology, 7*(1380).

Albertsen, K., Garde, A., Nabe-Nielsen, K., Hansen, Å., Lund, H., & Hvid, H. (2014). Work-life balance among shift workers: Results from an intervention study about self-rostering. *International Archives of Occupational and Environmental Health, 87*, 265–274.

Allexandre, D., Bernstein, A. M., Walker, E., Hunter, J., Roizen, M. F., & Morledge, T. J. (2016). A web-based mindfulness stress management program in a corporate call center: A randomized clinical trial to evaluate the added benefit of onsite group support. *Journal of Occupational and Environmental Medicine, 58*, 254–264.

Andersen, M. F., Nielsen, K., & Brinkmann, S. (2014). How do workers with common mental disorders experience a multidisciplinary return-to-work intervention? A qualitative study. *Journal of Occupational Rehabilitation, 24*, 709–724.

Arends, I., Bültmann, U., Nielsen, K., van Rhenen, W., de Boer, M. R., & van der Klink, J. J. L. (2014). Process evaluation of a problem solving intervention to prevent recurrent sickness absence in workers with common mental disorders. *Social Science and Medicine, 100*, 123–132.

Arends, I., van der Klink, J. J. L., van Rhenen, W., de Boer, M. R., & Bültmann, U. (2014). Prevention of recurrent sickness absence in workers with common mental disorders: Results of a cluster-randomised controlled trial. *Occupational and Environmental Medicine, 71*, 21–29.

Augustsson, H., Schwarz, U. V., Stenfors-Hayes, T., & Hasson, H. (2015). Investigating variations in implementation fidelity of an organizational-level occupational health intervention. *International Journal of Behavioral Medicine, 22*, 345–355.

Biron, C., Gatrell, C., & Cooper, C. L. (2010). Autopsy of a failure: Evaluating process and contextual issues in an organizational-level work stress intervention. *International Journal of Stress Management, 17*, 135–158.

Brakenridge, C. L., Fjeldsoe, B. S., Young, D. C., Winkler, E. A., Dunstan, D. W., Straker, L. M., & Healy, G. N. (2016). Evaluating the effectiveness of organisational-level strategies with or without an activity tracker to reduce office workers' sitting time: A cluster-randomised trial. *International Journal of Behavioral Nutrition, 13*(1), 115.

Brakenridge, C. L., Healy, G. N., Winkler, E. A. H., & Fjeldsoe, B. S. (2018). Usage, acceptability, and effectiveness of an activity tracker in a randomized trial of a workplace sitting intervention: Mixed-methods evaluation. *Interactive Journal of Medical Research, 7*(1), e5.

Byron, G., Ziedonis, D. M., McGrath, C., Frazier, J. A., deTorrijos, F., & Fulwiler, C. (2015). Implementation of mindfulness training for mental health staff: Organizational context and stakeholder perspectives. *Mindfulness, 6*, 861–872.

Carolan, S., & de Visser, R. O. (2018). Employees perspectives on the facilitators and barriers to engaging with digital mental health interventions in the workplace: Qualitative study. *JMIR Mental Health, 5*(1), e8.

Carolan, S., Harris, P. R., Greenwood, K., & Cavanagh, K. (2017). Increasing engagement with an occupational digital stress management program through the use of an online facilitated discussion group: Results of a pilot randomised controlled trial. *Internet Interventions, 10*, 1–11.

Chau, J. Y., Daley, M., Dunn, S., Srinivasan, A., Do, A., Bauman, A. E., & van der Ploeg, H. P. (2014). The effectiveness of sit-stand workstations for changing office workers' sitting time: Results from the Stand@Work randomized controlled trial pilot. *International Journal of Behavioral Nutrition and Physical Activity, 11*(1), 127.

Chau, J. Y., Engelen, L., Burks-Young, S., Daley, M., Maxwell, J. K., Milton, K., & Bauman, A. (2016). Perspectives on a "sit less, move more" intervention in Australian emergency call centres. *Aims Public Health, 3*, 288–297.

Coffey, M., Dugdill, L., & Tattersall, A. (2009). Designing a stress management intervention in social services. *International Journal of Workplace Health Management, 2*, 98–114.

Danford, A., Richardson, M., Stewart, P., Tailby, S., & Upchurch, M. (2004). High performance work systems and workplace partnership: A case study of aerospace workers. *New Technology, Work and Employment, 19*, 14–29.

Daniels, K., Watson, D., & Gedikli, C. (2017). Well-being and the social environment of work: A systematic review of intervention studies. *International Journal of Environmental Research and Public Health, 14*, 918. https://doi.org/10.3390/ijerph14080918

Daniels, K., Watson, D., Nayani, R., Tregaskis, O., Hogg, M., Etuknwa, A., & Semkina, A. (2021). Implementing practices focused on workplace health and psychological wellbeing: A systematic review. *Social Science and Medicine, 227*, 113888.

Edmunds, S., Stephenson, D., & Clow, A. (2013). The effects of a physical activity intervention on employees in small and medium enterprises: A mixed methods study. *Work, 46*, 39–49.

Fitzhugh, H., Michaelides, Connolly, S., & Daniels, K. (2019). *Mindfulness in policing: A randomized controlled trial of two online mindfulness resources across five forces in England and Wales*. College of Policing.

Foureur, M., Besley, K., Burton, G., Yu, N., & Crisp, J. (2013). Enhancing the resilience of nurses and midwives: Pilot of a mindfulness-based program for increased health, sense of coherence and decreased depression, anxiety and stress. *Contemporary Nurse, 45*, 114–125.

Fridrich, A., Jenny, G. J., & Bauer, G. F. (2016). Outcome expectancy as a process indicator in comprehensive worksite stress management interventions. *International Journal of Stress Management, 23*, 1–22.

Golembiewski, R. T. (1986). Contours in social change: Elemental graphics and a surrogate variable for gamma change. *Academy of Management Review, 11*, 550–566.

Greasley, K., & Edwards, P. (2015). When do health and well-being interventions work? Managerial commitment and context. *Economic and Industrial Democracy, 36*, 355–377.

Greasley, K., Edwards, P., Backer-McClearn, D., & Dale, J. (2012). Why do organisations engage in HR initiatives? A test case of a health and wellbeing intervention. *Employee Relations, 34*, 443–462.

Hadgraft, N. T., Willenberg, L., LaMontagne, A. D., Malkoski, K., Dunstan, D. W., Healy, G. N., Moodie, M., Eakin, E. G., Owen, N., & Lawler, S. P. (2017). Reducing occupational sitting: Workers' perspectives on participation in a multi-component intervention. *International Journal of Behavioral Nutrition and Physical Activity, 14*, 73.

Haslam, C., Kazi, A., Duncan, M., Clemes, S., & Twumasi, R. (2018). Walking works wonders: A tailored workplace intervention evaluated over 24 months. *Ergonomics, 672*, 31–41.

Healy, G. N., Winkler, E. A. H., Eakin, E. G., Owen, N., LaMontagne, A. D., Moodie, M., & Dunstan, D. W. (2017). A cluster RCT to reduce workers' sitting time: Impact on cardiometabolic biomarkers. *Medicine and Science in Sports and Exercise, 49*, 2032–2039.

Jenny, G., Inauen, A., Brauchli, R., Füllemann, D., Müllerm F., & Bauer G. (2011). *Projekt SWiNG—Schlussbericht der Evaluation: Management Summary* [online].

Gesundheitsförderung Schwiez. Available at: https://gesundheitsfoerderung.ch/assets/public/documents/de/5-grundlagen/publikationen/bgm/2011-07_Projekt_SWiNG_Schlussbericht_-_Management_Summary.pdf.
Jenny, G. J., Brauchli, R., Inauen, A., Füllemann, D., Fridrich, A., & Bauer, G. F. (2015). Process and outcome evaluation of an organizational-level stress management intervention in Switzerland. *Health Promotion International, 30*, 573–585.
Karanika-Murray, M., & Biron, C. (2013). The nature of change in organizational health interventions: Some observations and propositions. In G. Bauer & G. Jenny (Eds.), *Salutogenic organizations and change* (pp. 239–258). Springer.
Karasek, R., & Theorell, T. (1990). *Healthy work: Stress, productivity, and the reconstruction of working life*. Basic Books.
Kidger, J., Stone, T., Tilling, K., Brockman, R., Campbell, R., Ford, T., Hollingworth, W., King, M., Araya, R., & Gunnell, D. (2016). A pilot cluster randomised controlled trial of a support and training intervention to improve the mental health of secondary school teachers and students—the WISE (Wellbeing in Secondary Education) study. *BMC Public Health, 16*, 1060.
Kitchener, B. A., & Jorm, A. F. (2004). Mental health first aid training in a workplace setting: A randomized controlled trial [ISRCTN13249129]. *BMC Psychiatry, 4*, 1–8.
Martin, M. H., Nielsen, M. B., Petersen, S. M., Jakobsen, L. M., & Rugulies, R. (2012). Implementation of a coordinated and tailored return-to-work intervention for employees with mental health problems. *Journal of Occupational Rehabilitation, 22*, 427–436.
Martin, M. H. T., Nielsen, M. B. D., Madsen, I. E. H., Petersen, S. M. A., Lange, T., & Rugulies, R. (2013). Effectiveness of a coordinated and tailored return-to-work intervention for sickness absence beneficiaries with mental health problems. *Journal of Occupational Rehabilitation, 23*, 621–630.
Meade, A. W., Lautenschlager, G. J., & Hecht, J. E. (2005). Establishing measurement equivalence and invariance in longitudinal data with item response theory. *International Journal of Testing, 5*, 279–300.
Menzel, J., Wollesen, B., Fendel, R., & Mattes, K. (2015). Erfolgsfaktoren zur Umsetzung von Betrieblicher Gesundheitsförderung in kleinen und mittelständischen Unternehmen. *Gruppendynamik und Organisationsberatung, 46*, 245–264.
Moll, S. E., Patten, S., Stuart, H., MacDermid, J. C., & Kirsh, B. (2018). Beyond silence: A randomized, parallel-group trial exploring the impact of workplace mental health literacy training with healthcare employees. *The Canadian Journal of Psychiatry, 63*, 826–833.
Moll, S. E., VandenBussche, J., Brooks, K., Kirsh, B., Stuart, H., Patten, S., & MacDermid, J. C. (2018). Workplace mental health training in health care: Key ingredients of implementation. *The Canadian Journal of Psychiatry, 53*, 834–841.
Nielsen, K., & Randall, R. (2013). Opening the black box: Presenting a model for evaluating organizational-level interventions. *European Journal of Work and Organizational Psychology, 22*, 601–617.
Nielsen, K., Abildgaard, J. S., & Daniels, K. (2014). Putting context into organizational intervention design: Using tailored questionnaires to measure initiatives for worker well-being. *Human Relations, 67*, 1537–1560.
Page, K. M., & Vella-Brodrick, D. A. (2013). The working for wellness program: RCT of an employee well-being intervention. *Journal of Happiness Studies, 14*, 1007–1031.
Pawson, R., & Manzano-Santaella, A. (2012). A realist diagnostic workshop. *Evaluation, 18*, 176–191.
Saksvik, P. Ø., Faergestad, M., Fossum, S., Olaniyan, O. S., Indergard, Ø., & Karanika-Murray, M. (2018). An effect evaluation of the psychosocial work environment of a university unit after a successfully implemented employeeship program. *International Journal of Workplace Health Management, 11*, 31–44.
Saksvik, P. Ø., Olaniyan, O. S., Lysklett, K., Lien, M., & Bjerke, L. (2015). A process evaluation of a salutogenic intervention. *Scandinavian Psychologist, 2*, e8.

Schelvis, R. M., Wiezer, N. M., van der Beek, A. J., Twisk, J. W., Bohlmeijer, E. T., & Oude Hengel, K. M. (2017). The effect of an organizational level participatory intervention in secondary vocational education on work-related health outcomes: Results of a controlled trial. *BMC Public Health, 17*(1), 141.

Stansfeld, S. A., Kerry, S., Chandola, T., Russell, J., Berney, L., Hounsome, N., Lanz, D., Costelloe, C., Smuk, M., & Bhui, K. (2015). Pilot study of a cluster randomised trial of a guided e-learning health promotion intervention for managers based on management standards for the improvement of employee well-being and reduction of sickness absence: GEM Study. *BMJ Open, 5*(10), e007981.

Tafvelin, S., von Thiele Schwarz, U., Nielsen, K., & Hasson, H. (2018). Employees' and line managers' active involvement in participatory organizational interventions: Examining direct, reversed, and reciprocal effects on well-being. *Stress and Health, 35*, 69–80.

Tregaskis, O., Daniels, K., Glover, L., Butler, P., & Meyer, M. (2013). High performance work practices and firm performance: A longitudinal case study. *British Journal of Management, 24*, 225–244.

Undebakke, K. G., Innstrand, S. T., Anthun, K. S., & Christensen, M. (2015). *ARK: The ARK intervention programme; who—what—how*. Centre for Health Promotion Research.

von Thiele Schwarz, U., Augustsson, H., Hasson, H., & Stenfors-Hayes, T. (2015). Promoting employee health by integrating health protection, health promotion, and continuous improvement: A longitudinal quasi-experimental intervention study. *Journal of Occupational and Environmental Medicine, 57*, 217–225.

von Thiele Schwarz, U., Lundmark, R., & Hasson, H. (2016). The dynamic integrated evaluation model (DIEM): Achieving sustainability in organizational intervention through a participatory evaluation approach. *Stress and Health, 32*, 285–293.

von Thiele Schwarz, U., Nielsen, K. M., Stenfors-Hayes, T., & Hasson, H. (2017). Using kaizen to improve employee well-being: Results from two organizational intervention studies. *Human Relations, 70*, 966–993.

Zhang, Y., Flum, M., Kotejoshyer, R., Fleishman, J., Henning, R., & Punnett, L. (2016). Workplace participatory occupational health/health promotion program facilitators and barriers observed in three nursing homes. *Journal of Gerontological Nursing, 42*, 34–42.

Zhang, Y., Flum, M., West, C., & Punnett, L. (2015). Assessing organizational readiness for a participatory occupational health/health promotion intervention in skilled nursing facilities. *Health Promotion Practice, 16*, 724–732.

Chapter 4
Competing Logics

One of the conclusions of the previous chapter was that the failure or success of an intervention is dependent on a range of contextual factors, and that context should not be considered only as an issue where interventions have no or adverse effects. In this chapter, we focus on the wider context of the organisation and its environment (sometimes referred to as the omnibus context in the literature, following Johns, 2006). We uncover a range of factors that can aid or hinder implementation of workplace health and wellbeing initiatives, differentiating those factors internal to the wider context of the organisation and those of the context external to the organisation. Although the literature tends to indicate that adverse contextual factors (lack of resources, concurrent organisational changes) in almost all cases derail interventions (cf. Biron & Karanika-Murray, 2015; Roodbari et al., 2021), we argue adverse contextual factors in the wider organisational context reflect competing organisational logics (e.g. in respect of priorities for resourcing decisions). Therefore, how tensions between competing logics are managed and/or resolved may determine the effectiveness of interventions.

By organisational logics, we mean the ways in which organisational decision makers conceptualize the organisation and its environment, which are stored in decision makers' memories via cognitive schemas, and which influence decisions made about how the organisation runs, should run, organisational goals and priorities (after Prahalad and Bettis' conception of dominant logics in organisations, 1986). Some logics may emphasize the importance of wellbeing (e.g. for staff retention), yet others may emphasize, for example, long working hours as an important driver of productivity.

Such logics are not necessarily homogenous in any given organisation and may be subject to a range of influences (Daniels et al., 2002), therefore leading to the potential for multiple logics within the same organisation. However, we do not consider that competing logics are evident just between different groups of stakeholders and we consider it possible that the same individual can hold competing logics (after El-Sawad et al., 2004). Competing logics may be inevitable when it comes to implementing workplace health and wellbeing practices because worker

K. Daniels et al., *Achieving Sustainable Workplace Wellbeing*, Aligning Perspectives on Health, Safety and Well-Being, https://doi.org/10.1007/978-3-031-00665-4_4

health and wellbeing is, usually and at best,[1] a secondary organisational goal to the primary purposes of organisations to deliver services or products, for profit (privately owned businesses), as efficiently as possible (public sector organisations) or to specific targets (e.g., disadvantaged groups, voluntary sector organisations). Where logics lead to diverging conclusions, choices or priorities, then there are competing logics, and implementation problems may occur.

We begin the chapter by examining the evidence for competing logics in the literature and in our case data, before exploring in more depth the evidence for 'wellbeing' logics, and how organisations confront or otherwise address such logics.

What Are the Competing Logics?

The received wisdom and much of the reported evidence is that adverse 'omnibus' contexts affect the implementation of interventions or the activation of mechanisms in detrimental ways (Biron & Karanika-Murray, 2015; Daniels et al., 2021). The omnibus context itself may be divided into factors internal to the organisation and factors external to the organisation. However, to some degree, this is an artificial distinction, because internal organisational adjustments to changes in the external environment affect whether or how health and wellbeing interventions are implemented. In turn, organisational responses to the external environment are determined by how different organisational stakeholders perceive the external environment and judgements of appropriate responses, which themselves are influenced by stakeholders' logics and political processes that determine which logic prevails in a given situation (Johnson, 1987).

In relation to the internal omnibus context, our review of the evidence from interventions studies suggests the following factors are most prevalent in respect of adverse contexts:[2] Competing priorities that acted to limit opportunities for stakeholders to engage with the interventions and included workload, time constraints and concurrent organisational changes; lack of capacity or capability in the organisation to implement the changes required by the intervention; and lack of resources, including financial resources. Competing priorities, capability to implement changes and resourcing were also evident in our case data, as the following three quotes illustrate:

> Competing priorities: And I also think that just the busyness of life and of working life in particular. You know it's a danger that it could get crowded out, as I mentioned before there are lots of initiatives that are going on all the time within our industry you've got legislative issues which are very important. You've got government led things so post Grenfell (a major

[1] An exception would be 'lifestyle' businesses set up to provide an income for owner/managers. Even here, minimum thresholds of performance would be required to ensure the survivability of the business and ensure income for the owners and any employees.

[2] This classification is based on more in-depth analysis of the evidence from studies synthesised in Daniels et al. (2021).

> fire) there's a massive focus now on fire safety and rightly so. There's always a focus on health and safety generally for our workforce and that's always at the top of people's agenda There's lots and lots of different things that are vying for attention in the minds of our managers. So I think that's a risk that just gets crowded out by the busyness of working life. (**Medium construction, head of assurance**)
>
> Capacity or capability to change: There is always a resistance to change. This is predominantly an old-fashioned environment to work in, accountancy is what it is and tax is what it is, and there's always people who are resistant to change and our capacity to evolve is determined by so many different factors. But I think, as I mentioned earlier, I think generationally things are shifting and there will be a migration of people from a certain generation to be replaced by people who do really understand all this. (**Medium accountancy practice, senior manager**)
>
> Resourcing: Because I don't have a budget, as the wellbeing forum I don't have a budget, so it's very difficult for me to sit down in 2019 and say right, this is what we're going to do this year and it's going to cost me £50,000, [Name of director with responsibility for health and safety]. And he's going to say no, you just need to do what you're doing but not have a budget for it. (**Large infrastructure and construction, wellbeing lead**)

However, this last quote does indicate differences in access to resources according to positional power in the organisation, because our interview with the human resources director stated:

> Usually when I want to run things I'll go and say can I spend this money and I've never been told no so far. (**Large infrastructure and construction, human resources director**)

One other factor, which was articulated in relation to safety in our two case companies from the construction sector, was the difficulty in translating wellbeing outcomes in terms of hard metrics compared to performance outcomes. This is also reflected in the following quote from a large, multinational law firm. In this quote, the ease with which priority financial targets can be articulated is contrasted with the nature of wellbeing.

> I think also there is a part going back to the partners and line managers where we are setting objectives for people and setting objectives around must meet financial targets. Compared to a behaviour expectation or desirable behaviours, that's something you can deal with there. But it's more challenging to think of something a bit more nebulous than it is to simply say here is an output based on objectives. It needs more thought and probably more enlightenment in relation to people who are the performance reviewers when setting the objectives with the team member. (**Large, multinational law firm, partner**)

Although competing priorities and viewing wellbeing as a nebulous concept are clear examples of competing logics, issues relating to capability, capacity and resourcing reflect entrained ways of thinking and/or decisions about where to invest effort in recruiting or developing capacity as well as resourcing the intervention, and so also reflect competing logics.

Where studies reviewed by Daniels et al. (2021) reported favourable internal omnibus contexts, these tended to focus on capacity and capability to make changes or adequate resourcing levels (subsuming financial resources). We could infer that one feature of favourable internal omnibus context is the absence of competing priorities. Notwithstanding, an unfavourable internal omnibus context does not guarantee an intervention will fail, and a favourable internal omnibus context does not guarantee that an intervention will succeed. Indeed, the quotes from our informants on unfavourable contextual features above come from cases where programmes of health and wellbeing activities had been implemented. Rather, the favourability of the internal omnibus context simply increases the chances of intervention success or failure (Daniels et al.).

In respect of the external omnibus context, of the four studies in the review that mentioned unfavourable external contexts, three referred to adverse labour markets or recessionary pressures and one to restricted ability to make changes because of external political pressures on organisations (see Daniels et al., 2021). Similarly, our case companies mentioned factors related to labour markets (such as received practices for employing agency workers on temporary contracts in construction), pressures from clients and regulation by professional bodies:

> Unfortunately we do get quite a lot of transient work where they will come in for just a few weeks and then disappear again. So that's very hard to get a handle on really. But generally speaking I think everyone's, I'm just thinking, I can think of three or four examples while I'm sat here of people who over a period of time have sort of in their demeanour have become softer and don't feel like they've got to put up this hard face all the time. And are much more pro, sorry likely to open up and say something or talk about an experience in a way that then gives them the opportunity to bring out any problems that they've got. You do see some of that but it's quite hard to do when you've got a constantly changing workforce. (**Large infrastructure and construction, groundworks worker**)
>
> I think just the very environment we work in where there are very demanding clients and some very demanding projects in the sense of the type of locations they are in. And how some of those projects have to be delivered. A great example is we do an awful lot of work underground, rail, highways, tunnelling that sort of thing. Not always the best physical conditions to work in but there is not an awful lot of choice around that. (**Large infrastructure and construction, human resources director**)
>
> And I think you also look at the people on training contracts who are under pressures to, it could be a personal pressure or broader pressure, to get a series of passes at exams to go onto the next stage of their careers. I'm not saying careers are over if they don't pass but they can be compromising for people. So it's a huge pressure on people and you see evidence of it when the results day comes, when results are impending for ACCA or CTA exams, you see the people are struggling. It's a big moment to cope with. That's where we need to be supportive. Because there will be people who do well, and there will also be people who don't do quite so well who are the ones who are feeling very isolated. (**Medium accountancy practice, senior manager**)

Daniels et al. (2021) concluded that adverse external environments do have detrimental effects on the effectiveness of health and wellbeing interventions. However, some in our case companies recognize adverse features of the external environment, and yet these companies have implemented health and wellbeing programmes, and Daniels et al. did point to studies where concurrent organisational changes did not completely negate beneficial effects of the intervention, and so suggested internal adjustments to external changes may not always have detrimental effects on interventions. In this respect, one of these studies (reported in Abildgaard et al., 2016, 2018; Nielsen et al., 2014; von Thiele Schwarz et al., 2017) is particularly interesting, because it focused on an organisation undergoing a restructuring programme in response to a long-run decline for demand in its services: Specifically, the focal organisation was the Danish postal service which was downsizing in relation to declining use of traditional mail services. Therefore, there is evidence from at least one longitudinal study of a controlled intervention that health and wellbeing practices can be implemented against a backdrop of internal organisational adjustments to adverse external contexts. In this case, we would argue that the competing logic of downsizing was reconciled with the logic underpinning the health and wellbeing intervention. Moreover, two studies conducted during the COVID-19 pandemic (2020–2021), reported a maintained focus on wellbeing in work groups or organisations that had implemented workplace health and wellbeing initiatives (Dollard & Bailey, 2021; Nayani et al., 2021). In the case of COVID-19, the impacts on mental health due to social distancing measures and new working practices were well documented, in addition to economic impacts (ILO, 2020; ONS, 2020a–2020d). Therefore, these two studies of organisations during the pandemic provide further evidence that external shocks need not undermine implementation of health and wellbeing practices, provided health and wellbeing logics are salient.

Evidence for Wellbeing Logics

From the interventions literature, we can only infer the presence of organisational logics pertaining to health and wellbeing and that they may somehow come into competition with other organisational logics. More direct evidence of the logics that underpin decisions to implement health and wellbeing practices, and the logics that compete against them comes from our case studies.

Our case data revealed that organisational stakeholders could articulate wellbeing logics that formed at least part of the case, if not the whole case, for implementing health and wellbeing programmes. Some of these focused on internal factors and some on organisational responses to external circumstances. These wellbeing logics could be categorized around those focused on making a business case around performance (focused on internal context) and/or recruitment and retention (internal responses to external labour market factors), and those focused on care for employees or responding to perceived expectations to conform with changing societal norms.

In respect of the performance benefits of wellbeing programmes, the first quote from a senior human resources manager in a construction firm is illustrative of what might be called standard reasoning in relation to the performance benefits of wellbeing programmes:

> And when we started doing [name of wellbeing programme] and we looked at that cohort of people who do [name of wellbeing programme] their engagement is higher than anybody else in the business, their turnover is lower. These things we are doing are making a difference, absenteeism is down, turnover is down, engagement is up, all these people results are positive. And on the back of all of that the business is more profitable and turns over more than it did previously. (**Medium construction, human resources director**)

However, this second quote from a law firm illustrates other potential business benefits, in that a healthy and happy workforce is more productive, meaning that the same amount of work can be done by a smaller number of people than could be achieved with an unhealthy and unhappy workforce:

> It's probably good to pick up the business impact of that as well because as well as helping people and having a better working environment, to be blunt it allows us to use less office space, have less offices, and rent out floors that we don't need. So there's a direct business benefit to the health and wellbeing agenda as well. (**Large, multinational law firm, health & safety manager**)

Responses to labour market conditions tended to be articulated more often by informants working in sectors with skills shortages (e.g. construction) and/or a high skill requirements (e.g. accountancy, law), as illustrated in the following quotes from a senior partner in a medium-sized accountancy practice in relation to recruitment and the second from a manager in a medium-sized construction firm in relation to retention:

> One of the great things we're doing now is we can say to people actually if you want to come and work for us these are our credentials. I'm not just saying this, this is what's happening. We're recognised for the fact that we are a good employer to work for, which is massively important. And particularly important I think for grads (graduates) coming in because I think any firm now they're looking at their corporate responsibility policies, they're looking at their wellbeing policies, they're looking at the things which can be offered in terms of work/life balances. There's a lot of people in accountancy who are burnt out by the time they're 50, in the bigger firms, because they haven't had this sort of support, and I think we are doing something which I think makes us, not unique because I think a lot of firms are doing this but in the sector we are probably doing something which is beyond what other firms are doing currently. Currently, they'll catch up but the thing is it's an evolutionary process isn't it. (**Medium accountancy practice, senior manager**)
>
> the proof will be in the pudding and the staff retention, that's really the metrics you need to look at is the retention of staff and that's kind of the main reason for doing it I suppose. (**Medium construction, contracts director**)

However, other logics in relation to retention were also evident in the data. The next quote from a human resource manager in a medium-sized accounting practice illustrates the benefits of not having to recruit new staff:

> The skills market, for example, for qualified and part qualified accountants, is really tight. There's not enough resource coming through to do the jobs that we need them to do, so there are recruitment issues. And that was the other side of it, you know, actually, if you spent more on retaining and less on recruiting, then, you know, overall quality, happiness, everything would be much better. (**Medium accountancy practice, head of human resources**)

The next quote from a human resources manager in a medium-sized construction firm indicates another retention problem linked to risky lifestyle behaviours, namely serious illness:

> And it was because we send our staff, when they are over forty you go for a medical every year its voluntary but everybody goes. And what happens is we get that data back and what was happening about four or five years ago we were getting this data back where they were telling us that the majority of people who were going were either a heart attack or a stroke waiting to happen. We had high alcohol consumption, people weren't taking exercise, a lot of information was there and it was a risk to the business. So we have got a lot of the senior people in this business and because they were very professional basis on where we are going,

a lot of people could die, that knowledge is going to be going out of the business. So regardless of their the human side in terms of wanting to do the right thing there was a potential business issue here. (**Medium construction, human resources director**)

The last part of this quote in respect of '*wanting to do the right thing*' links both a business case (retention) with an ethical case concerned with care. This illustrates that wellbeing logics can cohere around multiple reasons for implementing a programme. The quote also illustrates one way in which programmes that provide benefits for the business can be implemented, but in a way that does not encourage employee cynicism and perceptions that health and wellbeing initiatives are introduced solely for the benefit of the business with no real regard for the welfare of employees. This point is also illustrated in the following quote from a large, multinational law firm, in the context of high fee earning lawyers:

frankly if you can't be bothered spending a bit of time looking after people there's something wrong. So as well as being the right thing to do there's obvious business benefits to us and as [name of co-worker] said the diversity inclusive stuff, you know, the more you go into that and the more diverse groups of people you employ, people talk to each other all the time and if Fred's looking for a job, they're not happy somewhere because they're not being treated well, oh why don't you come and see us. And we do recruit a lot of staff like that. (**Large, multinational law firm, health & safety manager**)

In the care sector, which is low skill and where, at least at the time of interviewing, the labour market was in employers' favour, a very different logic with regard to retention was articulated by one care home manager. In this quote, although high levels of turnover are accepted as an industry norm, staff in the home were encouraged to develop skills to move to better jobs, and so turnover is seen as a good thing if staff can develop and contribute positively while employed in the care home—again indicating concern for the individual worker rather than the business:

Not really because we always kind of have and it's just always happened naturally that one of the staff will say well I know somebody else isn't happy where they are or that's looking. It's obviously a bit of a pain for me when you've had someone that knows the job but a few years is not too bad for someone to be employed in a care home. There's a really high turnover of staff in care homes so if somebody stayed here three to four years while they were training themselves to do something different, that's not altogether bad I don't think. (**Small care provider, manager**)

One area linked to recruitment and retention was changing societal expectations around working conditions, wellbeing and employers' obligations in this regard, as illustrated in the following quotes from a manager in a large construction and infrastructure firm and one from a large, multinational law firm:

Slowly but surely over the last decade I think construction companies have realised that yes you can match people's wages, you can match their benefits as in a car, a health scheme and that, but actually the differentiator is probably all the softer issues that we can start introducing, like flexible working, extended parental leave, maternity leave, help with childcare and all that sort of stuff that is actually really important, especially to the millennials. Less so important to the older generation because they're thinking as long as I've got my pension then I'm alright and I've got my car. But the millennials are a slightly different culture and it's yes I can get a wage and I can get that wage pretty much wherever I go, and I can get a car and stuff like that, but it's working conditions and how you treat me which is important to me now. Will I get to get flexible working when my first child arrives or what care and consideration will you give to my working day when I have to go and look after my children on half term week and things like that. (**Large infrastructure and construction, wellbeing lead**)

So there has been a sea change but I think a lot of that happens with our competitors and I think it also reflects a lot of what has gone into society. So there are two strands to this, one is what do our clients expect of us, what do they want to see, they want to mirror, they would want us to mirror what they are doing. And so there is that, plus also being able to attract and retain the very best people. So there is that clearly commercial focus to it. (**Large, multinational law firm, partner**)

To summarise so far, wellbeing logics seemed to cohere around a business case in relation to enhanced performance, but logics appeared to be better developed and more nuanced in respect of recruitment and retention, especially in hard to recruit to sectors and in relation to meeting societal expectations. One key element that may be a critical condition for realizing health, wellbeing and performance benefits of health and wellbeing programmes may be genuine—or authentic—care for employees and a focus on realizing benefits for employees rather than benefits solely for the business. Indeed, in a systematic review of the effects of workplace interventions on wellbeing, Fox et al. (in press) found the interventions focused on employer rather than employee need uniformly had adverse effects on wellbeing. We will return to the topic of authentic care in the Chap. 8.

One curious omission from the wellbeing logics articulated by our informants was mention of regulatory requirements around health and safety. In the UK, there is no distinction in law between physical and psychological injury caused by work (Coleman, 1994), and so employers have a duty of care to ensure reasonable actions are taken to minimize risks to work-related psychological harm. In the three instances where health and safety legislation was mentioned by participants, it was in the context of contrasting managing wellbeing with managing physical risk, as this quote from a construction manager illustrates:

we give all these safety and health professionals lots of safety training, we don't actually give them much wellbeing training. We'll train them on control of hazardous substances because that's the legal requirement but do we give them any training on promoting wellbeing and what does wellbeing mean to us and what's the training associated with that. So I think we're playing catch up. They recognise that wellbeing is as important as safety because the two are intrinsically linked. If you've got good wellbeing then you're more likely as a human being not to do something that's going to put you at risk safety wise. But I'm not quite sure how we supplement the training. It's very easy in safety isn't it. You go on a health and safety work course, you do COSH training, you do work at height training, all these good things, what's the list of courses to make you a great wellbeing champion? And I'm not sure we've quite got the answer yet, which I guess is why we're having this conversation. (**Large infrastructure and construction, wellbeing lead**)

Management of Competing Logics

From our case data and the literature, there is evidence that implementing health and wellbeing practices and programmes of practices may be hindered, if not completely derailed, by logics that compete with the logics underpinning the management of health and wellbeing in the workplace. There is also evidence from our cases that organisational decision makers can articulate 'health and wellbeing logics' that can encapsulate organisational and individual benefits from implementing practices and/or programmes. In this section, we explore how tensions between health and wellbeing logics and other competing logics may be resolved or at least tolerated.

The most basic case of resolving tensions with competing logics is where prevailing power is with the organisational actors holding the health and wellbeing logic, such as where implementers have a great deal of autonomy or where implementers are supported by key decision makers (e.g. executive board level), as illustrated from quotes from two different care providers:

> Yes, we're a home in our own right. The company as a whole, we're the only learning disability home in the group and to be fair we're sort of, not treated different, we get support from Head Office but we are allowed to do our own thing as well. With the old people's home they like them to all be run on a similar level obviously but we're given a little bit more leeway to be a bit more, possibly sometimes, I don't know, quirky, and they respect the fact that we're doing something different to the other homes basically as well, which works for us. (**Small care provider, manager**)
>
> But the road map I think is there through the strategy of what we're trying to achieve and in fairness to the executive board they say we see you, we hear you, we know what you're trying to do and we're giving you the tools and also the funding to try and do that. Just keep coming back and reporting and tell us how that's going and how that's transforming. (**Large care provider, head of corporate facilities**)

However, in other cases, competing logics were recognized as a problem by some of our case informants, and competing logics need to be challenged and changed. In both the following quotes, challenging and changing relates to giving greater emphasis to staff wellbeing as a means to address high staff turnover rates related to historical ways of managing people:

> About four years ago really where the sector was coming out of I guess a huge recession that had seen [name of firm] in particular not make much money for quite a while. Lots of projects not turn out the way the sector wanted them, lots of changes in government funding levels, lot of people leaving the industry all of that sort of stuff. And the recognition that you can do OK if you do the same that you always did but you would never be good and certainly never exceptional. And it was just an opportunity to look at some of the core things that had always been the construction way of doing things fundamentally differently to make us different. And some of the things I have mentioned that we have been doing were part of that. We have a value which is called [label for company value which promotes questioning] and some of the things around working patterns and how jobs have to be delivered and how working conditions have to be were part of that challenge. And just asking some questions as to why, why have we always done it this way or why is it that people think like they do. Or why is that at that time we had a voluntary attrition rate of 24 percent, why. (**Large infrastructure and construction, human resources director**)

I think there is no doubt there are people in business still who would be listening to me thinking what a load of old tosh, I don't get this at all, but that's the type of stuff we have to re-educate people on, in my view. And it is a re-educational process and you're never too old to be re-educated, to learn. If employers could embrace all this to a greater extent they wouldn't be having those conversations with their HR (human resources) teams saying we've got another vacancy to fill. (**Medium accountancy practice, senior manager**)

Seeking to legitimate health and wellbeing logics and associated practices through external recognition was also evident in the data, whether the recognition was through gaining awards as in the first quote below or using practices approved by professional bodies or governments as in the second quote:

when we were starting to do work with IIP (recognised employment standard) or started to meet around or talk around going towards the IIP award in terms of the IOSH (standard approved by body for health and safety professionals) standard, the wellbeing standard, it was well actually we need to have a structure here. We are doing all these things and they are all good we think they are good but we not actually sure whether they are getting the results that we want. Are they exactly what people need, can we be more strategic, more coordinated in terms of wellbeing. (**Medium construction, human resources director**)

So I went to the CIPD (human resources profession) conference in Manchester last November and spoke to a gentleman who was on their (UK Government department) stand and I will be honest with you it all seemed too good to be true. Because it's a free service, it's at no cost to us as an employer. We sign up for it and we get access to these free resources which is brilliant. (**Large care provider, human resources business partner #2**)

One of the most frequently mentioned and elaborated factors in the case interviews was the use of evidence-based arguments, using data collected from the organisation. Many of these arguments were described in a factual manner by presenting dispassionate and logical business-focused arguments, for example:

I actually see it as being a business decision. I don't see this as actually being anything that is light and fluffy or anything like that. This is, as you've probably gathered, it's relatively systemised, it's relatively, in my mind, it's just obvious (**Medium accountancy practice, managing partner**)

But at the moment, it's kind of, you know, let's do what feels right based on our knowledge of the business. And the knowledge is strong, you know, we link in with the business on things like exit interviews and, you know, generally, you know, we're closely linked with the business. And so, I think, we're able to give a good steer to start with, but, obviously, this will evolve and this is incredibly early stages in many respects. (**Large, multinational law firm, human resources manager**)

Some of that information was coming back from [name of occupational health provider] that's coming back from the medicals that people were going to. Other information was coming back through employee engagement surveys. So we were identifying people who were having issues and as well as alongside that some of that was just the fact that people were talking to us and we knew that was a problem. We also look at people who are leaving, so we have a regular review of leavers, the reasons why people leave and actually being away from home was one, it was the top reason. So people were saying I can't hack it I can't deal with this any longer. (**Medium construction, human resources director**)

We also found in the data examples of using evidence to transfer practices from other sectors, but no direct evidence that practices in other sectors were used to legitimize implementing health and wellbeing practices per se. However, as the following quote illustrates, evidence from another sector was used to establish a pilot:

> the flexible working thing for example was a real challenge for some of our people to get their heads around. And I was able to show some examples from other sectors where how looking at jobs slightly differently in a lot of areas had paid real dividends. And the initial response I got if I am honest was well we don't think this will change the game but try it and see (**Large infrastructure and construction, human resources director**)

One thing that was apparent in the data was the use of evidence to address business problems that are salient for that organisation (for example turnover rates in both construction firms in our sample, evidenced in quotes presented earlier in this chapter). Addressing salient business problems through a health and wellbeing logic provides a counterpoint to competing logics that may pertain to ways in which the organisation should work and connects the health and wellbeing logic to the processes and practices that maintain organisational functioning rather than undermining that functioning. For example competing logics that are predicated on long working hours as a mean to secure profits can be challenged by health and wellbeing logics that link wellbeing to profit through promoting staff retention. The way in which health and wellbeing logics incorporate solutions to problems suggests that health and wellbeing logics are developed, at least in organisations that successfully implement health and wellbeing initiatives, by organisational actors with a good knowledge of how to address priorities particular to that organisation (a point also made by Daniels et al., 2019).[3] However, as also noted by Daniels et al., rational evidence-led arguments can be supplemented by 'stories' that help to provide compelling and tangible narratives. Such stories, if they have a 'shock' element may provide enough of a salient signal that cannot be undermined by questioning the credibility of other sources of evidence (cf., Johnson, 1987). Evidence of data-led arguments addressing salient business problems alongside narratives to shock other organisational actors comes from a series of inter-linked quotes from a human resources manager in a medium-sized accounting practice:

> Yes, shock tactics. And there might have been, the one thing I've learnt is, you know, the numbers are so, so important to them, that's their language. And I didn't want them to think oh it's HR (human resources) coming in with another fluffy initiative. So I made it real and you know, it's tangible then, isn't it? If you're talking about pounds, it's tangible.
>
> Well, yes, I mean, obviously, I've worked in different industries and acceptable staff turnover, for example, varies. But what I was able to say to them is, at that point in time, when I joined in early 2016, their staff turnover rate was higher than the turnover rate in the [name of well-known insurance company] call centres in the late nineties, when call centres were badged as Satanic mills of hell and all of that, and it was higher than the turnover in the call centre back in, you know, the bad days, if you like. And I think that was a real shocker to them.

---

[3]Interestingly, in our case data, there was no evidence of organisational actors using scientific/academic evidence to challenge competing logics. On the one hand, this may reflect general ignorance of this literature. On the other, it may (also) reflect that scientific evidence is too abstract and generic to make the case in any one given organisation.

> Yes. So it was about May 2017, I stood in front of them all and gave them the numbers and, I suppose, essentially, bribed them. And said, look, if you say you're not going to sign up to this, you're saying that you don't care about the wellbeing of your people. And I think it was the realisation, I think they all knew, they're all behind it, you know, they all support it. But I think it was the kind of, the jolt that was needed, the honesty that was needed. Because I think things had not been how they wanted it for some time but they didn't have that kind of catalyst, if you like. So I came in and just, you know, threw the rocket in and made it happen. (**Medium accountancy practice, head of human resources**)

To this point in this section, the data presented from our cases suggests health and wellbeing logics are promoted to supplant, or at least significantly diminish the power of, competing logics, and evidence is used in various ways to achieve this. However, another approach is for health and wellbeing logics to have an accommodation with competing logics, so that they are able co-exist. The following two quotes, from informants from the same large multinational law firm, indicate how health and wellbeing logics can be restrained. The second quote, in particular, indicates the restraints come from both resources available and because prevailing logics impose constraints on what businesses are expected to do for employee health and wellbeing.

> I think it's an important point, that we don't kind of force it down people's throats, if you like, because I think once you, you know, if you create that culture, then people feel, god, there's always something going on and I'm always being pressured to attend and get involved, then I think you can kind of lose it early on (**Large, multinational law firm, human resources manager**)
>
> You know if we had a never-ending amount of resource and budget we could do everything in the world but you know we can't physically do that and also as a business are we expected to be able to do this because we are just a business we're not you know we're not a person's friend who maybe you would have different expectations on to support you in a different way. (**Large, multinational law firm, responsible business associate**)

Conclusions

This chapter illustrates that implementation may be influenced not so much by the favourability of the wider (omnibus) context: Rather the favourability of the context is determined by the relative strength of the health and wellbeing logic to other competing logics. The power of organisational proponents of health and wellbeing, relative to proponents of competing logics, can be important. However, in some instances, it may be that proponents of health and wellbeing logics need to come to some sort of accommodation so that there is no threat to competing logics, logics that perhaps have more powerful proponents. Health and wellbeing logics can conflict with competing logics, and a variety of means, including but not limited to mobilization of evidence are used to resolve that conflict and create a favourable context for implementation. This later scenario was articulated more frequently and in greater detail by our informants. In this respect, it is worth repeating the following quote from earlier:

> I think there is no doubt there are people in business still who would be listening to me thinking what a load of old tosh, I don't get this at all, but that's the type of stuff we have to re-educate people on, in my view. And it is a re-educational process and you're never too old to be re-educated, to learn. If employers could embrace all this to a greater extent they wouldn't be having those conversations with their HR (human resources) teams saying we've got another vacancy to fill. (**Medium accountancy practice, senior manager**)

The quote from an interview post-implementation of a workplace health and wellbeing programme indicates that tensions between health and wellbeing logics and competing logics may never be fully resolved, and there is an ongoing process of conflict, negotiation and/or accommodation between logics and their proponents. Consequently, this ongoing process occurs not just before implementation of practices and programmes, but during and after implementation. Given that organisations evolve, the ongoing process of resolving tensions between logics may have several elements of dynamism. Moreover, because competing logics concern a wide array of organisational procedures, practices and structures, the tensions between health and wellbeing logics and competing logics illustrate one way in which (a) implementation of health and wellbeing practices and programmes can change the wider context (e.g. supplant the competing logic) and (b) are tied closely to the wider context (i.e. through the process of resolving tensions with competing logics).

References

Abildgaard, J. S., Nielsen, K., & Sverke, M. (2018). Can job insecurity be managed? Evaluating an organizational-level intervention addressing the negative effects of restructuring. *Work and Stress, 32*, 105–123.

Abildgaard, J. S., Saksvik, P. Ø., & Nielsen, K. (2016). How to measure the intervention process? An assessment of qualitative and quantitative approaches to data collection in the process evaluation of organizational interventions. *Frontiers in Psychology, 7*(1380).

Biron, C., & Karanika-Murray, M. (2015). From black and white to colours: Moving the science of organizational interventions for stress and well-being forward. In C. Biron & M. Karanika-Murray (Eds.), *Derailed organizational interventions for stress and wellbeing: Confessions of failure and solutions for success* (pp. 275–282). Springer.

Coleman, J. (1994). *Walker versus Northumberland County Council.*

Daniels, K., Delany, K., Napier, J., Hogg, M., & Rushworth, M. (2019). *The value of occupational health to workplace wellbeing*. Society of Occupational Medicine.

Daniels, K., Johnson, G., & de Chernatony, L. (2002). Task and institutional influences on managers' mental models of competition. *Organization Studies, 23*, 31–62.

Daniels, K., Watson, D., Nayani, R., Tregaskis, O., Hogg, M., Etuknwa, A., & Semkina, A. (2021). Implementing practices focused on workplace health and psychological wellbeing: A systematic review. *Social Science and Medicine, 227*, 113888.

Dollard, M. F., & Bailey, T. (2021). Building psychosocial safety climate in turbulent times: The case of COVID-19. *Journal of Applied Psychology, 106*, 951–964.

El-Sawad, A., Arnold, J., & Cohen, L. (2004). 'Doublethink': The prevalence and function of contradiction in accounts of organizational life. *Human relations, 57*, 1179–1203.

ILO (International Labour Organization). (2020). *ILO Monitor: COVID-19 and the world of work. Third edition updated estimates and analysis*. Available at: http://www.cnt-nar.be/DOSSIERS/

Covid-19/ILO-2020-04-29-Covid-19-and-the-world-of-work-(03)-EN.pdf. Accessed 10 July 2020.

Johns, G. (2006). The essential impact of context on organizational behavior. *Academy of Management Review, 31*, 386–408.

Johnson, G. (1987). *Strategic change and the management process*. Blackwell.

Nayani, R., Patey, J., Fitzhugh, H., Watson, D., Baric, M., Tregaskis, O., & Daniels, K. (2021). *Authenticity in the pursuit of mutuality during crisis*. University of East Anglia Working Paper.

Nielsen, K., Abildgaard, J. S., & Daniels, K. (2014). Putting context into organizational intervention design: Using tailored questionnaires to measure initiatives for worker well-being. *Human Relations, 67*, 1537–1560.

ONS (Office for National Statistics). (2020a). Coronavirus and anxiety, Great Britain: 3 April 2020 to 10 May 2020. Available at: https://www.ons.gov.uk/peoplepopulationandcommunity/wellbeing/articles/coronavirusandanxietygreatbritain/3april2020to10may2020. Accessed 10 July 2020.

ONS (Office for National Statistics). (2020b). Personal and economic well-being in Great Britain: June 2020. Available at: https://www.ons.gov.uk/peoplepopulationandcommunity/wellbeing/bulletins/personalandeconomicwellbeingintheuk/june2020. Accessed 10 July 2020.

ONS (Office for National Statistics). (2020c). Coronavirus and homeworking in the UK: April 2020. https://www.ons.gov.uk/employmentandlabourmarket/peopleinwork/employmentandemployeetypes/bulletins/coronavirusandhomeworkingintheuk/latest. Accessed 10 July 2020.

ONS (Office for National Statistics). (2020d). Coronavirus and the latest indicators for the UK economy and society: 23 July 2020. Available at: https://www.ons.gov.uk/peoplepopulationandcommunity/healthandsocialcare/conditionsanddiseases/bulletins/coronavirustheukeconomyandsocietyfasterindicators/latest. Accessed 10 July 2020.

Prahalad, C. K., & Bettis, R. A. (1986). The dominant logic: A new linkage between diversity and performance. *Strategic Management Journal, 7*, 485–501.

Roodbari, H., Axtell, C., Nielsen, K., & Sorensen, G. (2021). Organisational interventions to improve employees' health and wellbeing: A realist synthesis. *Applied Psychology: An International Review*. https://doi.org/10.1111/apps.12346

von Thiele Schwarz, U., Nielsen, K. M., Stenfors-Hayes, T., & Hasson, H. (2017). Using kaizen to improve employee well-being: Results from two organizational intervention studies. *Human Relations, 70*, 966–993.

Chapter 5
Actors and Implementation

In the previous chapter, we argued that the favourability or not of the wider organisational context reflects the degree to which health and wellbeing logics conflict with other competing logics, but that it is possible to resolve or accommodate conflicts where they do occur. Accordingly, it is not inevitable that an unfavourable context negates the implementation of workplace health and wellbeing practices. On the other hand, even in a seemingly benign context (e.g. resource munificence), health and wellbeing logics can be supplanted and implementation derailed if a competing logic prevails. As noted in the previous chapter, logics are held by organisational actors, and conflicts between logics can reflect conflicts between actors. Resolution or accommodation of health and wellbeing logics with competing logics therefore ties implementation into the political fabric of organisations.

In this chapter, we will look more closely at the influence of different organisational actors on the implementation of health and wellbeing practices. In so doing, our focus shifts to the discrete context of the intervention (Johns, 2006). In this chapter, we also introduce a new layer of context, which we label the delivery context and the pertains to the management of multiple health and wellbeing practices in a programme of activities. As noted in earlier chapters, guidance on best practice (ISO, 2018; LaMontagne et al., 2014) and research (Batorsky et al., 2016; Johnson et al., 2018; Jordan et al., 2003; Mattke et al., 2015) indicates many organisations adopt multiple practices in health and wellbeing programmes. The delivery context is one way within which the implementation, continuation and co-ordination of multiple practices can be managed. The delivery context is also an area, but not the only area, within which tensions with competing logics (and between actors) can be addressed.

K. Daniels et al., *Achieving Sustainable Workplace Wellbeing*, Aligning Perspectives on Health, Safety and Well-Being, https://doi.org/10.1007/978-3-031-00665-4_5

Actors

Daniels et al. (2021) identified five classes of actors that can be affected by and affect implementation. These are Recipients (usually workers) who can benefit from improved health and wellbeing; Recipients' managers (line managers) responsible for the day-to-day management of recipients and their performance; Senior managers responsible for the governance and functioning of the organisation; Service providers, or the specialist implementers of specific practices or activities, for example mindfulness practitioners or work redesign specialists; Expert or strategic implementers, practitioners with oversight of the entire programme of activities, usually human resources and/or occupational health specialists.

Each class of actors may hold competing logics to health and wellbeing logics. Examples of such logics from our cases were given in the previous chapter. Organisational actors may also hold logics or views about specific practices themselves, rather than just logics around health and wellbeing as a social good and/or means to achieve business goals. Studies reviewed by Daniels et al. (2021) indicated actors can have positive or negative attitudes towards the intervention, which can be regarded as elements of intervention-specific logics. Examples included: negative or positive perceptions of the intervention or the service provider (recipients, line managers); mistrust in the intentions or capability of others to deliver effective interventions (recipients' views of managers and vice versa); lack of self-confidence to make changes (recipients, line managers); perceptions of an unreceptive context within which to provide a service (service providers). Other examples of cynicism and mistrust in management from our cases were also given in Chap. 3.

Competing logics or negative perceptions of an intervention may lead to implementation problems that may become manifest through the behaviours of actors. In contrast, positive perceptions of the intervention may become manifest as behaviours that facilitate implementation. Examples from the literature (Daniels et al., 2021) include: Generic levels of support for the intervention (from co-workers, line managers, senior managers); Engagement and visibility with the intervention (senior managers, strategic/expert implementers); Lack of communications, vision or clarity about the intervention (senior managers, service providers); Specific active support (e.g. line managers monitoring progress); Imposing constraints on or terminating the intervention (senior managers). Some of these indicate more passive forms of support or resistance (e.g. generic support, visibility, not communicating) and others are more active (e.g. imposing constraints).

Data from our cases provides evidence that negative, neutral or even positive attitudes to wellbeing or a specific intervention influence implementation problems. The following quotes illustrate these points. The first indicates a level of passive resistance (deleting emails). The second indicates differences in of engagement by senior managers (partners in an accounting practice), ranging from high levels of active engagement and development of a programme of activities through to non-engagement, neither resisting nor actively supporting. The third quote illustrates how senior management positivity can lead to inaction without further guidance.

> But I think it was a bit of a topic of, it depended which office you necessarily sat in and also the dynamics in that office. So when I received the emails from wellbeing at HR (human resources) I'll read them whereas in some offices they'll just delete. (**Medium accountancy practice, auditor #1**)
>
> The partners, I would say, sit into three camps. So we've got the early adopters, who are really up for it. So one of our partners is a trained mindfulness practitioner and also, a mediator. So, and he has just rolled out sessions across the firm on mindfulness. So he's very, early adopter, very supportive. And some of our other partners, you know, they run regularly or cycle regularly and invite people to join them on whatever. So, and I would say, they're kind of in the middle camp. So they're not leading the way but they're happy to engage and do, embrace it. And then the third camp is, well it's just kind of there and, you know. They trust that it's doing what it needs to do and, therefore, we're looking after their people, but they don't really get too involved with it, and that's where my challenge is. I need to get that third group into the, at least the middle space. (**Medium accountancy practice, head of human resources**)
>
> But, you know, it is a big challenge getting the senior management to recognise, well they recognise wellbeing is key but I'm not quite sure without any guidance they know exactly what they should be doing to help it. (**Large infrastructure and construction, wellbeing lead**)[1]

We found less evidence of active resistance, possibly because our cases were drawn from organisations that had implemented some form of wellbeing approach and active engagement with various practices was evident (see Chap. 3). However, the need to accommodate health and wellbeing logics alongside competing logics means that there is potential for active resistance from various stakeholders, which was recognized by some of our informants. For example this recognition can be inferred from two quotes produced near the end of the last chapter concerning sometimes finding an accommodation between health and wellbeing logics and competing logics. This recognition is also evident in the following quote, which relates to senior managers having the power to block certain health and wellbeing initiatives if senior managers view those initiatives as disproportionate:

> So I think there's a risk, I wouldn't say a danger but there's a risk, that senior management might take a view OK we've done so much here but that's too far, whatever you're proposing that's one step too far. (**Medium construction, head of assurance**)

A small number of studies indicate that negative attitudes to health and wellbeing interventions can be overcome (e.g. Anderson & Sice, 2016; Tregaskis et al., 2013), and our cases also indicate negative attitudes can be consciously addressed and potentially overcome. Both the quotes below relate to changing workplace cultures that became more receptive to initiatives targeted at wellbeing:

> I've got a bit of a history, a turnaround history, of businesses and also of HR (human resources) functions. I've done a lot of HR transformation in my time and also uplifting HR teams and professionalism from really, really poor operational and strategic bases to, you know, transforming the cultures of businesses. And so that's what I'm trying to do here. I'm having to do it now and succeeding on the whole I think. It takes longer, it's more

[1] Another example is given in Chap. 3 in relation to a HR manager who did not make time to implement a wellbeing initiative.

> challenging, because of the limitations that I have in terms of resources and power but it's very intellectually stimulating. (**Large care provider, human resources director**)
>
> My boss when I first joined, who had the hundred KPIs, would walk through the office first thing in the morning and he wouldn't even talk to you. It was very much a schoolmaster's type of environment. He summoned you to his office sort of thing. And then when we merged and the less mature side of the business joined us, which was more relaxed, they looked at it and said why do you want 100 KPIs. Well because we've always had them. I don't even understand 50% of them, I don't even know what they're telling me. So there was a culture shock for both sides of the business I guess. And what that's meant is that the two sides of the business were managing their employees slightly differently. So that's come together over the years now. Like I say, it's been six or seven years so we've now got a quite relaxed culture. (**Large infrastructure and construction, wellbeing lead**)

The general conclusions from Daniels et al. (2021) and a review of job redesign interventions (Roodbari et al., 2021) are that positive predispositions towards specific health and wellbeing practices assist with implementation. Notwithstanding, our case evidence and Daniels et al. indicate negative dispositions can be overcome, that attitudes can become more positive and our case data indicate key actors can recognize the need to address negative attitudes and deploy strategies to achieve this (Chaps. 4 and 7).

The Delivery Context

The delivery context encompasses the processes of the management of an entire programme of activities, such as its governance, planning and evaluation, and whether and how stakeholders are consulted/involved in governance, planning and evaluation. Best practice guidelines (see Chap. 2) indicate the importance of steering groups, consultation, assessment and monitoring, and evidence from intervention studies indicates effective governance is associated with workplace health and wellbeing interventions delivering good outcomes (Daniels et al., 2021). However, studies and frameworks usually pertain to single initiatives (HSE, 2017/2019) or, in the case of one framework, ongoing work with a particular team of consultants or action researchers (von Thiele Schwarz et al., 2016), and so would form part of the discrete context. The delivery context sits between the omnibus context of the organisation and the discrete context of a specific intervention or initiative. The discrete context links health and wellbeing practices vertically to the wider organisation and horizontally links specific practices to each other.

Our case data reveal variety between organisations in the structure of and the co-ordinating functions in the delivery context. By structures, we refer to committees, working groups or other means of bringing actors together to implement workplace health and wellbeing practices. By co-ordinating functions, we refer to the purposes articulated in relation to the processes used to plan and implement workplace health and wellbeing practices. However, as we will see in the next section of this chapter, there are other functions that go beyond planning and implementation and that are focused on changing the organisational context to facilitate implementation.

In relation to structures, these varied between been cases. Here we provide three examples to illustrate this variety. In a small care home, there were informal processes of involving workers (and residents) in what wellbeing activities to pursue and informal monitoring of what worked and what did not. In a regional, medium-sized accountancy practice with several offices, the programme was co-ordinated by a human resources director with specialist support from another human resources professional, local wellbeing champions and an employee forum in a medium-sized accountancy practices. A large construction and infrastructure firm had a highly structured, hierarchical governance structure involving continuous improvement groups in linked areas (e.g. health, safety, inclusion) with the potential for smaller task and finish groups reporting to the continuous improvement groups, alongside regular discussion fora with workers on construction sites.

With the exception of the highly informal approach taken in a small care home, the more formalized governance structures were associated with a variety of co-ordinating functions. These are illustrated in Table 5.1. There are eight co-ordinating functions, which can be further categorized into strategy and planning (strategy, preparatory work, programme planning, resourcing), communications and information provision, and oversight of implementation (co-ordination, tailoring and standardization, monitoring).

Strategy and planning refer to the processes of setting up a new programme or substantially changing an existing approach. Organisations varied in their approach to explicitly articulating a health and wellbeing strategy, although the two where an overarching strategy was articulated did so through a small number of principles, as illustrated in Table 5.1. Preparatory work not only refers to needs assessments, but also to ensuring relevant (and powerful) stakeholders understand what needs to be done. All organisations had some form of programme planning, often linked into a calendar of activities, including the small care home that had regular activities with residents (e.g. annual trip on a narrow-gauge railway). Resourcing did not only refer to securing financial resources, but also using other resources to access services or support for services (e.g. using research students to investigate sector-specific problems such as fatigue in the large infrastructure and construction firm).

Communications and information provision most often related to one-way provision of information on the health and wellbeing services on offer, information on self-care, usually in an integrated place such as a web-portal (e.g. medium-sized construction firm, large, multinational law firm). Means for two-way communication and feedback were evident in monitoring processes and the composition of steering groups and other consultative processes. Consultative processes will be considered in more detail in the next section of this chapter. However, the large, multinational law firm did use its portal also as a means to access ideas for new initiatives, feedback on existing initiatives and as a support function.

Implementation comprised the co-ordinating functions of: Co-ordinating multiple activities or service providers, and in some cases provide oversight to locally initiated activities that were not necessarily included in central plans; and managing

Table 5.1 Structures and co-ordinating functions in the delivery context

Structures	*I've got a Group People leadership team to deliver and work on strategy that's made of my direct reports but also the business partners from the biggest businesses, so leisure, affordable housing, property services management, and the VP who represents group functions. And we've got a Group People strategy steering group. That's got representatives from all of the subsidiary businesses where we work together to cocreate products for the greater good of the group and to drive strategy through the wider group.* **Large care provider, human resources director** *And there were various little task and finish groups. What tends to happen with some of the CIGs* (continuous improvement groups) *is we set aside small task and finish groups to do a piece of work that might need doing as a subset of the overall strategy.* **Large infrastructure and construction, health and safety director**
Strategy	*Well the strands are the commitments, so that's the thing that we've signed up to. So making sure that people, you know, earn decent money, have got career opportunities, are supported in feeling well and all of that sort of stuff. Then the programme is designed sort of to bolster all of those strands. So the activities, [name of HR professional] is our coordinator, we've got champions on each site, wellbeing champions on each site, and [name of HR professional] meets with them and she'll talk to them about, right, so next month's topic, if you like, or external topic is x, so what are we going to do? And they've actually done that for the whole year now. So they've looked at that and there are things in place for that.* **Medium accountancy practice, head of human resources** *Yes so the enablers, we've got seven occupational health and wellbeing enablers that are [name of company] wide. So they are leadership, education, communication, healthy working environment, standards in design, engagement and improvement. So my strategy is split into those seven sections and then it's different actions basically that we'll do to try and work our way towards those different enablers.* **Large infrastructure and construction, senior safety adviser**
Preparatory work	*Yes we started, well part of the start of this whole journey was some very honest and frank workshops with all of the senior leaders around culture, what made us stagnate, what are some of their own personal issues and biases against trying certain things to try and draw that out. And they were very challenging to say the least but very necessary. Because people look to the role models at the top first of all and the direct reports under those leaders look up at the leaders and their willingness or not to change. So that was quite a pivotal starting point, and that wasn't a training session it was a workshop using a number of tools to draw out what is this reticence to try and do things differently.* **Large infrastructure and construction, human resources director**

(continued)

Table 5.1 (continued)

	And then our third category is a regional hub office which is very much more geared with a very little amount of permanent type desks but a large emphasis on agile facilities and agile type desk working and there are provisions to support the agile staff. We also then looked at, in these types of offices designations, what kind of wellbeing offering can we fit with inside that offering. And we've sort of subcategorised that to simple things like encouraging walking meetings, one to one meetings outside of the office located in and sort of close to where they might have some decent sort of catering or coffee type facilities at the simple end. **Large care provider, head of corporate facilities**
Programme planning	*And then, from there, we've developed a programme. So we've looked at each of those strands and we've said, right, what can we do to support financial wellbeing? What can we do to support physical wellbeing? What can we do to support community wellbeing? And so on. And we've then devised a programme, we've got an annual programme that we publish month by month, that is linked to external campaigns. So it might be national campaigns, such as breast cancer awareness, for example. And then there will be activities that we're doing across the firm that will support that.* **Medium accountancy practice, head of human resources** *So, typically, quarterly, but they're a bit more frequently when we've got some quite big things to agree. So what we were doing this morning, is agreeing a calendar for each month, so launching in May, each month will have a different focus. So things like healthy travel or, I've got it up in front of me, healthy eating, cancer awareness, drink awareness, and they kind of tied in with various things that are going on kind of nationally as well.* **Large, multinational law firm, human resources manager**
Resourcing	*We get most of our tools and things from [name of service provider] so [name of service provider] will come in and do talks for the guys about different things that we ask them to come in and do. We also have tie-ins through [name of service provider] with wearable tech around heart monitoring as well that we can use and make use of and we get them to come in and speak to them as well. So it just depends on what we're doing who we'll bring in.* **Large infrastructure and construction, senior safety adviser** *So current initiatives that we have been working with regards to mental health awareness, so we have recently been able to secure funding from our senior management, I report directly to the group executive director, [name of director], and I took a paper to her to get funding to get some mental health first aiders for the organisation. I originally asked for 12 and we asked for volunteers across the business, we got 146 people volunteering for 12 places. So that in itself told a story, painted a picture for us. So I went back and asked if she would be willing to increase that funding and we have now got 27 trained mental health first aiders across our business for the 1200 area of the affordable housing business that we work in, which was great news. So we have got*

(continued)

Table 5.1 (continued)

	those trained. **Large care provider, human resources business partner #2**
Communications and information provision	*I think this sort of whenever you're asking about what interests me. I think it's fair to say that we're always very well briefed on these things. So whenever you arrive at a workshop there's a booklet which has been properly thought through and drafted, you take that away. I always take it away and file it away so that I have something you know, as I said there when I was having my meetings with my direct reports and with my line manager I could pull that out and check right what is this, oh yes that's [name of programme] so this is what we're supposed to be doing.* **Medium construction, head of assurance** *And, I suppose, the other element to that, is when we launched the wellbeing strategy, on our micro site there's a, like a joint inbox, for emails with ideas, which they do actually, really frequently, or just their own views, or they'll say things like, you know, I've, actually, I'd just really like to speak to someone about this, I'm going through that, you know, I'm going through a divorce and, financially, I'm having a really difficult time, is there someone I can speak to? And that will come through to various members of that steering group, so that we can provide the support, and it's been really positive.* **Large, multinational law firm, human resources manager**
Co-ordination	*getting that early intervention on the mental health side is something that I need to pick up with the three providers once the contract is finalised for our new group income protection provider. And I think I need to make sure that I do what [name of colleague] done because I think she's done a fantastic job getting all these providers working together and the business partners engaged with it. So I'm really impressed coming in with what I've seen compared to you know what I've seen in other industries.* **Large care provider, payroll manager #2** *We basically reached out to all of the champions, mental health champions, all of network members and asked if anyone wanted to come forward and run any events locally. Because usually that's what we do is that us as the central team we'll run a couple of events that are aimed at the whole firm and then on the ground local people will run events in their offices. And we'll obviously just keep an eye on them and make sure the budget is allocated and that there's no health and safety issues that need to be thought about and keep an agenda together and advertise that via our intranet.* **Large, multinational law firm, responsible business associate**
Tailoring and standardisation	*Yeah and you know it's easy whenever you're sitting in an office and you've got a good strong internet connection and got all those resources available and it's clean and it's dry and comfortable. It's different whenever you're off site where maybe people, there is less, room, more noisy and all of that. So the ability to for example the hub we can now access on our mobile phones, smart phones and tablets. So the accessibility of information is much better than it would have been in the past.*

(continued)

Table 5.1 (continued)

	Medium construction, head of assurance *Because we class ourselves as an international law firm it's always been something in the back of our minds we want to try and make sure that it is international. The health and wellbeing hub the way we have set it up is that we have page per territory so not every territory will have the same information because not all our benefits work in those locations. But where possible we have tried to have a standard suite of health and wellbeing initiatives or information. So we have tried to make it applicable globally.* **Large, multinational law firm, assistant rewards manager**
Monitoring	*And we've said as part of our maturity assessment, which we're rewriting this year, and we will roll out quarter three this year, we ought to measure or get people to think about how we're doing on health, not just safety. So it's another way we're going to measure ourselves I think. And that's people looking within their own organisation against the sector's prompts if you like, how are we doing.* **Large infrastructure and construction, wellbeing lead** *So we set about, with a group pilot, where, it was kind of, it was a bit of a competition really. So there was, because there are a number of subsidiary businesses, then we did a pilot where ten Fit Bits were given to ten members of, or ten volunteers, within each of those businesses. And, initially, before the pilot started, there was a survey that was carried out via a kind of, I guess, some sort of activity coordinator, a kind of a personal trainer type thing. That you filled out all of your stats, you know, your height, your weight, your blood pressure, your cholesterol if you knew it, what your sleeping patterns were, etc., etc., and then we embarked on this sort of challenge.* **Large care provider, managing director of subsidiary business**

the tension between providing access to a standardized suite of services and providing localized services or solutions for specific groups with specific health and wellbeing concerns. All but one of our case companies was multisite, and the tension between standardization and tailoring was evident in all of these to some degree. There can be a variety of reasons for standardization, including quality control and assurance and economies of scale, but ones articulated included equity of provision (large, multinational law firm, regional accountancy practice) and reducing the burden of managing services (large care home provider). Monitoring pertains to having in places processes for checking on progress.

Political and Symbolic Functions of the Delivery Context

The co-ordinating functions of the delivery context can be thought of as functions that support changes to the administrative and technical aspects of the organisation, so that workers' health and wellbeing are influenced for the better through new ways of working or provision of various health and wellbeing services. However, because organisations are socio-technical entities (after Trist & Bamforth, 1951) and different groups of actors can affect implementation, implementation can involve influencing those actors. Accordingly, political, symbolic and cultural processes play a role in implementation. The role of political and symbolic action is known in the research literatures on the management of change and organisation theory (Gersick, 1991; Johnson, 1987, 1990; Westover, 2010). Political processes pertain to the facility to influence people into assisting implementation, or at least not hindering implementation (cf. Hardy, 1996; Kimura, 2015). Symbolic and cultural processes pertain to signalling the value of health and wellbeing to the organisation and thus providing a more supportive context for implementation (after Bowen & Ostroff, 2004; see also Huettermann & Bruch, 2019). Political processes themselves are symbolic, in that they convey what powerful stakeholders consider to be important (Hardy, 1996).

The conceptual literature on the implementation of workplace health and wellbeing practices does not consider such political, symbolic or cultural processes explicitly (see Chap. 2)[2] and, perhaps consequently, political and symbolic action is rarely considered in empirical studies of implementation (Daniels et al., 2021). Rather, as the models reviewed in Chap. 2 hint at, implementation is seen as a rational and planned activity that usually progresses in a linear and predetermined sequence of stages. These rational, planned aspects are echoed in the co-ordinating functions in the delivery context. However, our case data also show that the delivery context is also a locus of political and symbolic activity for legitimating health and wellbeing logics amongst multiple stakeholders.

Involving Others: Consultation and Coercion

The most direct means of persuading people is to involve them in the co-creation of health and wellbeing programmes and in the improvement and further development of programmes. By far this was the most frequently cited reason for various consultative processes with workers around health and wellbeing, including employee voice fora, various forms of survey and simply visiting workplaces to talk to workers. This bottom-up approach would help align managerial conceptions with worker conceptions of wellbeing and what to do about wellbeing, and so address some of the contested elements of wellbeing between different stakeholder groups (Chap. 1). The following quote illustrates how regular consultation with workers is used to refine health and wellbeing initiatives through both structured

[2]The importance of political and symbolic action is acknowledged tacitly in some models that indicate the importance of representative steering groups and securing commitments from senior management, although the political and symbolic nature of such prescriptions is not made explicit. See Chap. 2.

involvement mechanisms (voice meetings, suggestion scheme, toolbox talks) and informal involvement mechanisms (open door policy):

> We do something called a voice meeting which is normally once every two weeks or once a month depending on the timescale and how busy we are on site. But we'll try and get a select, a random selection of, it's normally a certain percentage of people on site to come and voice their opinions and that won't be all from one trade that will be from various different backgrounds from the whole of the site. To say right this is what we're doing, at the moment could we do any better, how could we improve and that's from their point to us so and we try that way and that works quite well. And again like I say we've got positive intervention cards for each, there's a little card which, I've probably got, I can't see any that's what I was looking around for. But I can show you one of them, they're on the board, they're on the wall out there when we get and they get submitted they can either be named or anonymous if they want to and then obviously they do toolbox talks most days about stuff. So there's always chance to voice your opinions and if not there's like also that open door policy where they can always, doesn't matter anytime just come and speak to one of us, if you don't want to say in front of someone let us know. I mean obviously you can always come into the meeting room down the side of me so. (**Large infrastructure and construction, site engineer**)

The following inter-linked quotes from two different informants from a large, multinational law firm illustrate how consultative devices are linked to the governance of a health and wellbeing programme through the steering group.

> Anybody can send emails to a generic email address that's been set up for the wellbeing steering group and make recommendations, suggestions, provide feedback and so on. So that group will help steer how we proceed in the future. (**Large, multinational law firm, facilities compliance manager**)
>
> So, you know, that steering group is really, like you said, a bit of a knowledge sharing. And, you know, it's probably the same with every company, but you're constantly being approached by people saying, oh have you thought about doing this? And we can help you and, I guess, sales really. And it's about kind of trying to wade through some of that and to think, well is some of this actually quite interesting, could we benefit from launching something like this? Or is it simply just, you know, another way to spend money really? (**Large, multinational law firm, human resources manager**)

A more far-reaching form of consultation is where workers were allowed to develop their own health and wellbeing practices in a bottom-up manner rather than being imposed from a centralized health and wellbeing co-ordinating structure.[3] This was evident in all of our cases in various ways. Examples included co-ordinated activities by 'wellbeing champions' for each office location in a regional accountancy practice and the informal approach taken in a small care home:

> Yes when we had a death last year of a gentleman he was 72 and he had been in the home since 1983 and that affected us all really really badly especially the older staff who had been there for years. And we were constantly in the office talking to [name of manager] over and over again about what we could do. In the end we arranged his funeral and we actually bought the coffin into work and we all decorated that for him. So that helped us losing him really. (**Small care provider, support worker #1**)

[3]As noted in Chaps. 1 and 2, existing models of implementation cannot normally capture these bottom-up initiatives, because their focus is on formally evaluated and top-down interventions.

A large, multinational law firm provides an example of how governance structures can co-ordinate or even encourage developing these 'bottom-up' health and wellbeing activities. The second quote in particular illustrates mapping various bottom-up initiatives, which in turn is used to identify gaps in provision and 'top-down' intervention to encourage those gaps to be filled:

> Most things in [name of firm] are driven from a policy perspective to start with I would say. So, we recognise the need to have a policy and that would be developed by a working group. So, we have a health and wellbeing group that's set up to coordinate those things. Below that, and the sort of go do it type stuff initiatives, ideas, how well are things working, that's very much done from my perspective at an individual level and individual lawyers or business ops people will stick their hand up and say I'd like to be involved in this or I've got an idea for that and then they help drive that forward. (**Large, multinational law firm, human resources manager**)
>
> **[Interviewer] These [networks] are up and running now but how do they kind of get off the ground? Do you have a sense of how they you know originated?**
>
> [Informant] Usually it's just from one or two people that have an interest, a personal interest that's generally where it starts from. I mean these networks have been around for a lot of years now so you know there's the LGBT one that's been around since 2007 and that got off the ground because there was just about six people I think that were all based in London at the time that decided that it was something we should be doing. So that and it's been a very similar practice for most of them you know a few key people that are you know have brought a personal interest that think that we need something and they've approached various people within the business and it's been driven from them. Or centrally as a team we've looked at any gaps or anywhere we think where there isn't representation for people that maybe requires the network. And we've maybe then gone out and approached specific people and said you know would you be interested in leading this and it's kicked off the ground from there. (**Large, multinational law firm, responsible business associate**)

However, consultative processes with workers served other functions. In two of our cases (a regional medium-sized accountancy practice and a large infrastructure and construction firm), consultative processes were also symbolic. The first quote below illustrates how consultative processes signal the importance of health and wellbeing in the accountancy practice through having the managing partner running a question-and-answer session in a smaller office. The second quote illustrates how consultative processes can be used to raise concerns but also used to demonstrate how concerns have been addressed through tangible actions.

> They're always telling us, they're always asking us what we'd like. There's lots of surveys being done, so when I first started I was based in [name of town] and I think only, I don't know how long after I started but the managing partner came and did a Q&A session with us all. So people could, and they were asking about what is going to go on with all of that. And that's not necessarily, I don't know if this is just an assumption, but it's not necessarily every, something every firm will do. Let the managing partner taking time out of his day to go, especially when he's generally based in [name of city] to go down to [name of town] to spend the day. Well not the day but a couple of hours sitting there being asked lots of questions, not knowing the questions beforehand. So you can kind of tell they are invested in their staff. (**Medium accountancy practice, auditor #1**)
>
> And we also have a thing called Voice reps which I always forget what this stands for but it's [name of consultation process]. So it's almost like our safety reps forum. So they're held on all the sites as well and it's a selection of people that attend them that have nominated themselves to be volunteers, not voluntolds, and they collect any issues or any positive

things that they see are happening from everybody on site. They bring it back and it gets passed up to management to say yes or no. We're quite honest with them that we won't be able to fix everything that they ask us to do. Then we feed it back to the people that attend the meeting and they can cascade it out to the rest of the team. So it allows people to raise concerns. If they don't want to come to the meeting themselves and put their hand up, they can get somebody else to do it, which is quite nice. And these meetings are quite successful actually. We get quite a lot of buy-ins from them because they see that we actually do things and it's not just a talking shop. (**Large infrastructure and construction, senior safety adviser**)

This last quote also illustrates a more straightforward political dimension to consultative processes, which is to explain why some things cannot be done. In this sense, there is a forum for discussing some of the contested elements of wellbeing. However, in this instance at least, they may have been settled in favour of the employer. This was also evident at the regional accountancy practice:

[Interviewer] You're right there's always ideas that perhaps won't meet that consistency bar that you talked about earlier. So how would you convey that feedback to employees about the things that you might take forward and then the things that you won't be able to follow through with?

[Informant] I think I'd probably discuss it in the employee forum for them to feed that back to their employees that they look after, because they have different areas that they look after and the representatives do. So I'd discuss it with them in the first instance and see what their thoughts are and for them to get feedback from the employees and to feedback in the next meeting. (**Medium accountancy practice, wellbeing coordinator**)

Workers are not the only actors consulted with. In our cases, those charged with managing programmes of activities would consult, variously with, with senior managers, external service providers, clients, suppliers and middle/line managers, as illustrated in the following quotes.

So we have a health and wellbeing steering group which is headed up by our HR (human resources) director. We have several different people in the group from different departments for example facilities, we have Responsible Business involved as well, the head of our disability and wellbeing group because we have various networking groups in the company. And I am part of that group from the reward basis because I have access to a lot of the management information on our health schemes such as our private medical insurance, income protection insurance. And we also have a health screening which we receive management information on. Within my role one of the things we do each year is we have a health con(ference) meeting which is with our benefits broker and we sit down with all our health care providers, such as occupational health, medical insurance providers (**Large, multinational law firm, assistant rewards manager**)

We're looking at the area of technology in the industry, both new technology and working changes due to improved equipment. So again we will have a board sponsor from our construction board to lead that. The purpose of them leading is, one, to make sure that we've got a plug in with the leadership but also we don't actually then have a meeting and then go and ask people for instruments or budgets if the right people are in the room. The expert leads then, so where we are now with a guy called [name] who's going to be heading that, who I had a meeting with yesterday, is to look at a cross-section of people who could best bring value to that group. So from a technology point of view we'd look at certainly an operational person across construction and infrastructure. We'd look at our Head of Procurement who has got an understanding of what our suppliers may bring to the party in terms of the work that we're trying to do. We'll look at technical experts. And we'll probably look at as well, although not necessarily part of the core group but as the ongoing group, is an end user group to test the thinking as well. So whilst we do internally with people, a cross-section, where appropriate the two things that we do also try and do is include supply chain or people who could bring another level of knowledge into the group in terms of outside ideas. We also look, if that particular area, I mean technology is a good example, and people/ plant interface which is another of the groups is a good example, there's a number of people who sit in our business that sit on industry forums as well. (**Large infrastructure and construction, health and safety director**)

As the second quote illustrates, the reason for wider consultation is not just about developing a programme, a specific initiative or being able to take decisions quickly through involving key actors early in the decision making. It is also about having a 'plug into leadership', which can also be taken to be a means of aligning health and wellbeing initiatives with wider business concerns (Daniels et al., 2019). In the following two quotes, first from a wellbeing lead and second from a human resources director, the involvement of senior managers or other organisational representatives illustrates how legal, budgetary or other constraints can limit choices about health and wellbeing practices and activities.

Yes, well we've got representatives from HR (human resources department) on our wellbeing forum now. Previously we didn't, so that was a gap that we identified, that we were discussing all this stuff but HR weren't there to either defend what we were suggesting or actually saying you can't do that because of legislation or whatever it is. So we've now got a member of the HR team on the wellbeing forum because we can sit as a group of individuals and say ah that would be great if we could do this and we could do that and do the other, we then go back to HR and they say well firstly we haven't got the budget for that and secondly we haven't got the resource. So ah ok, we thought it was a great idea, and it might well have been but it doesn't fit with our HR strategy. (**Large infrastructure and construction, wellbeing lead**)

[Interviewer] What has been the role of the HR (human resources) **business partners in this?**

[Informant] Making sure that people, there has to be governance around this sort of stuff so flexible working is a great example where you cannot accommodate everybody's personal circumstance because we do have a business to run. So we have added the sense of realism to some of this stuff but basically saying look everybody has different needs and requirements to support them to do well at work and most importantly feel mentally and physical well while they are at work. And actually we want to do as much as we can, we think we have got some great ideas but there will be ideas out there we don't know about. So it's that whole facilitation encouragement but keeping a sense of realism about stuff. Because like I say we want to do as much as we can to be a good employer here but everybody is different, we do have issues, some employees for whatever reason we can't accommodate their circumstance but more often than not we can. So facilitators adding structure and also keeping a sense of realism I would say. (**Large infrastructure and construction, human resources director**)

Other reasons voiced by our informants included using the involvement of senior managers to sense check what would be acceptable to the organisation, what would need more political support and to have a reciprocal influence on the organisation, as illustrated in two quotes from the same human resources manager in a large, multinational law firm.

Yes, exactly. And it's chaired by our HR (human resources) Director, so it's helpful, in the sense of, he has a very close link to the board. And so he's kind of able to give us a bit of a steer to say, look, this isn't going to work, you're not going to get this through or we need some more senior involvement, in order to, you know, influence and change here. So that's the benefit of that.

So yes, that's kind of, so I think probably the steering group was set up, I want to say, maybe June last year, maybe even a bit earlier, but as is the way, it takes a little while to get the sort of politics of these things sorted. And so we now meet quarterly, we had a launch of the wellbeing initiative or the wellbeing programme really, I would say, probably October last year. And our managing partner is very much kind of supportive of that. So he attends at least one of our steering group meetings every year. So that's helped, in terms of influencing the business. (**Large, multinational law firm, human resources manager**)

Another reason for consulting with multiple stakeholders, including at senior management levels, was to ensure stakeholders agreed with the proposed changes, as illustrated in the next two quotes, and to ensure a degree of standardization across different business units or location, as implied in the second of these quotes. The first quote relates to a change in performance and development appraisal processes to include a discussion about wellbeing needs. The second quote relates to setting up an oversight structure to ensure a global policy across all components of the organisation and across its different activities (including but not limited to health, safety and wellbeing).

So originally there was some survey centre around basically all of the personnel within [name of organisation] asking for some feedback on ways forward and trying to make this a better process. And there was obviously some examples given of the way forward in terms of that and certainly the [branded name of appraisal programme] was one that was put forward at that particular time. So there was a generalisation of feedback then it came and that was surveys that was sent out to everybody that worked for [name of organisation] at that particular time. So I think they got a very very good response at that particular time just from all employees. And certainly they all agreed with what [name of organisation] at that time, that the appraisal thing wasn't working at all. So there was a need out there so the end there was further survey in terms of the set up on how [branded name of appraisal programme] was then to be, was to be set up on and dealt with. And you were obviously offered suggestions, if this was put in place would you be acceptable to this sort of thing and would it be a step forward or a step back at that particular time. And I think it was again through all of this they seemed to be getting very good responses from everybody who worked in [name of organisation] to make sure that certainly everybody felt that there needed to be a change. And certainly everybody felt that [name of organisation] were putting us all in a position that we felt part of that decision on how this was going to be. So from that perspective I think that's certainly how I viewed it anyway from that perspective. (**Medium construction, operations manager**)

I will be looking to start a project board if you like, or a board of property and facilities management, it's a cooperative board across the group. And we will use that as our platform to talk about where we are as corporate facilities as the group facilities providers and talk to them about our ideas and the journey that we've been upon. Then we're going to open up the meeting to say this strategy we want to form a policy off the back of this office strategy and we want you guys to be part of this and we'd like and welcome your ideas to it. So we can start to set a standard policy that we all sign up to and we all work towards for the greater good of everyone that operates with inside this company. So that is the plan and it will be a policy that's supported by a number of standards that cover many different areas and they will link into areas like health and safety, health and wellbeing, environmental and all of the other things that go on with inside the business. So that's out next stage to get it out amongst our other property and facilities colleagues who look after those offices and get their buy-in

> to what we're doing and also look to then engage that as a set up global policy as standard. (**Large care provider, head of corporate facilities**)

However, in at least one instance, specific stakeholders were excluded (in the case below, human resources management) to make an initiative more acceptable to key implementers:

> What we don't want is to make it an initiative, so those mental health advocates do have informal networks because they are located in eleven different businesses around the country so they have their local networks, but they are not formal meetings or anything like that. But they will meet up as and when for a coffee when they see fit, and sometimes it might only be a couple of them have a chat. But we have deliberately kept the formal HR (human resources) role out of it because the minute you make it something as formal as that people see it as a bit like a referral to occupational health and that's exactly what this isn't meant to be. It's a totally different form of trying to help people's wellbeing. (**Large infrastructure and construction, human resources director**)

For the most part, our case data indicated that consultative processes were the most common way of using political means to influence different actors, either through finding out what is acceptable to the powerful, explaining to less powerful what cannot be done or sharing power through consulting on what to implement and how to improve it. We did, however, find some instances of less consultative and arguably more coercive practices, where power bases were used to ensure compliance with health and wellbeing logics. These relate to preventing staff gossiping about each other in a small care home, engaging with a new performance appraisal system with a wellbeing component in a medium-sized construction company, and the use of guidance to help managers meet management performance expectations around health and wellbeing rather than issuing mandatory performance requirements in a large infrastructure and construction firm.

> Yes I'd just come in and I made sure I didn't talk about people like that. If staff talked about other staff to me like that I had zero tolerance and told them not to. So that came from that. And then my senior, she was a carer here and I made her a senior, she became like that as well. So it's just the culture that kind of changed and getting people to know a bit more about each other as well and their lives and going out and this sort of thing. There was nothing on paper or training wise, it was just over time. (**Small care provider, manager**)
>
> Yes. And some of the [name of appraisal system] meetings that we have, two of them are informal so it could just be grabbing a coffee and sitting down and going well how's everything going. It's very informal but you have to let HR (human resources) know that you've had those informal chats and you just send an email and that is something I'd forgotten, send them an email. And they got back it's over two weeks and you need to have your [name of appraisal system] meeting with X employee. And I was whoops. I replied and said thank you very much. So it is good that they keep on top of it and then you don't actually forget yourself. (**Medium construction, financial controller**)
>
> The guidance is aimed to assist in business units and projects/offices to demonstrate they are meeting the minimum requirements of the [name of organisation] occupational health and wellbeing strategy and our integrated management system requirements. It talks people through the criteria and that this management tool is not intended as an audit but more of a self-assessment for people to use as an improvement tool. There's a bit more narrative that goes on that but basically it says then that if you've got to a level against, and I'll talk about that in a minute, if you're bronze you're meeting legal requirements, if you're silver you're meeting the bronze requirements plus exceeding some of the standards as listed. And then if

you're gold, you've met the bronze and silver but you're showing evidence of excellence and innovation.

It will be a performance expectation. We wouldn't do it as a mandatory. What I don t want to do, I think one of the things we have found with, possibly more so with occupational health, you sort of have to take a mandatory approach because of the legal requirements. I think on the wellbeing it's more about we build it into our expectations but use it as a little stick to hit people. Look at the work that we've done on mental health, and we're not all in [name of organisation] taking this route, is that if you start developing, or experience shows that if you start developing too many processes and procedures etcetera, running that or recording people that have had experience, what did they say etcetera, it will pretty much die in the water before it even gets up and running. So it's actually more of a framework for people to operate in than hard core procedures. That's the intention initially, is that yes there's an expectation for occupational health that you have your noise monitoring, that you have done your design work that you need to do to try and get rid of vibrating equipment etcetera, but on the wellbeing side it's more of an expectation to meet our standards. (**Large infrastructure and construction, health and safety director**)

Symbolism and Culture

As noted earlier, political action is symbolic by conveying what is important for a group of powerful stakeholders to other groups of stakeholders. The act of ceding (some) power by consulting employees is in itself a symbolic act conveying value for employees' views. Symbols and symbolic actions (e.g. content of senior manager speeches) encompass many aspects of organisational life. Schein (1985) and others (e.g. Johnson, 1987) have argued that organisational practices convey symbolic meaning of what is important and valued by the organisation, especially if those practices are routinised. So, for example the performance appraisal systems introduced into one of our case organisations (medium-sized construction firm) conveys the importance of health and wellbeing to the organisation.

So I think our guys have done a very good job in delivering a consistent message that you know this is the [name of old appraisal system] programme, this is [name of new appraisal system]. And giving people resources you know access to wellbeing coaches, access to training and proper support for staff members to think phew I actually I am invested in here and this is real and it's not just talk and that's very important. You don't just get an email this is happening and that's the last you hear of it, we actually say you know this person is going to get in contact with you and is going to have a meeting with you and you think oh hang on a minute but it's actually, they mean it you know. (**Medium construction, head of assurance**)

Other informants in other organisations alluded to the importance of the symbolic value of health and wellbeing practices. The first quote below illustrates how having multiple practices signals care, even if the specific practices are sub-optimal. The second of the two quotes relates to the symbolism of engaging in dialogue with people around a practice, rather than introducing the practice in a more passive manner.

So actually, you know, so something like EAP, it's something we can subscribe to. So something like the employee benefits system, we subscribe to it. And I think that some of this, you know, what have we done well, you know, have we got the best employee benefits system? No, we haven't. Have we got the best Employee Assistance Programme? No, we haven't. But the one thing is, I'd like to think [name of specific employee] would say to you, is that she feels we actually care about her. And actually, it doesn't, you don't have to have the best at that point in time because, you know, there are other policies as well that sort of sit alongside that. (**Medium accountancy practice, managing partner**)

I've noticed since we had the last toolbox talk there, I'm not sure if it's a direct consequence of that but not shortly after that had happened there was numerous people that did well one or two people that did come up and say to the people have you got five minutes. So I think that that shows that there are and it shows that they're taking it seriously because you can put these things in place and anybody can put the poster up saying I'm the mental health first aider but when you're actually holding talks and engaging with people that they take it a bit more seriously I think. (**Large infrastructure and construction, site engineer**)

Although we found no direct evidence in our cases, routinized monitoring systems may also convey the importance of health and wellbeing (cf. Johnson, 1987) and we did find evidence for the symbolism of routinized consultative processes (see above). Various other forms of symbolism were evident in the case data, including token gestures, visible artefacts and the work environment itself, as illustrated in the quotes below, relating variously to chocolates, fruit (token gestures), lanyards, cards (visible artefacts) and workspaces (work environment). However, as illustrated earlier in this chapter and elsewhere (see especially Chap. 8), such symbolic actions may complement rather than replace tangible action if programme implementation is to have benefits for worker wellbeing.

Yes, there's always something about wellbeing. And even yesterday, it was Valentine's day and they do try and have like something for a discussion point at the tea and coffee stations. So they had like little sweets and I suppose then when you're making a cup of tea you say oh are you going to have a chocolate. So you start a conversation with somebody you might not necessarily have had a conversation with. So it is nice because we are a big organisation and you don't know everybody and sometimes it can be difficult for people to go oh hi, I'm [informant's name], what do you do. So it's an easy way to start a conversation. (**Medium construction, financial controller**)

So the fruit for example, I know it seems ridiculous but just having the ability to go and get fruit from the kitchen is quite a nice touch and I think it makes people feel like... I think you spend a lot of time at work with the same people and I think trying to make it feel less corporate, you know, we all have our tasks, we all have our professionalisms and that kind of thing and I think having the ability to make it a bit more relaxed so that people can actually do their job better, I think it just helps. (**Medium accountancy practice, auditor #2**)

So they [mental health champions] have green lanyards and also the green ribbon pin badges. And in the very similar way to our physical first aiders that we have like an online, on our intranet you can do a people search and if you're a first aider it shows there's a little thimble or if you're a fire marshal there's a symbol, we got the symbol added for mental health champions as well. (**Large, multinational law firm, responsible business associate**)

So, yes, the continuous improvement group develop the strategy and action plan and they're called, like I said, the enablers. So the enablers are leadership, education, communication, healthy work environment, standards and design, engagement, and then improvement. I can send you over, we've produced a Z card to give to all our employees to tell people what we were doing. (**Large infrastructure and construction, wellbeing lead**)

> So it's facilities and looking at what's suitable in terms of having a good working environment. So the [name of organisation]'s approach is it doesn't matter which office you go into, it should be broadly the same. And we've gone over to agile working, or we are doing. So it's looking at those workspaces, what fits in, how you can make people feel good, you know, meeting places and everything around that really. (**Large, multinational law firm, health & safety manager**)

Symbols can convey in broad terms the value of health and wellbeing, and thus influence the culture of an organisation and collective attitudes to health and wellbeing practices. However, asides from articulating a general sense of the importance of wellbeing and/or care for workers, the symbolic aspects did not convey any specific reasons why individual workers should care about others' health and wellbeing. Without this, arguably health and wellbeing practices could become highly individualized and lose any sense of a connection to a wider collective (Davies, 2015; Hancock & Tyler, 2004) and therefore undermine a sense of organisational support or that co-workers are an important source of social support. However, in the case organisations, three major elements connected to health and wellbeing logics around a collective good or identity emerged from the data. These are illustrated in Table 5.2. The first of these was to create a sense that the core values of the business aligned with health and wellbeing logics. This was evidenced in four of our six case companies (care homes and professional services, but not the two construction firms). The second was about humanizing the workplace through recognizing individual needs and vulnerabilities, often evidenced through the actions of senior managers. We found examples in all of our case companies. The third element was creating dialogic processes through which people felt empowered to talk about health and wellbeing and were comfortable to do so. Again, we found examples in all case companies.

Alignment to business values, rhetoric around humanization of the workplace and establishing dialogic processes were all driven by management, so arguably reflect managements' and not workers' agendas, and thus establishing and health and wellbeing logic biased towards meeting organisational concerns through enhanced performance, retention of staff and reduced absence. Indeed, in the last chapter, we saw how health and wellbeing logics include such arguments. However, while it may certainly be the case in respect of alignment with business values, rhetoric around humanization and dialogic processes are focused specifically on recognizing individual needs and frailties and providing informal means of support for those struggling with wellbeing problems. Moreover, in the last chapter, we also saw that health and wellbeing logics can include a genuine concern for employees, and the widespread use of consultative processes in our organisations also mitigates against a purely one-sided, managerial, approach to health and wellbeing in our case organisations. However, managerial control of the wellbeing agenda and consultative processes therein does leave the balance of power with management (cf. Nechanska et al., 2020), and therefore the possibility that tensions between wellbeing and competing logics may be resolved in favour of a managerial agenda.

Table 5.2 Creating a sense of collective goods around health and wellbeing

Alignment with business values	*Our values are approachable, bold and connect, [name of appraisal system] definitely comes in there and I would hope that bold does in the fact that it is kind of a bold thing that we are doing. But I find a lot of things that we do, we did some work on a family portal a few years ago which I found quite bold. And that went down really well about support and coaching for any kind of family leave so it could be adoption, maternity, paternity. So yes I do think that whatever we do we have got to hope that it's backing up the values as well.* **Large, multinational law firm, policies and projects manager** *And I think from an HR* (human resources) *perspective as well, as I say we are such a diverse group with lots of separate entities we have, our values are quite strong as well. So the [name of organisational code] values that we use across all group companies is the common language across the board. And it's important in filtering that through from an HR perspective into everything we do so it's incorporated into the contracts. It's incorporated in induction, in the policies and the procedures. If we are doing some training it's about bringing the [name of organisational code] values into that as well. And I think as a general culture across [name of organisation] it is a very supportive culture and people are very aware of those [name of organisational code] values as well. So that all links into the wellbeing initiatives that we have.* **Large care provider, human resources business partner #1**
Humanisation of the workplace	*It makes you feel valued as a member of staff and a person really, if you are valued and you are told you are doing a good job on a day-to-day basis and things like that it makes you better and it makes you want to work better if you know what I mean. Where other care homes that don't bother, you are still just a number to them.* **Small care provider, support worker #1** *For me, actually listening to someone who is of partner level, or of manager level, speak about perhaps the struggles they have and the way that they have dealt with pressures and stress and taking time for themselves, that for me I think is a big thing. Knowing that other people, you know, it's so easy to just go hello and not think what someone else is going through and thinking to yourself oh I'm really busy and I'm quite stressed at the moment, and listening to, you know. It was everyone. It was people from trainees to partners, listening to how they deal with things and what they've learnt and what practices they've started integrating into their day, I think was really helpful for me. I liked that, yes.* **Medium accountancy practice, auditor #2**
Dialogic processes for health and wellbeing	*Oh there's often the things that are on, we have this portal called Yammer and we also have an intranet and we have a guy who's over in internal communications and he's often putting tips up about your mental health. It could be like coming up to Christmas, how to look after your family. It could be about cooking the turkey, those kind of things. They also launched this financial wellbeing for managing your money. I didn't actually go on it with me being an accountant but I know there's other people*

(continued)

Table 5.2 (continued)

	have used it and there was definitely a lot of discussion with people. **Medium construction, financial controller** *We've had no end of feedback, either verbally or written, from people in and around Head Office, to me personally, that says we're so pleased you're doing this, we're really pleased, it's really helping. And we did a wellbeing day around mental health last week, last Thursday, and the first time I did it, it was two years ago, I had three people come and talk to me, this time I've had 40 or 50 just come in the room and take leaflets, talk to me about their stories, their experiences. So that to me is the anecdotal effect of what we're doing, people are far more willing to talk about it. People come and talk to me, you know, in an open plan office or we'll go to a coffee shop and they'll talk about their experiences. But people generally are talking about it, particularly mental health, but now we've got to get that out as being wellbeing, let's talk about wellbeing openly rather than just mental health. So that's my focus for this year.* **Large infrastructure and construction, wellbeing lead**

The role of senior managers in symbolic actions was recognized as an important element in the delivery context and in creating a more favourable environment for implementation, as indicated in the following quote:

> One thing I would say is on a lot of the initiatives that we do have, the actual email about what's happening comes out from the senior partner. So it's not your local HR (human resources) person sending out something about the business has decided to invest in X, this is what it looks like to you and if you've got feedback blah, blah, blah. So it's seen to have sponsorship at the top. Senior leadership buy-in has been a really really important and useful backing for us. You know if you haven't got the buy-in from the top you've never going to get the people to take notice of it any further down. You know we always know we've got people I guess that maybe aren't in senior positions you know the wider range of people that have got a personal experiences of wellbeing whatever it might be that actually want to do things like run events or get something out across the business but if they haven't got the senior people they can actually approach to try and do it then again they're probably not going to get the momentum or it's not going to get the notice that we would want. So we've got really really lucky that we've got really good senior engagement with this pretty much across everything we do for responsible business and that's made a massive difference. (**Large, multinational law firm, responsible business associate**)

Although visible senior management support is recognized as an important lever in the change management literature (Michel, 2014) as well as in many conceptual models of implementing health and wellbeing practices (Chap. 2), the change management literature is focused on delivering change against primary organisational objectives (e.g., profit, efficiency), not secondary objectives around health and wellbeing. Therefore, specialist implementers working in the delivery context may need to spend some time and effort to obtain and maintain senior management support and to persuade senior managers to make actions visible and salient. The following quote illustrates the co-option of senior leaders into the delivery of a health and wellbeing programme, in this case, partners in an accounting practice. The quote also illustrates that it may be necessary to provide senior leaders some level of discretion in the level of their engagement. In this case, engagement at the lower end includes not questioning flexible working requests and active engagement in sports activities.

> And then, of course, getting partners involved with that as well has really helped, because, you know, we've got twenty partners at the moment, so that's twenty leaders, all have their own leadership style. So it can be very difficult getting a single kind of, a single initiative off the ground or a single voice to certain things. But we made sure that each of the partners was briefed on what was going on and how they could support it, even if it was just not making a big deal when someone says they want to leave at half four or someone puts in a flexible working request or the team want to drag them out for a rounder's match or whatever. And, you know, we have our partners taking part in the rounders and, you know, all sorts of things. (**Medium accountancy practice, head of human resources**)

Line and middle managers are also recognized in the change management literature as key enablers and blockers of change (Balogun, 2003; Currie & Procter, 2005), and this too was recognized as a key challenge to address in some of our cases. Earlier in this chapter, we saw that in a large infrastructure and construction firm, some line managers would not engage initially with helping to implement a health and wellbeing programme because they were sceptical that any benefits would be realized. To address this issue, early adopting line managers were used as role models and to provide proof of benefits. Educating line managers was also evident in a large care provider. In this instance, line managers became one of the key delivery mechanisms and therefore support for line managers was required as well as education:

> Because as I say we used to have a central HR (human resources) team up until 2016 and then there was a restructure and the HR business partners were devolved to the parts of the business. So there has been a shift very much in terms of managers taking ownership for managing employees, managing attendance and wellbeing so I think a lot of what we are trying to do is educating the, rather than us doing it all which is sometimes, a bit of hand holding as the central team used to do. It's much more about managers taking ownership of that and then being aware of what support they have and what support they can discuss with their direct reports. So I think there has been that shift there as well. Rather than HR driving it all its filtering through the managers as well. (**Large care provider, human resources business partner #1**)

The last quote also illustrates that multiple stakeholders may need to work together to implement health and wellbeing practices, in this instance, the human resources function supporting unit managers. In this respect, the role of actors in the delivery context may not just be focused on the implementation and co-ordination of various health and wellbeing services and practices in a technical sense of changing administrative or other procedures, but as we have seen, through the political and symbolic processes, actors in the delivery context can focus on changing the wider culture of the organisation, so that health and wellbeing logics become collectively held and sustained across the organisation. The first of the following quotes illustrates the importance of multiple actors for embedding health and wellbeing programmes, in this instance creating redundancy in case one particular actor leaves. The second quote relates more directly to a change in workplace culture that is more collective and transcends ownership of the health and wellbeing programme by a particular management function (in this instance, human resources).

> it's not just one person who's championed this wellbeing, it's a number of people. So it's not just the one person, say [name of managing director] or something, who champions it and then he leaves and the mojo and motivation for it then leaves, it's not that. It's really embedded into the organisation now so it's not just that one person that it's reliant on for it to actually happen, there's so many people working on it. (**Medium construction, financial controller**)
>
> I mean it's a bit of a cop out to say that we are very well connected, in terms of the responsible business team, it doesn't sit within HR (human resources). But it's about as close as it can get to HR without being the same team. So, you know, they attend our HR learning management meetings from time to time. So we are very in tune with that and, I guess I suppose, because we don't want it to be a series of initiatives, we don't want it to be like, great, now HR are launching, I don't know, bicycles on each floor or treadmills under the desk, we don't want it to be like that. We want it to be a slow kind of cultural shift towards, you know, feeling like the firm really cares about its employees and that they're supported when they're going through things like bereavement or, you know, with couples struggling to fall pregnant, for example, and kind of the stresses around that, and menopause. (**Large, multinational law firm, human resources manager**)

Conclusions

There is evidence from the implementation literature that any negative attitudes or predispositions by different stakeholders—senior managers, line managers, front-line workers—need not derail workplace health and wellbeing interventions. There is even evidence various stakeholders may change their attitudes over time. In this chapter, we have seen that the governance and other structures, which form the administrative basis for planning, implementing, co-ordinating and monitoring multiple health and wellbeing practices, also serves other purposes. Defining this as the delivery context that sits between the omnibus context of the wider organisation and the discrete context of a specific practice or intervention, we find evidence that actors in the delivery context deploy a range of political and symbolic strategies. To do so, specialist implementers in the delivery context (human resources, health and safety professionals) can persuade or co-opt other stakeholders (senior and middle managers, workers and various technical experts and other stakeholders) to support or facilitate actions within the delivery context. The strategies deployed may be focused on implementing a specific practice, such that feedback is sought on how to implement a specific practice so that is acceptable to stakeholders. Alternatively, strategies may be focused on securing changes in the wider organisational environment so that health and wellbeing logics become more embedded. In this way, the delivery context provides the link between the organisation on the one hand and a specific practice on the other.

The embedding of health and wellbeing logics through changes in organisational cultures should help organisations implement more health and wellbeing activities more easily over time and more extensively through the organisation (Dollard &

Bakker, 2010; Dollard & Karasek, 2010; see Chap. 8). One reason for this would be that decisions to introduce new practices would be consistent with existing logics, and so be more acceptable to stakeholders and be given less scrutiny (Johnson, 1987). In turn, cultural and political processes focused on embedding health and wellbeing logics may be one way to achieve sustainable wellbeing in organisations. In one of our case companies (medium-sized construction firm), a long-standing paternalism generated from a family run business with a history of employing people from a specific town in a specific area (Northern Ireland) translated into a favourable context within which to embed new practices:

> You have generations of people that have worked in the business and in the past that underlying philosophy that way of living is still there. So people matter and they understand that actually well we are going to do right by people and do good things for people. But in the same way we are doing that and we know that we are have an expectation of what we want people to deliver for us. So it's hard for me to describe but there is a vibrancy about that which can drive forward why we would do things. So when you say about me going talking to the senior team a lot of it's not difficult in terms of arguing what I would call the social value or the personal aspect of it. Because everybody at the top believes in that, everyone believes that we should treat people well. (**Medium construction, human resources director**)

However, as we argued in Chap. 1, and as seen in this chapter in respect of using consultative processes to explain why a particular course of action was not chosen, wellbeing can be a contested subject, and the grounds for contestation may change as stakeholders' concerns change. Therefore, we should not see the process of changing culture (and logics) as either a process of using political and symbolic means to unfreeze one culture to transition to another culture that is refrozen (after Lewin, 1944, see Johnson, 1990). Rather, it should be seen as an ongoing process that is inevitably 'messy'. In the next chapter, we will examine how organisations cope with this mess and sustain those practices that protect and/or enhance wellbeing.

References

Anderson, J., & Sice, P. (2016). Evaluating the possibilities and actualities of the learning process: How a school pilot wellbeing programme worked as an organisational learning process intervention. *The Learning Organization, 23*, 94–120.

Balogun, J. (2003). From blaming the middle to harnessing its potential: Creating change intermediaries. *British Journal of Management, 14*, 6983.

Batorsky, B., Van Stolk, C., & Liu, H. (2016). Is more always better in designing workplace wellness programs?: A comparison of wellness program components versus outcomes. *Journal of Occupational and Environmental Medicine, 58*, 987–993.

Bowen, D. E., & Ostroff, C. (2004). Understanding HRM–firm performance linkages: The role of the "strength" of the HRM system. *Academy of Management Review, 29*, 203–221.

Currie, G., & Procter, S. J. (2005). The antecedents of middle managers' strategic contribution: The case of a professional bureaucracy. *Journal of Management Studies, 42*, 1325–1356.

Daniels, K., Delany, K., Napier, J., Hogg, M., & Rushworth, M. (2019). *The value of occupational health to workplace wellbeing*. Society of Occupational Medicine.

Daniels, K., Watson, D., Nayani, R., Tregaskis, O., Hogg, M., Etuknwa, A., & Semkina, A. (2021). Implementing practices focused on workplace health and psychological wellbeing: A systematic review. *Social Science and Medicine, 227*, 113888.

Davies, W. (2015). *The happiness industry*. Verso.

Dollard, M. F., & Bakker, A. B. (2010). Psychosocial safety climate as a precursor to conducive work environments, psychological health problems, and employee engagement. *Journal of Occupational and Organizational Psychology, 83*, 579–599.

Dollard, M. F., & Karasek, R. A. (2010). Building psychosocial safety climate. In J. Houdmont & S. Leka (Eds.), *Contemporary occupational health psychology: Global perspectives on research and practice* (Vol. 1, pp. 208–233). Wiley.

Gersick, C. J. (1991). Revolutionary change theories: A multilevel exploration of the punctuated equilibrium paradigm. *Academy of Management Review, 16*, 10–36.

Hancock, P., & Tyler, M. (2004). "MOT your life": Critical management studies and the management of everyday life. *Human Relations, 57*, 619–645.

Hardy, C. (1996). Understanding power: Bringing about strategic change. *British Journal of Management, 7*, S3–S16.

Health and Safety Executive. (2017/2019). *Tackling work-related stress using the management standards approach: A step-by-step workbook*. http://www.hse.gov.uk/pubns/wbk01.pdf First published 2017, updated 2019.

Huettermann, H., & Bruch, H. (2019). Mutual gains? Health-related HRM, collective well-being and organizational performance. *Journal of Management Studies, 56*, 1045–1072.

ISO (International Organization for Standardization). (2018). *BS 45002-1:2018. Occupational health and safety management systems. General guidelines for the application of ISO 45001. Guidance on managing occupational health*. International Organization for Standardization.

Johns, G. (2006). The essential impact of context on organizational behavior. *Academy of Management Review, 31*, 386–408.

Johnson, G. (1987). *Strategic change and the management process*. Blackwell.

Johnson, G. (1990). Managing strategic change; the role of symbolic action. *British Journal of Management, 1*, 183–200.

Johnson, S., Robertson, I., & Cooper, C. L. (2018). *Work and well-being*. Palgrave Macmillan.

Jordan, J., Gurr, E., Tinline, G., Giga, S. I., Faragher, B., & Cooper, C. L. (2003). *Beacons of excellence in stress prevention: Research report 133*. HSE Books.

Kimura, T. (2015). A review of political skill: Current research trend and directions for future research. *International Journal of Management Reviews, 17*, 312–332.

LaMontagne, A. D., Martin, A., Page, K. M., Reavley, N. J., Noblet, A. J., Milner, A. J., Milner, A. J., Keegel, T., & Smith, P. M. (2014). Workplace mental health: Developing an integrated intervention approach. *BMC Psychiatry, 14*, 1–11.

Lewin, K. (1944) Constructs in field theory. In Cartwright, D. (1952). *Field theory in social science: Selected theoretical papers by Kurt Lewin* (pp 30–42). London: Social Science Paperbacks.

Mattke, S., Kapinos, K., Caloyeras, J. P., Taylor, E. A., Batorsky, B., Liu, H., Van Busum, K. R., & Newberry, S. (2015). Workplace wellness programs: Services offered, participation, and incentives. *Rand Health Quarterly, 5*, 7.

Michel, A. (2014). The mutual constitution of persons and organizations: An ontological perspective on organizational change. *Organization Science, 25*, 1082–1110.

Nechanska, E., Hughes, E., & Dundon, T. (2020). Towards an integration of employee voice and silence. *Human Resource Management Review, 30*, 100674.

Roodbari, H., Axtell, C., Nielsen, K., & Sorensen, G. (2021). Organisational interventions to improve employees' health and wellbeing: A realist synthesis. *Applied Psychology: An International Review*. https://doi.org/10.1111/apps.12346

Schein, E. H. (1985). *Organizational culture and leadership*. Wiley.

Tregaskis, O., Daniels, K., Glover, L., Butler, P., & Meyer, M. (2013). High performance work practices and firm performance: A longitudinal case study. *British Journal of Management, 24*, 225–244.

Trist, E. L., & Bamforth, K. W. (1951). Some social and psychological consequences of the longwall method of coal-getting: An examination of the psychological situation and defences of a work group in relation to the social structure and technological content of the work system. *Human Relations, 4*, 3–38.

von Thiele Schwarz, U., Lundmark, R., & Hasson, H. (2016). The dynamic integrated evaluation model (DIEM): Achieving sustainability in organizational intervention through a participatory evaluation approach. *Stress and Health, 32*, 285–293.

Westover, J. H. (2010). Managing organizational change: Change agent strategies and techniques to successfully managing the dynamics of stability and change in organizations. *International Journal of Management and Innovation, 2*, 45–51.

Chapter 6
Making Things Work: Learning, Adaptation and Continuation

In previous chapters, we have introduced the notion that sustaining wellbeing relates to an ongoing process (Chap. 1) of renegotiating conflicts between the wellbeing logics and competing logics (Chap. 4) of different actors (Chap. 5). We have introduced the delivery context (Chap. 5) as the arena for the co-ordination of activities in a workplace health and wellbeing programme (including bottom-up as well as top-down initiatives), which is also the locus of political and symbolic activity involved in the renegotiation of conflicts between logics and changing wellbeing priorities. As noted in the last chapter, this is by and large a 'messy' as well as an ongoing endeavour. The evidence from intervention studies also indicates political and symbolic action activity tends to favour intervention success, but does not guarantee success (Daniels et al., 2021). Moreover, Daniels et al. also concluded that effective governance is a necessary but not sufficient condition for intervention success. If politics, symbolic action and effective governance are important—and the last chapter indicates they are—then the question remains as to what other factors are critical for successful health and wellbeing programmes.

Daniels et al. (2021) concluded that learning structures and continuation of activities were two of these other factors. For Daniels et al., learning structures referred to processes and practices that enable organisations to monitor different health and wellbeing activities, and in so doing, provide a basis to adapt specific practices to enable continuation. Continuation referred to efforts at implementing, adapting and otherwise sustaining the intervention. We can expand on these definitions to reflect our focus on co-ordinated programmes of activities, so that: Learning structures refer to those processes and practices focused on monitoring health and wellbeing to provide a basis for adapting or terminating specific practices and introducing new practices; Continuation refers to the process of implementing and adapting practices in a programme to enable the continuation of the programme. Adaptation is the key element linking learning to continuation. Moreover, adaptation and continuation are embedded in the notion of sustaining wellbeing as an ongoing process of negotiating between different logics as those logics evolve.

K. Daniels et al., *Achieving Sustainable Workplace Wellbeing*, Aligning Perspectives on Health, Safety and Well-Being, https://doi.org/10.1007/978-3-031-00665-4_6

The purpose of this chapter is to explore in more detail the links between learning and continuation than has hitherto been the case in the literature, as well as the links to governance of a programme, and therefore the delivery context of multiple activities.

Learning Structures

In five out of our case organisation, there were formal monitoring procedures, such as staff surveys, monitoring of staff turnover and absence, running alongside various forms of consultation, that formed the learning structures used to make decisions on what to do, how to adapt it and what to stop. In one case, a small care home, all learning was done through informal, consultative processes. The formal procedures varied in their sophistication. Two of the more sophisticated approaches are illustrated in the following quotes. The first quote relates to running pilot projects in specific locations, and the second to using not just surveys, but also data from recruitment processes.

> We have also been looking very much around the work environment and we have currently got a trial going on the place of work where I work in [name of town] where we have got different colours across the different floors, we have got more comfortable seating areas. We have got some wellbeing stations, you know the buttons that you see when you come out of the loo and you press how did we do today, it's that sort of machine but there are lots of different questions. And you can do your own little online assessment about your own wellbeing which is great. And we have got some pods, so people can go off and book the pods where they are sound proofed and just get on with a piece of work. (**Large care provider, human resources business partner #2**).
>
> Well we have similar threads in terms of how we question and how we monitor across all of those things and we take that feedback both internally and externally. So a good example is when we recruit even if we don't recruit that particular candidate we ask them some of the things that prompted them to apply to us. And how they found the whole experience. And obviously flexible working is not the only thing but we have sort of picked that as a bit of a thread. We ask all the candidates was the fact that we have been externally recognised for having that type of culture was recognised as important to work life balance and health perspective one of the reasons why you applied. And so we have seen some quite good trends from that. And also our existing people are asked similar questions about the values they get from us offering those sorts of options to them which is where stuff like the employee survey comes in. (**Large infrastructure and construction, human resources director**).

Other examples of learning structures evident in the literature include embedding of continuous improvement processes, coaching (von Thiele Schwarz et al., 2017) and training (Mejías Herrera & Huaccho Huatuco, 2011) into the implementation of specific health and wellbeing interventions. Learning can form an intervention in its own right, as in the case of studies of communities of practice or even professional development (Mabry et al., 2018; Olson et al., 2016; Watson et al., 2018), and as evidenced in the informal, continuous improvement approach taken to staff wellbeing and other aspects of organisational functioning at a small care home:

That's changed a lot over the years, before we were just a number we were just a staff member we weren't allowed to have opinions or anything like that. We didn't, we weren't involved in the day to day running of the place. The management done that. But now since [name of home manager] has been manager which is I think six years we have been encouraged to take day to day things and if we can think of a better way of doing something we then discuss it with her and we put it into practice. And sometimes it works and sometimes it doesn't but as she has always said we won't know until we try. So we are all involved in the day to day running of the place really. (**Small care home, support worker #1**).

In the previous chapter, we saw that monitoring is one of the administrative functions in the delivery context, and so governance and learning are linked, with the former providing the infrastructure in which to embed learning and adapt different practices (von Thiele Schwarz et al., 2016). The following quotes illustrate how management of a whole programme of activities differs from management of standalone practices, as is the case in much of the existing literature (first quote) and how the political/symbolic aspects can be weaved into learning processes (second quote, involvement of senior managers).

It was a meeting between us and our broker at the time in that we have quarterly review meetings with lots of our different benefit providers, but it was quite segmented in that we would just receive some data from occupational health and some data from medical insurance. And sometimes it would be saying the same things and sometimes it would be slightly different and we just realised that actually if we all sat in the room together we would be able to look at our whole workforce rather than it just looking at particular workforce. With occupational health it's the people who are potentially already absent whereas the MI (medical insurers) we were getting from private medical insurance those people could still be actively at work. So it's a different target population really so that's what we tried to set up these meetings to consolidate the data and look at our whole population as a whole. (**Large, multinational law firm, assistant rewards manager**).

So we run half a dozen or so continuous improvement groups across the company based on key topics that the Board think we need to be doing better at and occupational health was an obvious winner really. So there was a continuous improvement group that started off and that would be representatives from around the business that would meet quarterly under the tutelage of a senior director, just seeing what we could do better, what we should be doing, and where the resources needed to go. That started a series of topics and projects, one being an occupational health and wellbeing training course, which we kicked off and the health and safety team rolled out. It was a one-day course and it was run internally by one of our safety managers. And there were a number of other initiatives. (**Large infrastructure and construction, wellbeing lead**).

Consonant with the interventions literature, our cases also evidence the use of learning structures in monitoring and adapting (first quote below), being prepared to adapt (second quote) or abandon specific practices if they are not perceived to be effective (third and fourth quotes).

I think initially maybe there wasn't probably enough of the line managers trained initially to be trained to be, and maybe we were trying to do [name of appraisal system] meetings with too many people at any particular time. And again that was, it was during that trial period at the start but again that was very very quickly recognised by everybody. And again as I said we trained up and we got all these trained in delivery [name of appraisal system]and then finding that [name of appraisal system] were needed to be delivered at different levels more. So that there was in sense in its own word, there was a connect then between a total connect then between certain individuals and their line manager as such. And I think that has probably helped along the way as well from getting those [name of appraisal system] meetings. And again I guess it's pretty much a fine tuning of anything that you put in place or any process that you put in place. You will put it in place you will come across difficulties and as long as people recognise that there will be difficulties and that there is a way to work through those and to make it better, and as long as that's done then the process then can only get better. (**Medium construction, operations manager**).

If anything, you know, when you take into account that sickness is down and everything else, the productivity's actually gone up. So the indications are all positive, you know, we know this is the right thing, the right track to be on. The activities that we offer and how that looks will vary. We will continue to evolve those as we get more and more feedback and information, and kind of, you know, monitor the stats. And if anything starts to slip we'll know we're not quite doing enough in that space. So we know we're in the right direction, it's just, yes, keeping it alive really. (**Medium accountancy practice, head of human resources**).

Yes because everybody brings something and we do take our life experiences with us wherever we go don't we. So obviously we apply it into the workplace as well and if it works it works it's a good thing and if it doesn't well we try something else. (**Small care home, support worker #1**).

OK, so two Christmas's ago, I thought it would be really good if we change pay day, because our pay day is the last day of the month, so people would get paid after Christmas. So I thought, it would be really good if we get approval from the board and talk to finance and pay people on the last working day before Christmas, so they've got the money before Christmas, and I thought that was a great idea. And we'd had a few people, only a handful, to be fair, talking to us about, you know, debt management over Christmas and all of that sort of thing, so we thought it would be a good way to help people. And the feedback that we got was so negative, it was like, well I'd already budgeted for not being paid until after Christmas and now I've got an extra week to go before January pay day. So all the negativity, and it was one of those things where I'd put quite a bit of work in to getting all the ducks in a row, you know, getting the sign up from the board, talking to finance, because all the BACS (bank payment system) crediting days had to be changed and, you know, that meant that we left the cut off dates the same, which meant both HR (human resources) and Finance had to work a little bit harder to get everything ready on time, which both teams signed up to. So we'd put all this extra effort in for the good of our employers, so we thought, and the feedback was awful. So I thought, right, I'm not doing that again. So I didn't. (**Medium accountancy practice, head of human resources**).

The second quote of the four produced alludes to not just adapting (or in that case being prepared to adapt) specific practices (in this case, flexible working) on the basis of feedback provided through learning structures, but also to adapting a whole programme of activities. The third quote about 'trying something else' also alludes to a programme of activities, although the approach to health and wellbeing and learning how to adapt practices taken in the small care home was much more informal than the overtly managed programmes in the other case organisations. An example of using formalized approaches of adapting programmes through learning structures is provided in the following quote:

So we use a RAG approach, red, amber, green, against each of the areas of the action plan. So for example on the last review that we did, we were doing some really strong evidence stuff around personal responsibility, strategic reviews, how we'd improve reporting both internally and externally, and how we'd improve the vision of people having a discussion around occupational health at a leadership level. So we were doing well in them areas. Our

> next level of discussion last week was how then do we push them down from the leadership team down into occupational teams if it's not happening already. But in other areas such as education, we found at the last review, which was April 2018, which was the last major review, we needed to do more about literacy, more about people talking about their experiences, the use of personal case studies etcetera. We've done a lot of work around that so that red now is definitely green in terms of what we've done in terms of improving literacy, the use of mental health toolkits through our academy platform etcetera. (**Large infrastructure and construction, health and safety director**).

In the same organisation, there was also evidence of learning to adapt monitoring systems:

> I was talking about the survey that we've just done that's on stress, the next stage of that survey is round about occupational health and wellbeing. So it's not just going to be stress concentrated, it's going to be a bit broader in terms of looking at everything occupational health and wellbeing. And we're hoping to put that out in April, kind of summertime. So that would give us a bit more information about what people's understanding is at the moment and it will also give us a bit of a focus for going forward. Because at the moment the focus that we've decided on is what we think is important but I'd like to know what everybody thinks is important within the company and look to see what trends are coming out. So I suppose that's the way we'll go going forward, is that the next survey that we do, which will be probably in the summer, will give us that kind of direction and it will tell us where people are at the moment and where they think we are as a company because that's obviously interesting. Because we do cultural surveys on the projects but it's usually round about safety. There's the odd question about occupational health and we tend to score quite low in it. So just doing a bit more directed one (survey) just about occupational health will give us a bit of understanding of where people are just now and where they think we are and what we need to look at next. (**Large infrastructure and construction, senior safety adviser**).

Learning structures were also used not just to check on progress and adapt specific practices or programmes of activities, but as means of persuading others to develop health and wellbeing activities. This is similar to the discussion in the Chap. 4 in relation to resolving tensions between health and wellbeing logics and competing logics by using evidence-based arguments. The difference in this instance is that it is an ongoing activity connected to delivery context rather than something that occurs when competing logics and health and wellbeing logics have not achieved some level of reconciliation, as might occur more frequently at the start of programme development. In the quote below, analysis is used not only to justify continued investment in one particular wellbeing service used in one part of the organisation but also to illustrate how that service could provide benefits in another part of the organisation.

> How we can develop strategies to work with our early intervention service so that's at a very early stage but we do have these regular quarterly meetings and ROI (return on investment) report was done last year and this is the second year we've done it. Just really to demonstrate for the business the impact of having that absence monitoring service and how cost savings etc. and it's also to try and demonstrate to our other parts of the business, like leisure who don't have this service how it helps to reduce absence, engage employees and also gives you a return on investment. (**Large care provider, payroll manager #1**).

In summary, we found evidence in our cases of learning structures being used to (1) adapt specific practices within the same overall programme; (2) adapting or changing whole programmes of activities and, in some cases refocusing programmes on specific issues; and (3) having in place learning structures that may be themselves adapted and which involve consultative elements that may themselves form a basis for developing or shifting shared understandings (cf. von Thiele Schwarz et al., 2017). In this respect, at a programme level, there is evidence of single loop, double (Argyris & Schon, 1978) and triple loop learning (Romme & Van Witteloostuijn, 1999). We reconsider learning in Chap. 8.

Continuation

Our analysis so far has indicated that learning structures facilitate adaptation of practices or programmes (and in the case of changing surveys, processes for programme management, and hence the delivery context). However, adaptation is insufficient for a practice or programme of practices: Rather practices must have continuity (i.e. longevity, Daniels et al., 2021), which implies an ongoing process of adaptation and embedding, as illustrated in the quotes below. In contrast to the second and third quotes below, the first quote links adapting, evolving and continuity of a health and wellbeing programme explicitly to a business case of based on recruitment, wherein the programme has to evolve to keep ahead of competitor businesses. In contrast, the second and third quotes, adaptation and continuation are linked to an ongoing process of embedding and culture change.

> I think it's because we believe we're not at the end of the journey. There continues to be the challenge that actually, we need to do more. Because actually, bear in mind, come back to why we're doing this, it's because we want to retain good people, we want to recruit good people. We want them at work as long as we can have them. And actually, as soon as our competitors, if you like, are competitive on some of this stuff, then actually, at that stage we are, we've got to move again. So I think it's, you know, work on the assumption that, you know, change is constant, well we've got to keep changing, we've got to keep getting better. (**Medium accountancy practice, managing partner**).
>
> But if we had started to try and implement all of the stuff and all of the challenges that came out of those workshops four years ago at once we would have failed. So I always use, when I describe our journey in this area I describe it as just that, it is a journey it's not an initiative because an initiative is where you just implement a series of things and then move on to the next. This is stuff that has to be continually worked on to embed it. (**Large infrastructure and construction, human resources director**).
>
> And I think, the culture doesn't change overnight. So it's, from my perspective, it's kind of, you know, dipping your toe in, trying something, see how it goes down, and then, you know, being prepared to adapt the approach throughout the sort of next few years probably. I think that's really important, rather than sort of snapping on some sort of initiative or, I hate the word, initiative, because it sounds like it's something that we sort of talk about and then you get over it. But some sort of project or some sort of kind of driver, which we then sort of get bored of and move on. So I think it's really important that it's reflective with what we choose to engage with. (**Large, multinational law firm, human resources manager**)

This last quote notes that specific practices that comprised that organisation's health and wellbeing programme should be linked into the intent for the whole programme and the continuation of that programme, thus linking specific practices together in a coherent strategy managed through programme governance in the delivery context. Another informant from the same organisation made specific links between governance, strategy and continuity. In the quote below, the informant indicates that some specific activities are linked into an agreed strategy, and these will form part of a rolling programme of activities, yet other, more localized activities would not form part of the strategy and so receive no financial support from the allocated budget.

> Yes we still get quite a few challenges about people wanting to do their own local initiatives which doesn't really tally with what we are doing as a wider scheme. But what we have said is we will have an agreed health and wellbeing strategy and we are rolling out a calendar which will have an initiative per month and that will be our overarching health and wellbeing strategy. But if local offices do want to do their own thing then we are happy for them to do that but it would just be a localised arrangement it wouldn't feed back into the health and wellbeing budget for example because it might not necessarily be something that would be applicable to all. (**Large, multinational law firm, assistant rewards manager**).

Alternatively, in a large infrastructure and construction firm, programme governance promoted adaptation and continuity in the form of reflexive consideration of programme goals and intent. This is illustrated in the next quote with relates to how a governance mechanism was used to reorient activities to the wider concept of wellbeing and away from a narrower focus on mental health:

> So our first six, half a dozen meetings or so, that wellbeing forum became around mental health and getting the structure around that. We've now realised, at the back end of 2018, that actually it was becoming a mental health forum not a wellbeing forum, so at the last meeting we had in November we refocused the group's attention on what we call seven enablers to wellbeing and making sure that the group didn't focus just on mental health but actually a bigger picture of wellbeing and that it was still in line with the original continuous improvement group. So that's where our focus is over the next three or four months, maybe the next two or three meetings, is to make sure that we widen our thinking, not just around mental health but overall wellbeing and then bring it in line with the wellbeing continuous improvement group. (**Large infrastructure and construction, wellbeing lead**).

The following quote from the same organisation illustrates how learning structures also feed into adaptation and continuity. In this instance, the learning that promotes adaptation and continuity comes not only from learning mechanisms focused on the organisation but also from examining practice in other sectors:

> I think sustaining and developing what we have already put into place. That whole continuing improvement thing, it's very easy to get to a point where things look great and you take your foot off stuff. So a great example is on the flexible working, we do need to get the odd 10–15% of line managers who are still not on board with this on board with it. And so its keeping working on that culture change. But I think it's extending our wellbeing offering where we can. And I think the best ideas come from within so that's people who have either joined us from other companies and seen things work well that we don't do. Or actually people suddenly seeing a gap either in how we think or how we work, how we operate and giving them the opportunity, whether that's formally or informally to tell us how we can improve. It's all of that really. And I think you have always got to look at other sectors as well. I think part of our culture change has been really, and it's still ongoing, the sector is very traditional and people do often refer to what others in our sector do. That's OK to a

> point but most people don't do things that differently to us, other sectors do have ideas that could be relevant. And I think we have got to encourage sensible benchmarking with other sectors that are not construction to move us forward. (**Large infrastructure and construction, human resources director**).

Daniels et al. (2021) found that one specific set of activities, linking governance and continuity, namely following a planned sequence of activities, was not associated with intervention success. This is despite many of the frameworks reviewed in Chap. 2 recommending specific and linear sequences of activities. This may reflect both the iterative and adaptive processes of implementing whole programmes of activities and specific activities, but also the intractability of detailed planning processes in some instances (Mintzberg, 1994), as illustrated in the following quote:

> But you do, and there's lots of, well this is HR (human resources), this is facilities, where would we put it? I don't know how we'd site it and all of those sorts of things. And you have to stop those discussions really quickly and just go forward and just say, look, we make a decision, if we get it wrong, we'll change it, but we'll, you know, just make it happen, at that stage. But it is just about trying to do lots of, as I say, lots of little things and just, otherwise, the little things will just overwhelm you because they never get done. (**Medium accountancy practice, managing partner**).

In the last chapter, we saw the importance of dialogic processes for implementing practices and programmes, and Daniels et al. (2021) did find some evidence that regular communication about health and wellbeing initiatives may assist with continuity efforts. Communication about activities may aid continuity through sensemaking/sensegiving (from the work of Weick, 1995), i.e. through visionary and symbolic leadership (Westley & Mintzberg, 1989) and experiential learning (Lewin, 1952; Burnes & Cooke, 2013). In this way, workers may be able to see how seemingly diverse organisational actions are connected to a singular aim to improve health and wellbeing. Moreover, regular communication may help to build an organisational culture within which health and wellbeing logics become accepted (cf. safety climate, Zohar, 2010) and, through ongoing, communication prevents health and wellbeing logics slipping in priority relevant to other logics (Goh et al., 2012).

The importance of co-ordinated communication, as part of programme governance, was evident in our case data, as illustrated in the following three quotes. The first quote relates to co-ordinated communication and communication as a process not just of signposting to support or making people aware of activities, but also to gather feedback on what issues are not addressing worker concerns—that is, the dialogic processes referred to in Chap. 5. The second and third quotes more explicitly acknowledge the importance of communication in bringing different activities together. The second quote relates to communication around policies being used as an opportunity to make people aware of the support available to line managers, and the third to promoting various activities as a coherent whole that transcend traditional ways of approaching health and safety.

> Yes, when we started that line, before that we were still doing things but they probably weren't in a coordinated fashion. So an example some of the things that we would be doing, we had a monthly focus upon a particular wellbeing topic so let's say it was prostate cancer

or it was wear pink or something. We have a focus space where there would be information there would be toolbox talks, there would be talks taking place on site. We could have a well man month and we had a health check taking place or bus turning up and people getting a simple health check done on site. Some sites would maybe go to their local GP round the corner and brought a nurse to come in and do things. Those sort of things are going on but we tried to put this in a more coordinated fashion so that there was a team that was actually managing the message, what we are doing when we are doing it. And consistently trying to look at what we were trying to get across to people, what were the issues. And if people came back and said we have an issue about maybe suicide or there is a mental health aspect issue in the industry we would be looking to build that into the annual calendar and that timetable. (**Medium construction, human resources director**).

So it was September/October last year I did it was a 2–2.5 hour session on managing attendance and wellbeing. So it was basically looking at obviously our sickness absence policy and attendance and managing attendance and return to work and discussions with people and absence reviews and things like that. But also making them aware of the support that they have available to them as managers when managing absence or mental health issues as well. (**Large care provider, human resources business partner #1**).

Well I think we've always recognised that we're called SHEQ (safety, health, environment and quality) but primarily we've got a lot more safety managers than we've got health managers if you like. We've got some occupational health specialists so they've focused their attention on things like COSH, control of hazardous substances and things like that where we've got a legal duty, again driven very much from a safety world. What we're trying to do is get them to think well actually you're a safety, health, environment and quality manager, you need to think about health, not just legal compliance but health as in wellbeing. And I've noticed over the last sort of 12, 18 months, the new appointments and things at some of the big projects such as [name of two large projects], they're no longer safety, health, environment, quality specialists, they're safety, wellbeing, environment, quality specialists. So, it's starting to get that certain recognition into the language as well. So, again it's one of these things that I think is growing because people recognise that you can do quite small things for great benefits just by advertising what's already out there. Like I say, we all have to give maternity and paternity leave, we all have to treat people fairly and with equality and diversity, it's just about sort of advertising it and promoting it. (**Large infrastructure and construction, wellbeing lead**).

Conclusions

In this chapter, we have argued that learning structures embedded in the delivery context facilitate adaptation of health and wellbeing practices, programmes of practices and even elements attached to the management of a programme of practices (i.e. the delivery context itself). However, adaptation is necessary yet insufficient for the maintenance and continuity of a programme. It also appears appropriate communication is important, and the dialogic processes embedded in the delivery context may provide the infrastructure to do so. The processes and structures therefore may have high levels of interdependences, as illustrated in the following quote, which pertains to learning structures, governance, communication and continuity of efforts:

About which ones we think are achievable and which ones actually we do have a duty of care as a business to focus on. We have communicated that across our mental health champions

> about what's come out of these sessions and what we're going to be looking to work on over the next 12 months and we've got a lot of actions from that with the various people that's involved. Whether it's HR (human resources), facilities, our team, [name of wellbeing lead], we're all working on it, the networks working on it and it was anything from you know key types of topics at events that they want to see us running to the training that's available for managers or line managers or you know people that are working with people directly. But there's a lot of actions so we're actually using the feedback that's come out of these sessions specifically to drive forward the next phase of work around the topic. (**Large, multinational law firm, responsible business associate**).

In this and the previous chapter, we have focused on how specific activities and programmes of activities can be implemented with reference to those practices and the delivery context of those practices. Although learning, adaptability and effective governance appears important for practice and programme continuity (Daniels et al., 2021 and this chapter), we have not considered how programmes of health and wellbeing practices are connected to the wider (omnibus) organisational environment, and how tensions between health and wellbeing logics on the one hand and competing logics on the other may be reconciled. This is the main topic of the next chapter.

References

Argyris, C., & Schon, D. A. (1978). *Organizational learning: A theory of action perspective*. Addison Wesley.

Burnes, B., & Cooke, B. (2013). Kurt Lewin's field theory: A review and re-evaluation. *International Journal of Management Reviews, 15*, 408–425.

Daniels, K., Watson, D., Nayani, R., Tregaskis, O., Hogg, M., Etuknwa, A., & Semkina, A. (2021). Implementing practices focused on workplace health and psychological wellbeing: A systematic review. *Social Science and Medicine, 227*, 113888.

Goh, Y. M., Love, P. E., Brown, H., & Spickett, J. (2012). Organizational accidents: A systemic model of production versus protection. *Journal of Management Studies, 49*, 52–76.

Lewin, K. (1952). Constructs in field theory [1944]. In D. Cartwright (Ed.), *Field theory in social science: Selected theoretical papers by Kurt Lewin* (pp. 30–42). Social Science Paperbacks.

Mabry, L., Parker, K. N., Thompson, S. V., Bettencourt, K. M., Haque, A., Luther Rhoten, K., ... Olson, R. (2018). Protecting workers in the home care industry: Workers' experienced job demands, resource gaps, and benefits following a socially supportive intervention. *Home Health Care Services Quarterly, 37*, 259–276.

Mejías Herrera, S. H., & Huaccho Huatuco, L. (2011). Macroergonomics intervention programs: Recommendations for their design and implementation. *Human Factors and Ergonomics in Manufacturing, 21*, 227–243.

Mintzberg, H. (1994). *The rise and fall of strategic planning*. Free Press.

Olson, R., Thompson, S. V., Elliot, D. L., Hess, J. A., Rhoten, K. L., Parker, K. N., Wright, R. R., Wipfli, B., Bettencourt, K. M., Buckmaster, A., & Marino, M. (2016). Safety and health support for home care workers: The COMPASS randomized controlled trial. *American Journal of Public Health, 106*, 1823–1832.

Romme, A. G. L., & Van Witteloostuijn, A. (1999). Circular organizing and triple loop learning. *Journal of Organizational Change Management, 12*, 439–454.

von Thiele Schwarz, U., Lundmark, R., & Hasson, H. (2016). The dynamic integrated evaluation model (DIEM): Achieving sustainability in organizational intervention through a participatory evaluation approach. *Stress and Health, 32*, 285–293.

von Thiele Schwarz, U., Nielsen, K. M., Stenfors-Hayes, T., & Hasson, H. (2017). Using kaizen to improve employee Well-being: Results from two organizational intervention studies. *Human Relations, 70*, 966–993.

Watson, D., Tregaskis, O., Gedikli, C., Vaughn, O., & Semkina, A. (2018). Well-being through learning: A systematic review of learning interventions in the workplace and their impact on Well-being. *European Journal of Work and Organizational Psychology, 27*, 247–268.

Weick, K. E. (1995). *Sensemaking in organizations*. Sage.

Westley, F., & Mintzberg, H. (1989). Visionary leadership and strategic management. *Strategic Management Journal, 10*, 17–32.

Zohar, D. (2010). Thirty years of safety climate research: Reflections and future directions. *Accident Analysis and Prevention, 42*, 1517–1522.

Chapter 7
Putting the Workplace Back into Workplace Wellbeing

> So I think that user need evaluation, that deep conversation with the heads of service for those departments and also the people throughout the teams is extremely important. There's a balance off in how much we react to either of those parties as well because there's always a group policy and a strategy to think of as well. Because people will tell you that they want and need many things and it's not necessarily the case that that fits with the actual business plan. But I think that's probably the one of the fundamental things that we've found that to make sure that we are talking and regularly talking because people's needs and thoughts are changing quite rapidly as the environment changes and technology changes around us. (**Large care provider, head of corporate facilities**).

In the previous chapter, we argued that one of the key factors associated with workplace health and wellbeing programmes that achieve sustainable wellbeing is the adaptation of those programmes. This begs the question of adapting to what? The quote above illustrates it is not just adaptation to account for unforeseen issues with implementation or changing preferences and needs of employees, but an ongoing adaptation to the wider organisation, that is itself changing and evolving, possibly in response to changes occurring in the organisational environment.

Figure 7.1 is the same model we first introduced in Chap. 1 (Fig. 1.1), for which we have been developing each of the elements throughout the other chapters. In this chapter, the purpose is to provide an account of how programmes of health and wellbeing activities are connected to the wider organisation, its procedures, practices and structures, and in so doing ways in which health and wellbeing logics are reconciled with the competing logics that sustain those procedures, practices and structures. We make the assertion that wider organisational procedures, practices and structures represent other logics, because those procedures, practices and structures are a consequence of those logics and are sustained by those logics (Johnson, 1987; Schein, 1985).

In Chap. 5, we introduced the notion of the delivery context, which sits between the wider omnibus context of the organisation and the discrete context of specific health and wellbeing practices (Johns, 2006). In the previous chapter, we examined the processes that sustain wellbeing (Daniels et al., 2021): These are learning from

K. Daniels et al., *Achieving Sustainable Workplace Wellbeing*, Aligning Perspectives on Health, Safety and Well-Being, https://doi.org/10.1007/978-3-031-00665-4_7

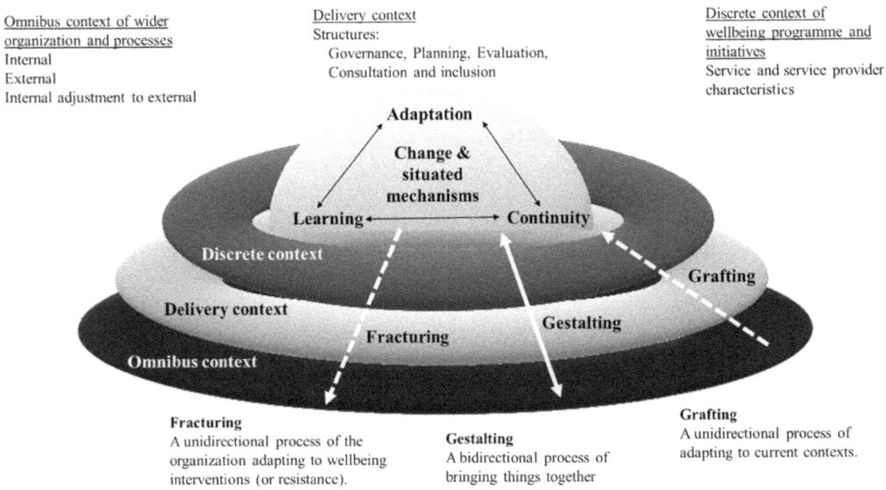

Fig. 7.1 A model of how organisations implement and sustain workplace health and wellbeing programmes

implementation of specific activities, so the practice can be adapted to the context or *vice versa*, thus enabling continuity of both specific practices if appropriate and the wider programme of health and wellbeing practices.

In the last chapter, effective governance in the delivery context was examined as a condition for learning, adaptation and therefore continuity, or the sustaining of wellbeing. Learning, adaptation and continuity are conceptually distinct from those processes—physical, psychological or social—that explain the effectiveness of any given health and wellbeing activity. As outlined in Chap. 3, any given practice may come to have effects on health and wellbeing through a variety of mechanisms that may or may not have been part of the plan for how the practice was intended to work. However, learning, adaptation and continuity are factors that sustain health and wellbeing activities and programmes of activities so that they are implemented and have a level of durability to allow the potential for those activities to enhance different elements of health and wellbeing.

In this chapter, we examine the last three elements of the model. These three elements relate to how organisations connect health and wellbeing practices to other organisational procedures, practices and structures. These process, practices and structures are manifestations of other logics that can compete with health and wellbeing logics. Therefore, to allow for implementation and continuation of health and wellbeing practices, there needs to be in place some way in which the implementation of health and wellbeing practices can be reconciled with other organisational procedures, practices and structures.

We propose three such process. (1) Grafting, which refers to adapting health and wellbeing practices, so they are compatible with other organisational procedures, practices and structures. Grafting pertains to reconciling logics by ensuring they do not compete so that competing logics remain intact. (2) Fracturing, which is changing the organisation to be compatible with the health and wellbeing practice by replacing old processes, structures and structures with new ones. Fracturing pertains to creating conflict with competing logics so that competing logics become either extinct or at least subservient to health and wellbeing logics. (3) Gestalting, which is bringing different health and wellbeing practices and other organisational procedures, practices and structures together for simultaneous change in order both to meet common goals or interpretation and hence reduce conflict. Grafting and fracturing have received some attention in the literature (see Chap. 2 and below) yet are considered only superficial ways, if at all as in the case of fracturing in particular. Grafting, fracturing and Gestalting are not considered in combination in existing conceptual approaches to implementing workplace health and wellbeing practices.

Grafting

Grafting relates to implementing health and wellbeing programmes and activities so that they are compatible with or build upon existing procedures, systems and structures (which may include existing health and wellbeing and activities). It relates to layering of health and wellbeing programmes and activities on top of existing procedures, practices and structures or integrating health and wellbeing programmes and activities with existing procedures, practices and structures. The consequence is minimal conflict with existing procedures, practices and structures and the logics underpinning them. Therefore, the purpose of grafting enables multiple objectives to be pursued in ways that are compatible with each other, yet without changing how existing objectives are pursued.

Maximizing compatibility with existing processes, practices and procedures has been recommended in prior reviews focused on workplace wellbeing interventions (Daniels et al., 2017; Knight et al., 2019; Nielsen & Noblet, 2018), recommended in some implementation models (see Chap. 2) and is one of a set of ten principles developed to guide 'researchers in designing, implementing, and evaluating organisational interventions that are both scientifically rigorous and practically relevant' (von Thiele Schwarz et al., 2021, p. 416). Maximizing compatibility is also a principle in several models of organisational change (Armenakis & Bedeian, 1999; Armenakis et al., 1993; Kotter, 1995; Rafferty et al., 2013) and change in complex systems more generally (Cherns, 1987; Clegg, 2000; Davis et al., 2014).

Examples of grafting in the implementation literature include using existing continuous improvement processes to discuss how to improve health and wellbeing (von Thiele Schwarz et al., 2017) and existing meeting structures to discuss how to improve health and wellbeing (Fridrich et al., 2016; Jenny et al., 2011, 2015). Grafting was also evident in our case study data. Most examples pertained to repurposing existing resources for staff wellbeing, as illustrated in the following three quotes. The first quote relates to staff joining yoga classes intended for social care residents, yet staff joining the classes incurred no additional costs. The second involves using an existing staff intranet site for communication about health and wellbeing resources. The third quote illustrates how existing facilities (meeting rooms) were used for yoga classes.

> Oh we do yoga on a Tuesday, we have a yoga teacher come in of a Tuesday. That's nice, that's lovely actually.
>
> **[Interviewer] And is that for staff and residents or staff?**
>
> Yes we all do it together, yes. And then at the end of the yoga we do like this relaxation session on the floor. So yes we do that now actually, I'd forgotten about that.
>
> **[Interviewer] That's interesting.**
>
> And she only charges 30 quid actually. It doesn't matter how many people join in, it's an hour. (**Small care provider, manager**)
>
> Well I think what we would say; I was struggling last year to sort of get a handle on everything that was in one place so that managers could access what actually is available. So I put a really simple document together really and put on our intranet site and our people services which is our shared point site for this service. So managers go in and access lots of information, forms and policies etc. So I'd put on there a sort of absence, health and wellbeing guide. (**Large care provider, payroll manager #1**).
>
> So that's one of the things that we found from there and then just taking that wellbeing further again with one of our large existing meeting room spaces which is a boardroom that boards a large meeting room behind it. We have what's called the collapsible acoustic wall so you can actually open up the space already to form an even larger space. And they used to use that maybe boardrooms, maybe running a large conference and what we've done with that is we've actually just started some of the yoga sessions with inside the office. We went out to people and said would they be interested for that. We had a decent response and we've actually opened that up and we've run two sort of yoga sessions through the week that has literally just started and we've had a reasonable response to that. And more and more people are asking about it but they're asking can you do them, run them at different times. So we're going to have to go back and revisit that one. But you know we think it's something that if we maybe think about it a bit more, look at the times and look at availability of those spaces maybe we can get a bit more take-up from that. And it is people with inside the workspace but also people who are regularly visiting the office, these agile workers who are going why actually I'm going to gear my week so I can pick up some business in the afternoon and then when you've done that there's a yoga session on a Thursday at 4.30 I can actually get into that. (**Large care provider, head of corporate facilities**).

In one instance, we also found evidence of grafting in relation to ongoing projects, rather than existing meeting structures or resources.

> Well I will be honest with you, so one of the heads of service that I support is the head of corporate facilities so whilst he reports into one of the group executives for affordable housing the actual work that he does is group wide. So he looks after the estates that we have and he had been having, there had been a conversation by our group executive around the estate what do we need to do. And also our direct health and safety they had jointly put a paper together around how we can review our estate and what we need to do. And so they had a strong wellbeing element just around with regards to the work environment. So that's been fantastic because it's very much dovetailed into the work that I was doing (**Large care provider, human resources business partner #2**).

We also found evidence of incorporating discussions around health and wellbeing into appraisal processes, both in a large care home provider, a medium-sized construction firm and an accountancy practice, for example:

> So I am not pushing against a closed door, we have health and wellbeing as part of our [internal brand name], which is what we call our appraisal document, so [internal brand name] document. And there is a section on there that talks about health and safety, health and wellbeing. So it's a natural part of our discussions as well. (**Large care provider, human resources business partner #2**).

Only in one case company did we find evidence grafting processes that related to competing logics that were explicitly articulated by an informant. This may be because institutional logics are largely tacit and out of awareness for many organisational members (Johnson, 1987; Schein, 1985), reflecting taken-granted assumptions about the organisation. It may also be because, in this particular instance, the examples relate to institutional logics that pervade an entire profession rather than a single organisation, in this instance, the accountancy profession that is used to compliance with procedures and hence are salient to non-accountants working in accountancy practices:

> We have got a, because people are quite timesheet focussed so we have got a wellbeing code on our timesheets because obviously the financial group are trying to get people to do lots of chargeable time. But we're actually saying that actually they need to focus on their wellbeing as well.
>
> **[Interviewer] So if they take time out for a wellbeing activity they can charge it effectively?**
>
> They can do yeah. We've got a group wellbeing code. (**Medium accountancy practice, wellbeing coordinator**)

The example indicates that wellbeing activities could be recorded on time sheets, within which timesheets comprise the main process for capturing engagement in legitimate workplace activities. A further change, again which reflects grafting health and wellbeing activities onto existing processes and an underlying institutional logic focused on compliance, was that the same accountancy practice introduced formalized job descriptions for 'mental health champions'.

Grafting relates to introducing practices in a way that attempts minimum disturbance to other organisational procedures, practices and structures. Where such practices are introduced by workers, yet without seeking the permission of managers, it may be the case that the health and wellbeing activities are 'underground' activities to be hidden from managers because of potential conflict with competing logics. For example this can occur with job crafting where workers self-initiate changes to their jobs not necessarily with managerial awareness (Wrzesniewski & Dutton, 2001), provide themselves with self-initiated support communities (Korczynski, 2003) or introduce practices themselves, such as mindfulness (Braganza et al., 2018). Whether hidden from management or not, where competing logics encourage procedures, practices and structures incompatible with health and wellbeing logics (long working hours, abusive management styles), grafting may not lead to sustainable wellbeing. This is because some underlying problems may be left unaddressed and/or the presence of competing logics incompatible with health and wellbeing may confuse signals relating to any symbolic effects of health and wellbeing practices (see Chap. 3 and next chapter). In this latter case, employees may question the authenticity with which the organisation prioritizes employee health and wellbeing.

Fracturing

Fracturing pertains to creating (open) conflict when introducing health and wellbeing practices and existing procedures, practices and structures, in order, in the long run, to replace those procedures, practices and structures incompatible with health and wellbeing logics, and therefore to render competing logics less influential. Fracturing is most discernible where there is active pursuit of conflict or confrontation between stakeholders and where active pursuit of open conflict serves the symbolic purpose of signalling the importance of health and wellbeing (Gersick, 1991; Johnson, 1990). Conflict may therefore be viewed as a necessary, but manageable (Westover, 2010), means of questioning competing logics (Reger et al., 1994). Indeed, in the related area of safety, speaking out against unsafe norms and behaviours is regarded as desirable for improving safety (Tucker et al., 2008; see also Tregaskis et al., 2013, in which workers were trained to challenge unsafe behaviours in a high hazard manufacturing environment). Therefore, fracturing may be a more viable approach to sustaining wellbeing than grafting in environments where competing logics underpin prevalent behaviours and norms that are harmful to health and wellbeing (Chapleau et al., 2011).

Although conflict is seen as a part of organisational change, sometimes a necessary part (Johnson, 1990), it is not considered explicitly in best practice frameworks to guide implementation (Chap. 2), rather grafting is seen as the better option. Von Thiele Schwarz et al. (2021) have maximizing compatibility between interventions and pre-existing procedures, practices and structures as one of their ten principles to guide intervention researchers and do consider sometimes that '*it is not always feasible to follow this principle [of compatibility]. For example, it is not applicable when the existing processes are part of the problem. That may be the case when the content of the intervention calls for changes of the system, rather than within the system*' (p. 421). In this instance, challenging existing procedures, practices and structures is not established as one of the ten principles, but rather as a qualifier of one principle.

Nevertheless, we did find evidence of fracturing. In a small care home provider, this was in the form of a new care home manager challenging employee norms in relation to how they felt valued by the organisation and how they behaved towards each other:

> There's a lot in care of people accusing each other of being lazy. Don't ask me why, they love it in care homes. But to think about why that person actually might be tired, you know, you don't know what's gone on in their home life or you don't know about their home life, you don't know what's going... So before you automatically make comments about people, maybe ask them how they are. They're not firing on all cylinders today, are you tired, is there

> something happening? And that slowly started happening here where people did then do that as opposed to just making accusations towards each other. (**Small care provider, manager**).

In a medium-sized construction company, fracturing was evidenced through replacing an old appraisal system with a new one that involved more informal meetings and had a significant element focused on employee health and wellbeing. This contrasts with examples of appraisal systems that were modified within existing frameworks to incorporate health and wellbeing matters, as illustrated in the section of grafting.

> And then coming out of that with an issue was about our appraisals so there were two things, first of all we wanted our employees to align better with what the business was doing. So the business was ambitious we were progressing we wanted to go in a certain direction and we wanted to bring our employees to that point. We wanted to bring them with us. And we wanted them to be fully engaged, so we knew there was a direct correlation between high engagement and high productivity so we needed to look at well how are we going to make people more engaged. And one of the things that was coming back to us was about our appraisal system. So people hated it managers hated it, employees hated it. And it was the usual sort of tick this box once a year and you have to meet your manager and score people. And our guys just didn't get it. So we decided that we were going to look at what we were going to do and we come up with this concept of [new internally branded name of appraisal system].
>
> So [new internally branded name of appraisal system] is very much about there is no scoring it's all about let's say [name of co-worker] works for me and I am her manager I meet her on a regular basis informally. It was actually about getting managers and employees to sit down and talk to each other, have a relationship. Understand where that person was trying to go what their ambition was for [name of company] in the business in life. What the company ambition was and to try and marry those two together. (**Medium construction, human resources director**)

In other instances, there is evidence of grafting and fracturing co-occurring. In the following two examples, existing human resource management practices were replaced by new ones more focused on health and wellbeing. In both organisations, we presented evidence in the previous section of grafting.

> Yes, the trouble is though, what I found when I first started here, being all professional people, being accountants, being very keen on detail, if something was written in policy, they will follow it to the letter. It's in black and white, so we follow it, regardless of the individual, the circumstances, anything else that might be going on. So you had a one size that, basically, was used to fit all. And that doesn't play to 'passion for our people', it doesn't recognise people as individuals and it doesn't recognise that everyone's got different needs. So that needed to go and I suppose that was really my driver. That actually, we were creating the wrong culture. Because they're very good at following rules and very, and not so good at seeing grey areas. Very good at seeing the black and white, not so good at the grey areas, and a lot of people stuff is grey. So that's why the policies needed to go and that's why I replaced them the way I did. (**Medium accountancy practice, head of human resources**).
>
> We're an organisation that up until about four years ago, maybe slightly longer, had the breadth and depth central HR (human resources) team that you would probably expect for an organisation of our scale but we had a succession, I understand, of HRDs (human resources directors) over... We had eight in eight years pretty much prior to me, just couldn't work out how to engage with the organisation as it's evolved, because it's evolved quite significantly over the last ten years. And so the HR function was blown to the four corners of the wind and I'm the first. (**Large care provider, human resources director**).

Fracturing may be easier to achieve than existing implementation and evaluation frameworks acknowledge (see Chap. 2, von Thiele Schwarz et al., 2021). First, this is because fracturing is not mutually exclusive with either grafting or Gestalting (see next section). Second, where there is a sufficient power or evidence base (Chap. 4) from which to argue for an alternative approach, it might be possible for new health and wellbeing logics and activities to prevail over dysfunctional procedures, practices, structures and their underlying logics. However, as implied in the idea that sustaining wellbeing is an ongoing process requiring learning, adaptation and continuation, the examples given in this section all took some time and effort to implement (measured in years, not months). For this reason, existing frameworks, focused on discrete interventions rather than evolving programmes of interventions, may prioritize implementation processes that take the route of least resistance.

Gestalting

Gestalting relates to making different logics compatible. Gestalting is a way of negating conflict through a process of connecting social and technical procedures, practices or structures in a way that creates a common purpose or interpretation. It may include integrating procedures, practices or structures into a smaller number of procedures, practices or structures, or introducing something new to act as a bridge to connect two (or more) existing, but previously unconnected, features of the organisation with workplace health and wellbeing practices. In an extreme form, it may even relate to integration of health and wellbeing logics with competing logics to form a new organisational logic: As we saw in Chap. 4, health and wellbeing logics tended to cohere around a business case, although genuine care for employees may also need to present in the organisational health and wellbeing logic (see next chapter).

Gestalting processes may be focused on sensemaking/sensegiving (Weick, 1995) to create shared understandings of how health and wellbeing fit into the wider purposes of the organisation, and could include symbolic leadership (Westley & Mintzberg, 1989, see Chap. 5) and experiential learning (Lewin, 1952; Burnes & Cooke, 2013) in which organisational stakeholders learn through doing connections between health and wellbeing and other organisational processes. In this respect, grafting of health and wellbeing practices onto existing Kaizen processes (von Thiele Schwarz et al., 2017) may also have been an example of Gestalting. Other examples in literature include co-opting stakeholders onto governance structures (Csiernik & Csiernik, 2012; Csiernik et al., 2012) and convening integrative workshops (e.g. Mabry et al., 2018).

As with some of the examples in the literature, our case organisations also provided evidence of creating common purpose and, in this example, creating steering group that bridges activities and, through internal branding, is a sensegiving mechanism to signal what wellbeing is according to the organisation and that there is a coherent approach to wellbeing:

So my suggestion was to have a steering group that brought together all of those different elements, so responsible business or CSR (corporate social responsibility), you might call it yes, HR (human resources), facilities, the various diversity networks, to bring them together so that we're doing something that's kind of joined up and that's got almost like a sort of internal brand. So people know what wellbeing means, rather than just kind of the bits that touch them, whether it's, you know, flexible working or, I don't know what it might be using the physio on site, that kind of thing. (**Large, multinational law firm, human resources manager**).

The following quote is also another example of sensegiving, in this instance how different processes are used to generate consistent communication of wellbeing as being a part of the values espoused formally within the organisation.

And I think from an HR (human resources) perspective as well, as I say we are such a diverse group with lots of separate entities we have, our values are quite strong as well. So the [branded name of organisational values statement] that we use across all group companies is the common language across the board. And it's important in filtering that through from an HR perspective into everything we do so it's incorporated into the contracts. It's incorporated in induction, in the policies and the procedures. If we are doing some training it's about bringing the [branded name of organisational values statement] into that as well. And I think as a general culture across [name of organisation] it is a very supportive culture and people are very aware of those [branded name of organisational values statement] as well. So that all links into the wellbeing initiatives that we have. (**Large care provider, human resources business partner #1**).

Gestalting can occur with either grafting or fracturing, as exemplified in the following quotes. The first quote relates to the co-occurrence of Gestalting and grafting. The first quote illustrates 'everyday conversations' both as a sensegiving mechanism but also as an implementation mechanism based on further grafting. The second quote relates to Gestalting and fracturing, where the fracturing relates to changing the processes for inducting new starters into the organisations. The third and fourth quotes are interlinked quotes from the same informant. These quotes relate to replacing the old health and wellbeing governance structure with a new one (fracturing) as a means of establishing a coherent health and wellbeing strategy (Gestalting) based on an existing and known set of competences (grafting).

I guess it's not necessarily always singling it out as a separate thing but actually weaving it into normal conversations. You know everyday conversations you're having rather than it being a standalone topic that sometimes looks like you're just adding lip service to it. If it's part of everyday conversations that you're having on a consistent basis it just becomes the nature of the firm that you know these things are things we talk about all the time. So I think we're very keen to make sure that wherever possible you know we don't also want to shoehorn it into something where it isn't appropriate but you know making sure that things like wellbeing is picked up in key day to day messages where it might make sense to do it and that it's a part of you know agendas for people meeting, team meetings and making sure that it does start to become something that is expected across the business all the time. (**Large, multinational law firm, responsible business associate**).

I would say it's keeping the profile high, it's about what we have also done is we also have introduced inductions for all of our new starters they come to one of our offices and they all have the face-to-face induction. But what we also do is not only are we telling them about the group, so within that induction there is many things that we cover but we also cover and reiterate the wellbeing support that's available to them as a new employee. We also have cascaded out to all existing colleagues, because we have some feedback and a lot of people have been in the business a long time and the business has grown and changed a lot over the last 3–5 years. So we have also done an abridged version of the induction which again just helps remind people about all the support that is available. There are regular updates throughout the year about what things we do offer as a business. (**Large care provider, human resources business partner #2**).

Because I was chairman of the group, I was writing my minutes up following a meeting and I thought where are we going with this. Just because of how I work I needed a structure to fit in the minutes and I thought I'm just writing down lots of different actions. So we'd gone very much into task mode. So, yes, we need more mental health first aiders, we need to produce some communications, we need to get a plan out, we need to emphasise EAP, we need to emphasise [name of wellbeing service provider]. It was just a long list of tasks that we were doing, which was all well and good but I thought there's no sort of structure or strategy to what we're achieving.

Our next meeting is on the 15th of March and what we've restructured the whole meeting around our [short list of core organisational competences] so we've got a clear focus on where we should be going. (**Large infrastructure and construction, wellbeing lead**).

Conclusions

This chapter has been focused on how health and wellbeing activities and programmes operate alongside other organisational procedures, practices and structures, and how either health and wellbeing activities and programmes or the wider organisation are adapted to allow implementation and to negate any potential conflict. Health and wellbeing activities can be adapted to fit how the organisation currently operates (grafting) or *vice versa* (fracturing), or attempts can be made to find common purpose (Gestalting). These three processes are not mutually exclusive, and we have provided evidence they can occur together.

Our case organisations provided more examples of grafting and Gestalting than fracturing, suggesting creating conflict is usually avoided. Similarly, the literature provides few examples of implementers deliberately creating conflict (Chapleau et al., 2011 is an exception), and in one case implementers withdrew an intervention rather than engage in a potentially conflictual environment (Zhang et al., 2015, 2016). Examples in the literature relate to organisational outsiders conducting research studies on specific and pre-planned interventions: Therefore, knowledge of how to navigate the political realities of organisations and power to effect change through conflict may be limited. For organisational outsiders with relatively little power, such as research teams, perhaps accommodation with existing procedures, practices and structures is all that can realistically be achieved (i.e. grafting) in most circumstances. Notwithstanding, although it may be the case that fracturing is a rare occurrence, our data indicate it can happen.

The most extensive data provided by informants in larger organisations was on Gestalting. Indeed, all the data presented in this chapter on Gestalting was from the three largest organisations in our sample. That this is so may simply reflect the complexity of co-ordination in larger organisations. In our smallest case (a care home), the informal approach to wellbeing, the manager's 'open door' and that the manager participated with staff in various activities would have made the approach to wellbeing visible to staff. In the two other organisations, there was evidence of various procedures to bring together various health and wellbeing initiatives in a coherent approach (e.g. office wellbeing champions co-ordinated by a central wellbeing lead and an employee voice forum in the regional accountancy practice; a performance appraisal system that incorporated wellbeing in the discussion in addition to normal performance and development considerations in a medium-sized construction firm). Gestalting may therefore act, in some instances at least, as the means through which health and wellbeing logics are reconciled with competing logics through integrating health and wellbeing into the organisation's dominant logic of how the organisation works effectively to achieve its primary goals (e.g. profit, efficient use of public funds, charitable mission).[1] As we saw in Chap. 4, health and wellbeing logics contained arguments around benefits for core organisational goals (e.g. retention of skilled staff to provide client service in the regional accountancy practice).

References

Armenakis, A. A., & Bedeian, A. G. (1999). Organizational change: A review of theory and research in the 1990s. *Journal of Management, 25*, 293–315.

Armenakis, A. A., Harris, S. G., & Mossholder, K. W. (1993). Creating readiness for organizational change. *Human Relations, 46*, 681–703.

Braganza, S., Young, J., Sweeny, A., & Brazil, V. (2018). oneED: Embedding a mindfulness-based wellness programme into an emergency department. *Emergency Medicine Australasia, 30*, 678–686.

Burnes, B., & Cooke, B. (2013). Kurt Lewin's field theory: A review and re-evaluation. *International Journal of Management Reviews, 15*, 408–425.

Chapleau, A., Seroczynski, A. D., Meyers, S., Lamb, K., & Haynes, S. (2011). Occupational therapy consultation for case managers in community mental health: Exploring strategies to improve job satisfaction and self-efficacy. *Professional Case Management, 16*, 71–79.

Cherns, A. (1987). Principles of sociotechnical design revisited. *Human Relations, 40*, 153–161.

Clegg, C. W. (2000). Sociotechnical principles for system design. *Applied Ergonomics, 31*, 463–477.

Csiernik, R., Chaulk, P., & McQuaid, S. (2012). A process evaluation of a Canadian public sector employee assistance program. *Journal of Workplace Behavioral Health, 27*, 160–180.

Csiernik, R., & Csiernik, A. (2012). Canadian employee assistance programming: An overview. *Journal of Workplace Behavioral Health, 27*, 100–116.

[1] Exceptions here might be organisations that are set up to promote employee health and wellbeing as a social good, as might be the case in some lifestyle businesses or organisations set up to create employment for disadvantaged groups. By way of analogy, Salaman and Storey (2016) discuss the evolution of the John Lewis partnership and concluded that the industrial democracy embodied in employee ownership of John Lewis was the reason for the organisation (dominant logic) rather than employee ownership being a way to achieve superior productivity or profit.

Daniels, K., Gedikli, C., Watson, D., Semkina, A., & Vaughn, O. (2017). Job design, employment practices and Well-being: A systematic review of intervention studies. *Ergonomics, 60*, 1177–1196.

Daniels, K., Watson, D., Nayani, R., Tregaskis, O., Hogg, M., Etuknwa, A., & Semkina, A. (2021). Implementing practices focused on workplace health and psychological wellbeing: A systematic review. *Social Science and Medicine, 227*, 113888.

Davis, M. C., Challenger, R., Jayewardene, D. N. W., & Clegg, C. W. (2014). Advancing socio-technical thinking: A call for bravery. *Applied Ergonomics, 45*, 171–180.

Fridrich, A., Jenny, G. J., & Bauer, G. F. (2016). Outcome expectancy as a process indicator in comprehensive worksite stress management interventions. *International Journal of Stress Management, 23*, 1–22.

Gersick, C. J. (1991). Revolutionary change theories: A multilevel exploration of the punctuated equilibrium paradigm. *Academy of Management Review, 16*, 10–36.

Jenny, G. J., Brauchli, R., Inauen, A., Füllemann, D., Fridrich, A., & Bauer, G. F. (2015). Process and outcome evaluation of an organizational-level stress management intervention in Switzerland. *Health Promotion International, 30*, 573–585.

Jenny, G., Inauen, A., Brauchli, R., Füllemann, D., Müllerm, F., & Bauer G. (2011). *Projekt SWiNG – Schlussbericht der Evaluation: Management Summary* [online]. Gesundheitsförderung Schwiez. Available at: https://gesundheitsfoerderung.ch/assets/public/documents/de/5-grundlagen/publikationen/bgm/2011-07_Projekt_SWiNG_Schlussbericht_-_Management_Summary.pdf.

Johns, G. (2006). The essential impact of context on organizational behavior. *Academy of Management Review, 31*, 386–408.

Johnson, G. (1987). *Strategic change and the management process*. Blackwell.

Johnson, G. (1990). Managing strategic change; the role of symbolic action. *British Journal of Management, 1*, 183–200.

Knight, C., Patterson, M., & Dawson, J. (2019). Work engagement interventions can be effective: A systematic review. *European Journal of Work and Organizational Psychology, 28*, 348–372.

Korczynski, M. (2003). Communities of coping: Collective emotional labour in service work. *Organization, 10*(1), 55–79.

Kotter, J. P. (1995). Leading change: Why transformation efforts fail. *Harvard Business Review, 73*(2), 59–67.

Lewin, K. (1952). Constructs in field theory [1944]. In D. Cartwright (Ed.), *Field theory in social science: Selected theoretical papers by Kurt Lewin* (pp. 30–42). Social Science Paperbacks.

Mabry, L., Parker, K. N., Thompson, S. V., Bettencourt, K. M., Haque, A., Luther Rhoten, K., . . . Olson, R. (2018). Protecting workers in the home care industry: Workers' experienced job demands, resource gaps, and benefits following a socially supportive intervention. *Home Health Care Services Quarterly, 37*, 259–276.

Nielsen, K. M., & Noblet, A. (2018). Organizational interventions: Where we are, where we go from here? In K. Nielsen & A. Noblet (Eds.), *Organizational interventions for health and Well-being: A handbook for evidence-based practice* (pp. 1–22). Routledge.

Rafferty, A. E., Jimmieson, N. L., & Armenakis, A. A. (2013). Change readiness a multilevel review. *Journal of Management, 39*, 110–135.

Reger, R. K., Mullane, J. V., Gustafson, L. T., & DeMarie, S. M. (1994). Creating earthquakes to change organizational mindsets. *Academy of Management Perspectives, 8*, 31–43.

Salaman, G., & Storey, J. (2016). *A better way of doing business? Lessons from the John Lewis Partnership*. Oxford University Press.

Schein, E. H. (1985). *Organizational culture and leadership*. Wiley.

Tregaskis, O., Daniels, K., Glover, L., Butler, P., & Meyer, M. (2013). High performance work practices and firm performance: A longitudinal case study. *British Journal of Management, 24*, 225–244.

Tucker, S., Chmiel, N., Turner, N., Hershcovis, M. S., & Stride, C. B. (2008). Perceived organizational support for safety and employee safety voice: The mediating role of coworker support for safety. *Journal of Occupational Health Psychology, 13*, 319–330.

von Thiele Schwarz, U., Nielsen, K., Edwards, K., Hasson, H., Ipsen, C., Savage, C., . . . Reed, J. E. (2021). How to design, implement and evaluate organizational interventions for maximum impact: The Sigtuna principles. *European Journal of Work and Organizational Psychology, 30*, 415–427.

von Thiele Schwarz, U., Nielsen, K. M., Stenfors-Hayes, T., & Hasson, H. (2017). Using kaizen to improve employee Well-being: Results from two organizational intervention studies. *Human Relations, 70*, 966–993.

Weick, K. E. (1995). *Sensemaking in organizations*. Sage.

Westley, F., & Mintzberg, H. (1989). Visionary leadership and strategic management. *Strategic Management Journal, 10*, 17–32.

Westover, J. H. (2010). Managing organizational change: Change agent strategies and techniques to successfully managing the dynamics of stability and change in organizations. *International Journal of Management and Innovation, 2*, 45–51.

Wrzesniewski, A., & Dutton, J. E. (2001). Crafting a job: Revisioning employees as active crafters of their work. *Academy of Management Review, 26*, 179–201.

Zhang, Y., Flum, M., Kotejoshyer, R., Fleishman, J., Henning, R., & Punnett, L. (2016). Workplace participatory occupational health/health promotion program facilitators and barriers observed in three nursing homes. *Journal of Gerontological Nursing, 42*, 34–42.

Zhang, Y., Flum, M., West, C., & Punnett, L. (2015). Assessing organizational readiness for a participatory occupational health/health promotion intervention in skilled nursing facilities. *Health Promotion Practice, 16*, 724–732.

Chapter 8
Synergies, Capability and Authenticity

Continuity of effort, coupled with effective governance and learning structures in the delivery context, appear to lead to successful implementation of workplace health and wellbeing activities and programmes (see also Daniels, Watson, et al., 2021), alongside processes that adapt the programme to the organisation or *vice versa* through grafting, fracturing and Gestalting. In Chap. 3, we presented evidence that specific activities can come to have effects on health and wellbeing in multiple ways, some that may reflect how a specific activity or initiative was intended to work and others that are unintended and potentially emergent from how the activity or initiative was implemented. In this chapter, we focus on how health and wellbeing programmes, comprising multiple activities, may come to have effects on workers' health and wellbeing. That is, in this chapter, the unit of analysis is the programme. Our analysis focuses on main areas: (1) If and how programmes of activities come to have effects on health and wellbeing above and beyond the sum of the effects of specific initiatives that comprise health and wellbeing programmes (i.e. synergies between parts of a programme); (2) if and how health and wellbeing programmes come to have effects on the future effectiveness of new activities implemented as part of the evolution of those programmes (i.e. development of implementation capabilities); and (3) how any beneficial effects of health and wellbeing programmes could be undermined (i.e. inauthentic compared to authentic action).

Synergies

In the human resource management (HRM) literature, it has long been established that bundles of specific practices (e.g. training, performance appraisal) confer advantages by mutually reinforcing each other (Combs et al., 2006), with worker health and wellbeing sometimes being included amongst the benefits (Ogbonnaya et al., 2017). In the HRM literature, the major differentiation is between the extent to which organisations use a coherent set of HRM best practices that are mutually

K. Daniels et al., *Achieving Sustainable Workplace Wellbeing*, Aligning Perspectives on Health, Safety and Well-Being, https://doi.org/10.1007/978-3-031-00665-4_8

reinforcing compared to organisations that make less use of best practices (Boon et al., 2019; Combs et al., 2006). That is, in general organisations are differentiated on a continuum.

Similarly, for health and wellbeing practices, we may expect that organisations that decide to invest in worker health and wellbeing would take a strategic and programmatic approach and invest in mutually reinforcing health and wellbeing practices (e.g. as recommended in the normative literature on occupational health, ISO, 2018), to invest in practices that are considered best practice, and/or to invest in practices that are tailored to meet the specific concerns or needs of their workers. Our case companies also provide evidence for this strategic approach. Although the specific practices adopted in each case are different,[1] each case includes a range of practices in its programme of health and wellbeing activities. Therefore, it may be the case that (a) organisations can be differentiated by a continuum from adoption of no or only a small number of health and wellbeing practices through to extensive adoption of a wide range of practices and (b) that organisations that adopt the widest range of practices should have workers that report better health and wellbeing than workers employed by organisations that adopt a smaller range of practices, especially where there is an evolving programme that changes according to changes in employee health and wellbeing needs and concerns.

In respect of whether organisations are differentiated by a single continuum of lower to higher levels of adoption, two studies provide evidence that this may be the case (Daniels, Fida, et al., 2021; Huettermann & Bruch, 2019). Both studies were based on surveys of organisational practices and statistical aggregation techniques (i.e. factor analytic and cluster analytic methods). Although Huettermann and Bruch's analysis focused on practices targeted at psychological health, Daniels, Fida, et al. examined a wide range of practices targeted at psychological health (e.g. resilience training), physical health (e.g., health screening), health behaviours (e.g. smoking cessation) and supporting infrastructure (e.g. service promotion, governance structures). Moreover, Daniels, Fida, et al. examined whether patterns in the data could be better accounted for by a single continuum or discrete categories representing different configurations of practices. Daniels, Fida, et al. found that a single dimension could account for many differences between organisations and that there was limited evidence that organisations could be classified according to a small number of discrete categories. This finding would support the idea that organisations that adopt the most extensive range of health and wellbeing practices do so in a co-ordinated and strategic manner. Daniels, Fida, et al. also found evidence that at least one other continuum of practices, although much less dominant than the continuum of low to extensive adoption of practices, could explain some of the differences between organisations. However, it was not clear what this other continuum represents in terms of health and wellbeing practices.

---

[1] We do not mean to suggest that there is a single and universal 'best' combination of practices. Our cases do evidence consultation with employees on what practices suit their health and wellbeing concerns and tailoring practices to the needs of employees as well as the organisation itself.

With regards to the effects of multiple practices combined into coherent programmes, three studies have provided evidence for benefits (Batorsky et al., 2016; Daniels, Fida, et al., 2021; Huettermann & Bruch, 2019). However, only one of these studies directly assessed employee reports of psychological and physical health (Daniels, Fida, et al.), with the two other studies using proxy measures (service use, perceptions of programme effectiveness, Batorsky et al.; perceptions of others' psychological health, Huettermann & Bruch). Daniels, Fida, et al. was also the only study to assess whether the extensiveness of workplace health and wellbeing programmes could predict changes in health. Both Huettermann and Bruch and Daniels, Fida, et al. used multisource data, in which data on practices were supplied by human resources or other relevant managers and data on outcomes supplied by employees. Although there were differences between the three studies, there was convergence for health and wellbeing benefits for more extensive adoption of practices. However, although psychological benefits appear to have been transmitted through programmes enhancing workers' ability to cope with workplace stressors (Huettermann and Bruch), these appeared to be specific to aiding recovery from poor psychological wellbeing (Daniels, Fida, et al.) rather than aiding workers to put in place personal, preventive strategies to prevent deterioration of poor wellbeing in the first place.

There may be multiple reasons why a co-ordinated programme of activities can confer benefits for employee health and wellbeing (Chap. 3, Table 3.2). Using theoretical frameworks from the HRM literature (Bowen & Ostroff, 2004), Huettermann and Bruch (2019) argued that organisations that adopt an extensive range of health and wellbeing practices send strong signals to employees of organisational care. Indeed, three of the mechanisms listed in Table 3.2 relate to the symbolic elements of health and wellbeing programmes: Feeling invested in, inclusivity, removal of stigma. The signalling elements of workplace health and wellbeing practices could therefore stimulate such symbolic mechanisms. Extrapolating from Bowen and Ostroff, signals may be more likely to be interpreted as organisational commitment to worker wellbeing through extensive provision of health and wellbeing practices, that is supplemented through clear communication about those practices, the legitimate authority of those with responsibility for implementing practices and through congruence between the messages and actions of key decision makers (see below). In turn, signalling organisational commitment to worker wellbeing may create a climate through which, for example people feel invested in activities targeted at their health and wellbeing, included regardless of health status or other characteristic that may otherwise confer 'outsider' status and able to disclose to others any health concerns through removing the stigma associated with disclosing. Removing stigma and promoting disclosure may be particularly beneficial for people seeking help with problems that may not always be visible to others, such as mental health problems (Daniels, Fida, et al., 2021).

The delivery context and imbuing actors within the delivery context legitimate authority to act (which can be done symbolically through visible provision of budgets as well as involvement of senior managers) may be key means of reinforcing signals from extensive adoption of practices and that those practices are integrated into a coherent strategic approach to worker health and wellbeing. Similarly, continuity of activity provides consistent signalling over time. Signalling may also be aided by grafting and Gestalting processes, that signal congruence between health and wellbeing goals and other organisational goals, thus communicating congruence, or at least not conflict, with other actions taken by the organisation and key stakeholders. However, fracturing may also play a key signalling role. A highly visible break from previous organisational practices may play a key role in signalling a change in approach more oriented to worker health and wellbeing (Johnson, 1990).

Learning and Developing Implementation Capabilities

Continuity of effort and introducing new components of health and wellbeing programmes may lead to an acceleration of the extent to which newer components have beneficial effects on wellbeing relative to earlier components. We believe this to be the case, provided workers' health and wellbeing in an organisation are not approaching across the workforce uniformly a state of maximum health and wellbeing, where in which improvements would be harder and harder to achieve as the maxima is approached. However, it is unrealistic to imagine a workforce with uniformly high levels of wellbeing at any given time for two reasons. First, no matter how good work is, events happen to people outside of work that affect health and wellbeing and that have work-relevant implications, for example in relation to symptoms affecting wellbeing and performance during working hours (Kendall et al., 2015). Second, as environments change, so do employees' concerns around wellbeing: As the Covid-19 pandemic and the financial crash of 2008 indicate, catastrophic events can have very serious consequences for employee health and the financial viability of organisations with all the attendant issues associated with job insecurity.

One reason for expecting synergies between older and newer components of a health and wellbeing programme is tied to the starting conditions that employers may find themselves in. The need to address employee health and wellbeing concerns may stem from a high incidence of health and wellbeing problems in the workforce and/or working conditions that put employees at some risk. In these instances, it may be the case that workers with poor health or wellbeing may be a barrier to implementing health and wellbeing practices (e.g. Carolan & de Visser, 2018), because workers may be particularly disengaged and/or cynical about management intentions (Tregaskis et al., 2013), resulting in resistance to changes (Nielsen et al., 2010). Therefore, making small improvements in health and wellbeing may make it is easier to implement future initiatives, thus facilitating worker engagement with health and wellbeing activities with less effort expended in service promotion and overcoming passive or active resistance from workers to any initiatives.

However, we believe there is another mechanism through which synergies between components are achieved across time. Our model positions learning as a key component for sustaining wellbeing in organisations. On the basis of the evidence from the literature (Daniels, Watson, et al., 2021) and our case studies, learning mainly relates to adapting different activities for implementation. However, is it also possible that learning can leverage the resources invested into workplace health and wellbeing programmes, such that the learning accumulated through implementation of previous health and wellbeing activities enables future activities to have a greater effect on wellbeing that would otherwise be the case if that learning had not been accumulated.

Learning from implementation improves an organisations capability to implement further health and wellbeing practices, wherein the improved capability can reside in individuals, procedures and structures and interactions between these components (Felin et al., 2012). For health and wellbeing programmes, individuals may improve organisational capability through accumulated experience and knowledge of what worked well and what did not amongst specialist implementers in the human resources or occupational health functions. For procedures, this could mean adaptations to service procurement, promotion or communications. For structures, this could pertain to changes of governance arrangements in the delivery context, so that communication between different stakeholders is improved.

The principle at play in respect of developing capabilities is that every time a new health and wellbeing initiative is introduced into an organisation, the organisation builds its capability of introducing new initiatives in the future, meaning less resource (time, effort, funding) is required for implementation or the reach of the initiative becomes greater for the same level of resourcing. This would imply that the hardest phase of implementing a health and wellbeing programme is in the initial phases, not just because resistance is likely to be stronger and health and wellbeing logics have less traction, but also because there is limited capability in the organisation because procedures and structures have not been established and become routinized (cf. Felin et al., 2012) and individuals may not have gained relevant knowledge. Even for expert implementers bought in from outside of the organisation with advanced knowledge of health and wellbeing programmes, there is a need to develop understanding of the specific organisational context, stakeholder concerns and sources of power and influence, as well as to develop capabilities in others to assist with implementation (e.g. local wellbeing champions, senior managers).

Some organisations may face particular problems in developing implementation capabilities. These include organisations with transient workforces, project-based organisations, those that rely on specialized services provided by expert consultants or those that completely outsource health and wellbeing services. For those with transient workforces, although capabilities may develop internally on how to communicate, consult with and involve temporary workers, the capabilities of the workers themselves to engage with health and wellbeing programmes may be limited because the workers may not have had the time to develop a deep understanding of the programme, how the different elements fit together or the health and wellbeing logics underpinning the programme. For the other kinds of organisations listed, the problems with developing capabilities in implementation relate to the temporary nature of the organisation (project), temporary engagement with the organisations (consultants) or distance from the organisation (outsourced), all of which limit knowledge of the organisation, its culture, politics and underpinning health and wellbeing logics. The last factor is important because health and wellbeing initiatives need to be consistent with the prevailing health and wellbeing logic. For example introducing flexible working patterns is consistent with a health and wellbeing logic focused on retention of working parents; introducing resilience training is less consistent and may have less influence on retention than flexible working.

Much of the evidence we found in relation to learning in our case studies pertains to single-loop learning (Argyris & Schon, 1978). That is, organisations adjusted their health and wellbeing activities and implementation to be consistent with the prevailing health and wellbeing logic. Therefore, we expect, by and large, most capabilities will build through implementing activities consistent with the prevailing health and wellbeing logic. However, we did see evidence of double-loop learning in two ways. First, in so far competing logics were questioned and challenged by health and wellbeing logics (Chap. 4). Second, we did find some evidence of double-loop learning in relation to participants questioning whether their health and wellbeing logics themselves need to be adapted. This did not pertain so much about questioning the business case for wellbeing (e.g. staff retention), but more shifting conceptions of what constitutes wellbeing, as the following quotes reproduced from earlier chapters illustrate:

> So our first six, half a dozen meetings or so, that wellbeing forum became around mental health and getting the structure around that. We've now realised, at the back end of 2018, that actually it was becoming a mental health forum not a wellbeing forum, so at the last meeting we had in November we refocused the group's attention on what we call seven enablers to wellbeing and making sure that the group didn't focus just on mental health but actually a bigger picture of wellbeing and that it was still in line with the original continuous improvement group. So that's where our focus is over the next three or four months, maybe the next two or three meetings, is to make sure that we widen our thinking, not just around mental health but overall wellbeing and then bring it in line with the wellbeing continuous improvement group. (**Large infrastructure and construction, wellbeing lead**).
>
> And consistently trying to look at what we were trying to get across to people, what were the issues. And if people came back and said we have an issue about maybe suicide or there is a mental health aspect issue in the industry we would be looking to build that into the annual calendar and that timetable. (**Medium construction, human resources director**).

Double-loop learning in relation to what constitutes wellbeing would be consistent with the idea that sustaining wellbeing is a continual process through which organisations develop, evolve and continue to address workers' wellbeing priorities and is a continuous process of (re)negotiation. Nevertheless, because we found no discernible evidence of changes to health and wellbeing logics in relation to the business case, we expect at least some elements of health and wellbeing logics to become crystalized (Lewin, 1952) and subject to little or minor incremental change unless there is signal from a salient event that the underpinning health and wellbeing logic needs considerable revision (Johnson, 1987). This may relate to a change in senior organisational leadership (cf. Tregaskis et al., 2013) or a major shock such as the Covid-19 pandemic (Nayani et al., in press).

Undermining Health and Wellbeing Activities

Our model assumes effective implementation leads to beneficial outcomes for a variety of reasons. So far in the chapter, we have also argued that the activities that comprise health and wellbeing programmes may have synergistic effects both contemporaneously and over time. We put forward one reason for these synergistic effects to be related to the symbolism of adopting an extensive range of practices. However, these symbolic aspects may be undermined because of the attributions employees make about employer actions (Nishii et al., 2008; Van De Voorde & Beijer, 2015). Specifically, if employees attribute employer actions around health and wellbeing to genuine employer concern for employee health and wellbeing, the symbolic effects of extensive workplace health and wellbeing programmes are likely to be realized, and through a sense of social exchange (Gouldner, 1960: 171), employees may respond to such genuine signals of care with higher levels of motivation and commitment to the organisation, in turn producing beneficial effects for performance (Ogbonnaya & Messersmith, 2019). On the other hand, if employees attribute employer actions around health and wellbeing to be self-serving and a means purely to increase productivity without genuine care for employees, symbolic effects may become undermined. In other words, any symbolic effects of workplace health and wellbeing programmes may be undermined if employer actions are perceived by employees to be inauthentic.

The extent to which an organisation is perceived to be authenticity or inauthentic reflects the degree to which espoused organisational values are perceived to be aligned with organisational actions and practices (Lehman et al., 2019; Kovacs et al., 2014; Hahl, 2016; Cording et al., 2014). In the case of workplace health and wellbeing programmes, the perceptions and interpretations that matter are those of employees. In a more or less steady and benign environment, organisations may be able to engage easily in the kind of activities within which business prerogatives (e.g. productivity) can be aligned with employee concerns (e.g. health and wellbeing) and to do so in a sustained way, this exhibiting consistency of action with espoused values. In some cases, where there are competing logics and associated norms and behaviours that are harmful to health and wellbeing, grafting and/or Gestalting may be seen as inauthentic and fracturing the more authentic response to those competing logics. Even so, stable environments may make it relatively easy for organisations to be perceived as authentic in their concern for employee health and wellbeing or at least not inauthentic.

However, during times of crisis, tensions are more likely to emerge between health and wellbeing logics and competing logics (cf. Dobbins & Dundon, 2017). For example during the financial crash of 2008 and the Covid-19 pandemic, tensions would have emerged between actions required for organisational survival, and in response to the pandemic Government mandates to provide key services in health, retail and education, for example on the one hand, and actions required to address employee concerns about health and wellbeing on the other hand. In a study of organisational responses to the Covid-19 lockdowns in the UK, Nayani et al. (in press) found that organisational responses to employee concerns around health and wellbeing were perceived to be more or less authentic according to the extent to which: (a) organisations had a history of consistent action around employee health and wellbeing prior to the pandemic; and (b) had in place dialogic processes with employees (see Chap. 5) that enabled organisations to (c) notice, understand and act on employee concerns about the pandemic and, as it evolved, the effects on employee mental health of enforced homeworking, social isolation and perceived risk of infection. Critical to being perceived by employees as authentic or inauthentic is not just the consistency of action around health and wellbeing, reflecting continuity, but also being able to respond to shifts in employee concerns, reflecting adaptation. During a crisis, these shifts are likely to be large, although we would argue it is the case that one element of the learning that is important for successful implementation concerns learning how to notice and respond to shifts in employee concerns, regardless of the scale of those shifts. More importantly, being able to respond to employee shifts in concerns reinforces the importance of consultative processes embedded in programme governance and the delivery context (Chap. 5).

Summary and Conclusions

This chapter has been focused on how health and wellbeing programmes come to have effects on wellbeing that may transcend the effects of single practices. For beneficial effects, these relate to the symbolic effects of extensive health and wellbeing programmes that convey strong signals of employer care for employee wellbeing and the accumulated learning that builds organisational capability in effective implementation. However, even where programmes have an extensive range of activities and services available to employees, if employers do not consistently act to reinforce employee wellbeing as a legitimate organisational goal in its own right and are not able to respond to shifts in employee concerns around health and wellbeing, shifts that may be accentuated during crises, then any benefits conferred through symbolism, and even employee motivation to engage with the health and wellbeing programme, may be undermined by employees viewing the organisation as inauthentic in its efforts to sustain employee wellbeing.

Nevertheless, existing research on synergies between health and wellbeing practices, developing capabilities in implementation and (in)authentic action around health and wellbeing is sparse at best and therefore in need of more extensive consideration. For each topic, we have outlined potential for roles at some parts of our model, variously learning, adaptation, continuity, the delivery context, grafting, fracturing and Gestalting. However, additional research is needed to understand how the elements of our model can help understand further synergies, capabilities and authenticity, or how our model or other models of programme implementation need to be developed to include these considerations.

References

Argyris, C., & Schon, D. A. (1978). *Organizational learning: A theory of action perspective.* Addison Wesley.

Batorsky, B., Van Stolk, C., & Liu, H. (2016). Is more always better in designing workplace wellness programs?: A comparison of wellness program components versus outcomes. *Journal of Occupational and Environmental Medicine, 58*, 987–993.

Boon, C., Den Hartog, D. N., & Lepak, D. P. (2019). A systematic review of human resource management systems and their measurement. *Journal of Management, 45*, 2498–2537.

Bowen, D. E., & Ostroff, C. (2004). Understanding HRM–firm performance linkages: The role of the "strength" of the HRM system. *Academy of Management Review, 29*, 203–221.

Carolan, S., & de Visser, R. O. (2018). Employees perspectives on the facilitators and barriers to engaging with digital mental health interventions in the workplace: Qualitative study. *JMIR Mental Health, 5*(1), e8.

Combs, J., Liu, Y., Hall, A., & Ketchen, D. (2006). How much do high-performance work practices matter? A meta-analysis of their effects on organizational performance. *Personnel Psychology, 59*, 501–528.

Cording, M., Harrison, J. S., Hoskisson, R. E., & Jonsen, K. (2014). Walking the talk: A multistakeholder exploration of organizational authenticity, employee productivity, and post-merger performance. *Academy of Management Perspectives, 28*, 38–56.

Daniels, K., Fida, R., Stepanek, M., & Gendronneau, C. (2021). Do multicomponent workplace health and wellbeing programs predict changes in health and wellbeing? *International Journal of Public Health and Environmental Research, 18*, 8964. https://doi.org/10.3390/ijerph18178964

Daniels, K., Watson, D., Nayani, R., Tregaskis, O., Hogg, M., Etuknwa, A., & Semkina, A. (2021). Implementing practices focused on workplace health and psychological wellbeing: A systematic review. *Social Science and Medicine, 227*, 113888.

Dobbins, T., & Dundon, T. (2017). The chimera of sustainable labour–management partnership. *British Journal of Management, 28*, 519–533.

Felin, T., Foss, N. J., Heimeriks, K. H., & Madsen, T. L. (2012). Microfoundations of routines and capabilities: Individuals, processes, and structure. *Journal of Management Studies, 49*, 1351–1374.

Gouldner, A. (1960). The norm of reciprocity. *American Sociological Review, 25*, 161–178.

Hahl, O. (2016). Turning back the clock in baseball: The increased prominence of extrinsic rewards and demand for authenticity. *Organization Science, 27*, 929–953.

Huettermann, H., & Bruch, H. (2019). Mutual gains? Health-related HRM, collective Well-being and organizational performance. *Journal of Management Studies, 56*, 1045–1072.

ISO (International Organization for Standardization). (2018). *BS 45002–1:2018. Occupational health and safety management systems. General guidelines for the application of ISO 45001. Guidance on managing occupational health.* International Organization for Standardization.

Johnson, G. (1987). *Strategic change and the management process.* Blackwell.

Johnson, G. (1990). Managing strategic change; the role of symbolic action. *British Journal of Management, 1*, 183–200.

Kendall, N., Burton, K., Lunt, J., Mellor, N., & Daniels, K. (2015). *Development of an intervention toolbox for common health problems in the workplace*. HSE Books.

Kovács, B., Carroll, G. R., & Lehman, D. W. (2014). Authenticity and consumer value ratings: Empirical tests from the restaurant domain. *Organization Science, 25*, 458–478.

Lehman, D. W., O'Connor, K., Kovács, B., & Newman, G. E. (2019). Authenticity. *Academy of Management Annals, 13*, 1–42.

Lewin, K. (1952). Constructs in field theory [1944]. In D. Cartwright (Ed.), *Field theory in social science: Selected theoretical papers by Kurt Lewin* (pp. 30–42). Social Science Paperbacks.

Nayani, R., Patey, J., Fitzhugh, H., Watson, D., Baric, M., Tregaskis, O., & Daniels, K. (in press). Authenticity in the pursuit of mutuality during crisis. *British Journal of Management.*

Nielsen, K., Randall, R., Holten, A.-L., & Rial-Gonzalez, E. (2010). Conducting organizational-level occupational health interventions: What works? *Work & Stress, 24*, 234–259.

Nishii, L. H., Lepak, D. P., & Schneider, B. (2008). Employee attributions of the "why" of HR practices: Their effects on employee attitudes and behaviors, and customer satisfaction. *Personnel Psychology, 61*, 503–545.

Ogbonnaya, C., Daniels, K., Connolly, S., & van Veldhoven, M. (2017). Integrated and isolated impact of high performance work practices on employee health and Well-being: A comparative study. *Journal of Occupational Health Psychology, 22*, 98–114.

Ogbonnaya, C., & Messersmith, J. (2019). Employee performance, Well-being and differential effects of human resource management subdimensions: Mutual gains or conflicting outcomes? *Human Resource Management Journal, 29*, 509–526.

Tregaskis, O., Daniels, K., Glover, L., Butler, P., & Meyer, M. (2013). High performance work practices and firm performance: A longitudinal case study. *British Journal of Management, 24*, 225–244.

Van De Voorde, K., & Beijer, S. (2015). The role of employee HR attributions in the relationship between high-performance work systems and employee outcomes. *Human Resource Management Journal, 25*, 62–78.

Chapter 9
Conclusions and Extensions

The model we have developed focuses on the processes through which organisations do or do not embed and evolve workplace practices that lead to sustainable wellbeing for workers. Here, we refer to sustainable wellbeing as attaining and maintaining a good level of worker wellbeing *and* how organisations respond to workers' shifting priorities and concerns in relation to their wellbeing. We view sustaining wellbeing as a continuous process of (re)negotiation, because: workers' wellbeing priorities and concerns change; organisations and their environments change; and even where different stakeholders' wellbeing concerns and priorities may have reached a level of acceptable accommodation, changing circumstances may lead to subsequent divergence between stakeholders. The model therefore relates to an ongoing process of implementing and evolving a programme of activities targeted at wellbeing rather than a single and discrete intervention regardless of whether they are relatively simple (e.g. mindfulness instruction) or complex (e.g. multifocal intervention encompassing job redesign, workplace health promotion and resilience training). Our intention is that the model is explanatory rather than normative, and is focused on the processes through which organisations adapt to or are adapted by workplace health and wellbeing programmes.

The model does not give primacy to specific elements of programmes as in some existing models (e.g. steering groups, see Chap. 2) in explaining how specific practices or programmes come to be implemented, because there are a variety of means through which a programme can come to be implemented and success depends on context. We do not need to assume the presence of specific structural features (e.g. an inclusive steering group may contribute to effective governance, but the explanatory principle is effective governance). That is, the model accommodates equifinality of different ways to achieve the same end, or indeed that the same entity (e.g. inclusive steering group) can achieve different or multiple ends (effective governance and/or symbolism).

The model has three major areas, each of which in turn has three major concepts embedded in those areas. First, there is the context, that can be divided into three parts. Second, there are three processes that sustain wellbeing. Third, there are three

K. Daniels et al., *Achieving Sustainable Workplace Wellbeing*, Aligning Perspectives on Health, Safety and Well-Being, https://doi.org/10.1007/978-3-031-00665-4_9

processes through which health and wellbeing practices are connected to or accommodated with other organisational processes, structures and systems. Underpinning all of this is the notion that within a given organisation, the logics underpinning the health and wellbeing programme can be (almost inevitably will be) in conflict with competing logics (e.g. around productivity), and these conflicts have to be negotiated and resolved somehow. Like all elements of the model, this process of negotiation is ongoing.

In relation to context, the three elements are: (a) the omnibus context of the wider organisation and its environment; (b) the discrete contexts of implementation of specific health and wellbeing practices and activities; and (c) the delivery context that encompass the processes involved in the management of an entire programme of activities, including governance, planning, evaluation, and stakeholder consultation/involvement. Like Russell et al. (2016), we see the omnibus context as dynamic and open to change by the discrete or delivery contexts. Although the omnibus and discrete contexts will be familiar through the adoption of Johns' typology (2006) in the existing implementation literature, the delivery context is unique to this model because it encompasses multiple, evolving and connected activities. Nevertheless, we see the boundaries between adjacent layers as fuzzy and permeable.

The three processes that lead to sustainable workplace wellbeing are: (a) learning during implementation to allow (b) adaptation of a practice or practices to the omnibus context or vice versa, in turn leading to (c) continuity of any changes made. These three processes pertain to implementation and are separate to the mechanisms (intended or emergent) that single practices may activate to influence worker health or wellbeing.

Adaptation to, or of, the omnibus context is critical to successful and sustained implementation. The three processes that relate to adaptation of practices and the omnibus context are: (a) grafting, through which practices are made compatible with other organisational procedures, practices and structures; (b) fracturing, through which the omnibus context is changed to be compatible with new health and wellbeing practices; and (c) Gestalting, through which health and wellbeing practices and parts of the omnibus context are linked together to meet common goals or interpretation. Each of these practices, grafting, fracturing or Gestalting are means of managing conflict between health and wellbeing and competing logics. Two (grafting and Gestalting) are focused on finding common ground between logics, but the other (fracturing) is focused on managing conflict through enabling the health and wellbeing logic to dominate and subjugate competing logics. The ways in which organisations manage these tensions and logics are acknowledged in some of the literature (Chap. 2), but the processes through which they are managed have not be examined in any depth in the literature (Daniels et al., 2021).

The model developed in this book gives greater prominence to the organisation as a unit of analysis, rather than the individual or intervention, compared to existing models and frameworks. Another point of departure from many existing frameworks on implementation is the explicit acknowledgement that wellbeing and what to do about wellbeing can be contested and conceptualized as socially constructed. Unlike prior approaches, acknowledging the socially constructed nature of wellbeing and the need for different logics (Chap. 4) to be reconciled provides a platform for analyzing how different decision options come to be perceived and acted upon by organisational stakeholders.

Implications for Research Methodologies

For research on the evaluation of workplace health and wellbeing interventions, as we have noted previously in Chap. 2, realist evaluation (see e.g. Pawson & Manzano-Santaella, 2012, Greenhalgh, 2014, Moore et al., 2015) provides a suitable framework within which to evaluate the effectiveness and implementation of interventions, that can incorporate both inductive and deductive methods, and that can also be applied to synthesizing evidence from multiple studies (Daniels et al., 2021; Roodbari et al., in press). Incorporation of inductive methods is important because a given intervention may activate multiple mechanisms, not all of which could be anticipated *ex ante* in a programme theory (Chaps. 2 and 3). Although not prominent in the workplace literature, realist evaluation approaches may be gaining in popularity in intervention research.

For researchers involved in the evaluation of specific interventions using traditional evaluation methods (e.g. randomized control trial with qualitative process implementation), our model suggests researchers need to ask seven fundamental questions about interventions in order to delineate how implementation had affected findings in relation to whether changes were made and mechanisms activated. These are:

1. What efforts were made to adapt the intervention to its context, and how did these efforts change over time? (Principle of adaptation, Chap. 6)
2. What processes or procedures were in place to capture learning from implementation to inform adaptation? (Principle of learning, Chap. 6)
3. Were changes made and sustained over time? (Principle of continuity, Chap. 6)
4. Where there any existing workplace health and wellbeing initiatives (including bottom-up initiatives) and how was the focal intervention co-ordinated in its own right and in relation to other initiatives (Examination of delivery context, Chap. 5)
5. Was any conflict between the intervention and other organisational procedures, practices and structures reconciled by adapting the intervention to fit the organisation? (Principle of grafting, Chap. 7)
6. Was any conflict between the intervention and other organisational procedures, practices and structures reconciled by adapting these procedures, practices and structures to fit the intervention? (Principle of fracturing, Chap. 7)
7. Was any conflict between the intervention and other organisational procedures, practices and structures reconciled by bringing together procedures, practices and structures to create a common purpose between the intervention and other elements of the organisation? (Principle of Gestalting, Chap. 7)

8. What factors led to the wellbeing outcomes of the interventions? These are: (lack of) substantive changes; activation of mechanisms as hypothesized by the theoretical perspective underpinning the intervention; activation of mechanisms not anticipated as part of the interventions; activation of mechanisms that cause adverse effects (mechanisms in the discrete context, Chap. 3)

These eight questions can be used as a simple checklist for researchers where the primacy is given to effectiveness evaluation and resources for conducting a process evaluation are limited. However, for researchers with more extensive resources for process evaluation, we would recommend more detailed examination of the principles of the model, elaboration of these eight questions and investigation of the nature of presence of health and wellbeing logics and competing logics. Questions 1 and 8 may be particularly important in the context of evaluation research, where the goal is to determine whether a specific class of interventions has beneficial effects and require interventions to be implemented as planned (intervention fidelity attained). Adapting and changing the intervention reduces fidelity, thus rendering it difficult to determine whether any (intended or otherwise) mechanisms activated are due to the nature of the intervention or through the processes of adaptation (see Fikretoglu et al., in press). On the other hand, it is important to understand how different processes pertaining to implementing specific practices (learning, adaptation, continuation, grafting, fracturing and Gestalting) interact with the component parts of specific interventions in conferring benefits to wellbeing (or not). Understanding such interactions helps to enhance theoretical understanding of how the workplace may influence wellbeing by extending existing models (e.g. those based on psychosocial job/work characteristics or psychosocial hazards, Chap. 1). Incorporating implementation processes explicitly in such models may not only bridge a gap between theory and practice but enhance theory by providing better understanding of how to operationalize changes in key constructs.

Our model can guide process evaluation of discrete interventions because it makes explicit processes that sustain health and wellbeing practices (adaptation, learning, continuity) that connect these practices to each other (delivery context) and to the wider organisational context (grafting, Gestalting, fracturing). However, its point of departure from existing models and frameworks is that the model relates to explaining how programmes of activities may come to be implemented. In this respect, methods used in traditional intervention research (randomized control trials, quasi-experimental methods) may not be appropriate, because the focus of the model is on how programmes of activities evolve and are adapted rather than time-limited studies of discrete interventions but also because not all of the processes we outline may be amenable to quantitative analysis.

In considering the focus of the model on implementing whole programmes of activities, Patey and colleagues (2021) recommended that researchers focus on using longitudinal, qualitative case study designs of the kind deployed in organisational change research, ideally using multiple cases for cross-case analysis. Their reasoning is that these methods are well placed to capture the planned and unplanned nature of implementation, that programmes of activities can evolve in unpredictable ways, that implementation of programmes of practices is continuous and ongoing, implementation is influenced by a range of factors related to the political and cultural contexts of organisations, and multiple logics are in play: In particular, the nature of these logics may be highly idiosyncratic to organisations and could not be known *ex ante*.

Extensions: Implications for Other Areas of Enquiry

Enhancing worker wellbeing is a means of creating social value through enhancing public health and quality of life and potentially reducing spend on disability benefits and healthcare costs allowing allocation of public funds to other social goods (e.g. Bilsker et al., 2005). However, much of the mainstream organisational change literature is focused on how organisations change to meet primary organisational goals. For many organisations, the primary organisational purpose entails creating economic value (profit in the private sector, efficient use of public money to provide services in the public sector). For charitable organisations, the primary purpose may be creating social value (e.g. housing the homeless), but not social value in terms of the health and wellbeing of salaried or voluntary staff. Moreover, in the absence of either political will or even the means to enact strong regulatory frameworks for employee mental health concerns (Mishiba, 2020), then any regulatory influences on organisational practices for health and wellbeing are likely to be influenced by 'soft regulation' (government guidance, voluntary codes of practice). Therefore, although enhancing worker wellbeing beyond minimum regulatory requirements is a means of creating additional social value, it is in almost all cases a secondary organisational goal subservient to productivity variously defined and measured and as illustrated in Chap. 4, wherein which health and wellbeing logics incorporated solutions to business problems.

In these respects, our model could provide a useful platform for other areas of research on how work organisations could create social value through pursuing secondary organisational goals that are subject to soft regulation or no regulation and may include a raft of activities. Examples could include action on climate change and addressing diversity and inequalities through charitable, community actions (e.g. volunteering). Empirical work in these areas could be guided by the model and in turn lead to adaptations to the model that have relevance to improved understanding of how to implement workplace health and wellbeing initiatives and programmes of activities. Moreover, research on how organisations pursue multiple sources of social value (worker health and wellbeing, addressing climate change) alongside primary organisational goals may provide explanations of how organisations attempt to reconcile multiple competing logics rather than just two competing logics.

Overall Conclusions

In this book, our aim has not been to provide an alternative to existing research on workplace health and wellbeing interventions. There is value in this line of research, insofar that the focus on discrete interventions of varying complexity provides rigorous assessments of what interventions provide benefits, why they do so, and in the circumstances and for whom they do so (the oft quoted what works, for whom and in what circumstances). Instead, our aim has been to complement and augment this line of research by addressing a key question related to what organisations do in practice, which is to implement multiple health and wellbeing practices in programme of activities that are more or less well co-ordinated, rarely supported by teams of researchers or consultants and to explain the process of implementation of these multiple activities.

Although our research has been motivated by what happens in practice, neither have we aimed to provide best practice guidelines for practitioners. Our aim has been to provide an explanatory model, which can inform practice but does not direct it through prescribed actions. Beyond the three processes of adaptation, learning and continuity, we have no evidence for an optimal approach to implementing practices that would predictably lead to successful implementation. That is, the model is not simplistically normative. That is not to say the model has no practical implications: There is potential value in simply making organisational practitioners aware of processes underpinning implementation, that commitment and continuous improvement are prerequisites for successful implementation, there is likely to be conflict that will never fully be resolved and that there is no one best approach to implementation.[1] Making practitioners aware of these complexities may have more value than staged and planned approaches that neither reflect what happens in practice or give little credence to processes through which conflict and shifting employee concerns are negotiated and renegotiated.

Our model indicates that understanding of how organisations achieve and sustain workplace wellbeing necessitates thinking deeply about how specific health and wellbeing practices and programmes of practices are influenced by and influence the wider organisational context. Such thinking requires researchers to consider organisations as political and cultural arenas within which stakeholders seek to promote different logics. Such thinking is not prevalent in most existing research on workplace health and wellbeing interventions. Therefore, understanding of how organisations achieve and sustain workplace wellbeing requires a necessary shift away from the dominant logic in existing research in this field, wherein implementation matters because it affects the fidelity of intended interventions, to a logic within which implementation matters because it affects how workers' wellbeing is enhanced and maintained amidst shifting and competing concerns that need to be accommodated and resolved.

[1] As part of the funding requirements for this project, we have developed evidence-led guidance on implementation for organisational practitioners.

References

Bilsker, D., Gilbert, M., Myette, T. L., & Stewart-Patterson, C. (2005). *Depression and work function: Bridging the gap between mental health care and the workplace*. Mental Health Evaluation and Community Consultation Unit, University of British Columbia.

Daniels, K., Watson, D., Nayani, R., Tregaskis, O., Hogg, M., Etuknwa, A., & Semkina, A. (2021). Implementing practices focused on workplace health and psychological wellbeing: A systematic review. *Social Science and Medicine, 227*, 113888.

Fikretoglu, D., Easterbrook, B., & Nazarov, A. (in press). Fidelity in workplace mental health intervention research: A narrative review. *Work & Stress*.

Greenhalgh, J. (2014). Realist synthesis. In P. K. Edwards, J. O'Mahoney, & S. Vincent (Eds.), *Studying organizations using critical realism: A practical guide* (pp. 264–281). Oxford University Press.

Johns, G. (2006). The essential impact of context on organizational behavior. *Academy of Management Review, 31*, 386–408.

Mishiba, T. (2020). *Workplace mental health law: Comparative perspectives*. Routledge.

Moore, G. F., Audrey, S., Barker, M., Bond, L., Bonell, C., Hardeman, W., . . . Baird, J. (2015). Process evaluation of complex interventions: Medical Research Council guidance. *British Medical Journal, 350*, h1258.

Patey, J., Nasamu, E., Nayani, R., Watson, D., Connolly, S., & Daniels, K. (2021). Evaluating multicomponent wellbeing strategies: Theoretical and methodological insights. In T. Wall, C. Cooper, & P. Brough (Eds.), *The SAGE handbook of Organisational wellbeing* (pp. 478–493). SAGE.

Pawson, R., & Manzano-Santaella, A. (2012). A realist diagnostic workshop. *Evaluation, 18*, 176–191.

Roodbari, H., Axtell, C., Nielsen, K., & Sorensen, G. (in press). Organisational interventions to improve employees' health and wellbeing: A realist synthesis. *Applied Psychology: An International Review*.

Russell, J., Berney, L., Stansfeld, S., Lanz, D., Kerry, S., Chandola, T., & Bhui, K. (2016). The role of qualitative research in adding value to a randomised controlled trial: Lessons from a pilot study of a guided e-learning intervention for managers to improve employee wellbeing and reduce sickness absence. *Trials, 17*, 396.

Technical Appendix

In this technical appendix, we provide an overview of the methods used to review existing frameworks and models (Chap. 2), and for the qualitative empirical research that has informed the development of model and presented throughout the book.

Systematic Review of Intervention Studies and Review of Reviews

Daniels et al. (2021a, Daniels, K., Watson, D., Nayani, R., Tregaskis, O., Hogg, M., Etuknwa, A. & Semkina, A. (2021). Implementing practices focused on workplace health and psychological wellbeing: A systematic review. *Social Science and Medicine 227,* 113888) produced a systematic review of intervention studies. This review provides some background for this book as well as material for more detailed analysis of primary studies cited in this book. The review was registered with PROSPERO: The International Prospective Register of Systematic Reviews (ID: CRD42019119656).

A review of models and other reviews was completed initially at the end of 2018. The review was updated in May 2021 with additional searches and also included publications we knew had been published since 2019 (e.g. through journal tables of contents of alerts). After May 2021 until the end of October 2021, we only added to the review publications we had become aware of through journal tables of contents of alerts.

The substantive search terms for the review of models/reviews were the same as those used for the systematic review of implementation of workplace health and wellbeing interventions conducted by Daniels et al. (2021a). The substantive search terms used for primary empirical papers were:

Population/Sampling keywords= (occupational OR organisational* OR organizational* OR industrial* OR work* OR employ* OR job)

K. Daniels et al., *Achieving Sustainable Workplace Wellbeing*, Aligning Perspectives on Health, Safety and Well-Being, https://doi.org/10.1007/978-3-031-00665-4

AND

Intervention keywords = (*program* OR *intervent* OR prevent* OR *stress_manage* OR health_promot* OR health_aware* OR health-screen* OR well*eing_promot* OR well*eing_aware* OR mindfulness* OR resilienc* OR well*eing_program* OR counsel* OR coach* OR *therap* OR employee_assistance_program* OR return_to_work OR stay_at_work OR vocational_rehab* OR job_craft* OR job_enlarge* OR job_enrich* OR job_rotat* OR job_redesign OR work_redesign OR task_redesign OR flexible_work* OR flexibil* OR *train* OR high_commitment_manage* OR high_performance_work* OR human_resource_dev* OR human_resource* OR employment_practice* OR HRM OR SHRM OR strategic_human_resource OR high_involvement_manage* OR management_develop* OR leadership_develop*)

AND

Outcome keywords = (stress OR well-being OR wellbeing OR well_being OR mental_health OR mental_ill* OR emotions OR affect* OR mood OR job_satis* OR anxiety OR depress* OR burnout OR job_engagement OR work_engagement OR employee_engagement OR life_satis* OR job_strain OR psychological_health OR employee*healt* OR worker_healt* OR organi*ational_health OR occupational_health OR job_quality OR job_design OR job_redesign OR job_characteristic* OR job_feature* OR psychosocial_risk* OR employment_quality OR work_quality OR work_design OR work_redesign OR work_characteristic* OR work_feature* OR meaningful_work* OR work_environ* OR return_to_work* OR worker_welfar* OR employee_welfar* OR functioning OR quality_of_life OR quality_of_work*_life OR effort-reward_imbalance OR wellness OR work_ability OR life_style OR lifestyle)

AND

Study design/Methods keywords =(process* OR implement* OR change_manage* OR change_process* OR *interv* OR realis*_evaluat* OR intervention)

These search terms were discussed and developed by the authors of Daniels et al. (2021a) with input from Nick Pahl (Society of Occupational Medicine), Ewan MacDonald (University of Glasgow), Kristy Sanderson (University of East Anglia), Johannes Siegrist (Dusseldorf University), Mike Whitmore (RAND Europe), Karen McDonell (RoSPA) and Paul Montgomery (University of Birmingham).

Study design and methods keywords were not used in the review of models/ reviews. To identify relevant theoretical or conceptual frameworks as well as existing reviews, additional search terms included:

(best_evidence_review * OR systematic_review * OR meta-analys* OR narrative_review OR theory OR theoretical_frame* OR theoretical_model OR concept*_review OR concept*_frame* OR concept*_model OR).

For the review of models/existing reviews, Martin Hogg (co-author of Daniels et al., 2021 and a technical report for the What Works Centre for Wellbeing) conducted searches in 2018 in the Web of Science (to detect peer-reviewed papers) and PsycINFO (additionally to detect books and book chapters) databases. No time restrictions were placed on the searches. Some 1509 titles were identified. Of these, an initial title sift, to identify obviously out of scope papers (e.g. empirical investigations), left 218 sources for further review. Martin Hogg and Kevin Daniels examined the abstracts of the remaining sources. Additional publications known to the review team not identified through the electronic searches were included as necessary. This left a total of 37 publications to be included in the review, plus a further four publications specifically on realist evaluation methods. These publications were read by Kevin Daniels, Rachel Nayani and David Watson, who made notes on the publications. Publications that did not focus on implementation (e.g. had a focus on methods or identifying gaps in research around an outcome) were excluded. This left a total of 34 publications in the review. Subsequently, Rachel Nayani developed a summary of main themes in the publications and grouped those publications into a smaller number of classes. Kevin Daniels then developed a narrative synthesis of the publications, finalized in July 2019 as the first chapter of an internal technical report for the What Works Centre for Wellbeing. Up until 2021, a further six publications were incorporated into the synthesis, which has been amended accordingly. A seventh publication (Roodbari et al., in press) is a realist evaluation of job redesign studies and findings from this review have been incorporated elsewhere in this book.

Qualitative Case Studies

Data were collected from six organisations. Data were collected over a two-month period in 2019, through a mixture of telephone ($N = 28$) and face-to-face interviews ($N = 13$). Interviewing was undertaken by each of the book's authors in pairs as a verification procedure to ensure completeness of data. Interviews lasted approximately an hour and, in all but one case, were voice recorded and transcribed verbatim by a professional transcription service. In some instances (noted below), we interviewed two people at once.

Recruitment and Sample

Recruitment of organisations reporting good practice in wellbeing interventions were was made via a call for interest and contacts of the research team, using a purposive sampling strategy. Six organisations of varying sizes were recruited from three sectors (construction, professional services, and care/social), representing different levels of pay and job skill (i.e. high and low) for ecological validity of findings. Interviewees represented multiple stakeholders involved in developing, delivering and experiencing the wellbeing programme in each case study organisation.

Cases, sector, size and interviewees comprised:

'Large infrastructure and construction'. Eight interviewees from a large construction company, employing many thousands of staff and sub-contractors. Interviewees included senior human resources and safety managers, mid-level managers and onsite workers. One interview was not recorded, and data were recorded as notes.

'Medium construction'. Seven interviewees from a construction firm with less than 500 employees. Interviewees included a senior human resources manager, mid-level managers and technical professionals.

'Large, multinational law'. Seven interviewees from a large, multinational law firm with many thousands of employees. Interviewees included a senior human resources manager, mid-level managers and technical professionals. Two interviewees—both health and wellbeing managers—were interviewed together.

'Medium accountancy practice'. Six interviewees from a regionally based accountancy practice with around 500 employees. Interviews included senior managers, human resources and wellbeing leads, technical professionals.

'Large care'. Nine interviewees from a multidivisional business specializing in properties for social care and other social purposes with many thousands of employees. Interviews included senior and mid-level managers and human resources managers. There were two joint interviews. One involved two payroll managers. The other involved a human resources business partner and the managing director of a subsidiary business.

'Small care'. Four interviewees with a small care home that was part of a larger group. Interviewees included the care home manager, another manager and two care workers (interviewed at the same time).

Table A1 summarizes the case companies and interviews.

Data Collection

Semi-structured interviews were the primary means of data collection. In addition, organisational documents were reviewed. We developed interview guides, which were devised according to interviewee type: For the leader/sponsor (i.e. those responsible for directing the programme); for managers/agents (i.e. those involved in putting the programme in place); and for the recipients of the programme. Questions were focused on understanding the what, how and why of the organisation's approach to health and wellbeing and the initiatives encompassed within that approach. Leader/sponsor interviews also covered how the internal and external contextual factors may have influenced the choice and implementation of health and wellbeing activities, as well as factors that may have affected implementation or the choice of approach toward implementation. Manager and worker questions were also directed at experiences and perceptions of the initiatives, as well as views on the processes of how these interventions may have affected wellbeing and performance.

Table A1 Case summary and interviewees

Case study	Case Description	Interviewees	Summary of approach and initiatives
Large infrastructure and construction	Large construction and infrastructure firm. Early adopter of new international standard for health and safety. Two mental health first aiders on site, various signs/leaflets of wellbeing toolbox around site office and facilities. Very transient and shifting workforce, also highly international.	Leader/sponsors: Wellbeing lead; Human resources director; Health and safety director Manager/Agent: Senior Safety Adviser; Site Manager Worker: Groundworks Worker; Site Engineer; Electrician	Many different initiatives, but most high profile is mental health, which has dominated wellbeing activities. Also employee perks/rewards, employee assistance programme, health surveillance organized around an evolving strategy and seven key enablers: (1) leadership, (2) education, (3) communication, (4) healthy working environment (5) standards in design, (6) engagement and (7) improvement. Continuous improvement group on occupational health and wellbeing.
Medium construction	A family-owned construction and civil engineering company with 300 employees. Workforce is mainly male, middle-aged. Mobile workforce and multi-site locations, with around 100 'live' sites at any one time.	Leader/Sponsor: Human resources director Manager/Agent: Contracts director; operations manager; head of assurance Worker: Bid co-ordinator; financial controller; marketing officer	Cultural value of doing the right thing by employees embedded in family ethos of the firm. Provision includes various resources (e.g. employee assistance programme, educational/training and support tools and information) and initiatives (e.g. employee led volunteering, embedding wellbeing training within managerial training). Core is an appraisal and personal development programme using coaching techniques and designed to foster personal health and wellbeing alongside work-based competencies.
Large, multinational law	An international law firm with over 2,500	Leader/Sponsor: Human resources manager	Approach articulated around three pillars of

(continued)

Table A1 (continued)

Case study	Case Description	Interviewees	Summary of approach and initiatives
	employees and 25 offices globally.	Manager/Agent: Health and safety manager; facilities compliance manager; policies and projects manager; responsible business associate; assistant rewards manager Worker: Partner	wellbeing: Health, financial and environment. Informed by the pillars, a mental health and wellbeing strategy, and governance structures co-ordinate and mobilize action including a health and wellbeing steering group. Wellbeing resources organized through an intranet hub, which includes policies and procedures as well as advice and signposting to support. External partners and provider organisations are important in delivering wellbeing services and understanding employee need. Employee interest groups inform bottom-up initiatives, but emphasis on integrating localized actions into comprehensive practices across firm.
Medium accountancy practice	An audit and accounting partnership, employing over 300 employees across multiple sites and run by 20 partners. Working at client site, in office, some travel. Not highest payers in industry.	Leader/sponsor: Head of human resources; managing partner Manager/Agent: Senior manager; wellbeing co-ordinator Worker: Auditor; auditor	Broad range of activities organized under six different strands: Financial, social, mental, physical, career and community. Examples of activities include wellbeing champions, mental health awareness training, healthy eating initiatives, debt management advice, charitable and community work as well as a social fund for team-based social activities. Existing human resources policies and processes re-configured

(continued)

Table A1 (continued)

Case study	Case Description	Interviewees	Summary of approach and initiatives
			under the six strands. Employee wellbeing seen as fundamental to core business services and in supporting their talent framework.
Large care	A commercial business for social purpose. Group organisational structure, encompassing a wide range of 20 businesses, including: leisure centres, care and support services, facilities management, property management, construction (e.g. social housing), housing associations. Total 13,000 employees, 9,000 in leisure centres. Company is acquisitive, pursuing growth strategy—need to be competitive in attracting workers ('future-proof') as well as 'driving productivity.'	Leader/Sponsor: Human resources director; health and safety director Manager/Agent: human resources business partner; head of corporate facilities; human resources business partner Worker: Payroll manager; payroll manager; human resources business partner; managing director of subsidiary business	Wellbeing strategy across groups within organisation is configured around five pillars (employee physical wellbeing, employee mental wellbeing, employee safety and external facing: community wellbeing and place making wellbeing). Attempting to generate a joined-up wellbeing strategy, delivery and governance structure, while also accommodating subsidiary-led and tailored wellbeing initiatives and facilitating cross-group learning. Consistency across organisation through strategic communication and establishment of mental health first aider/champions. Partnering with wellbeing service providers to ensure there is evidence to make informed decisions about wellbeing priorities and assessment of initiatives.
Small care	A learning and disability care home under the umbrella of care provider. The home is single site, with around 20 residents and 22 staff (full and part time). Management structure is	Leader/Sponsor: Care home manager Manager/Agent: Deputy Manager Worker: Support worker; Support worker	Recruitment according to fit and mindset aligned to the inclusive and supportive culture. Role modelling by leadership, consideration, and support for staff alongside no

(continued)

Table A1 (continued)

Case study	Case Description	Interviewees	Summary of approach and initiatives
	manager, deputy manager, 2 seniors. 24-hour shifts.		tolerance of bullying or power plays. Other-career encouragement and support for individual progression beyond the organisation and sector. Employees encouraged to bring own interests into work and integrate caring for residents' wellbeing with their own.

Data Analysis

We developed a coding framework derived from our knowledge of the literature. Following a reflexive and iterative process (Miles & Huberman, 1994; Miles, M.B. & Huberman, A.M. (1994). *Qualitative Data Analysis: An Expanded Sourcebook*. Thousand Oaks: Sage) and moving between the themes, extracts and the transcriptions to ensure comprehensive treatment of the data, the coding framework was refined through within case analysis and cross-case comparison. Applying abductive reasoning and moving between data and literature, we explored the extent to which the themes had been adequately reflected in the literature and what our data could add to that literature by providing more detail, adding new perspectives or reinterpreting existing frameworks as appropriate. Coded data were used both to generate new knowledge and illustrate, refine and/or nuance existing knowledge.

As a sense checking process, data synthesis and the new model were discussed extensively within the research team and presented at internal and external seminars and workshops. These discussions included practitioners, policy makers and academic researchers.

GPSR Compliance
The European Union's (EU) General Product Safety Regulation (GPSR) is a set of rules that requires consumer products to be safe and our obligations to ensure this.

If you have any concerns about our products, you can contact us on

ProductSafety@springernature.com

In case Publisher is established outside the EU, the EU authorized representative is:

Springer Nature Customer Service Center GmbH
Europaplatz 3
69115 Heidelberg, Germany

www.ingramcontent.com/pod-product-compliance
Ingram Content Group UK Ltd.
Pitfield, Milton Keynes, MK11 3LW, UK
UKHW020820290926
15470UKWH00003B/1281
* 9 7 8 3 0 3 1 0 0 6 6 4 7 *